IZU ISLANDS
(JAPANESE)
NDS
URACAS
MARIANA ISLANDS
SAIPAN
TINIAN
ROTA
GUAM (U.S.)
WAKE Is.
(U.S.)
JAPANESE MANDATE
C R O N E S I A
FEYS
TRUK
ENEWETOK
MARSHALL
ISLANDS
EAURIPIK
PONAPE
ROLINE ISLANDS
KUSAIE
JALUIT
GILBERT Is
ESE MANDATE
GREENWICH Is.
EQUATOR
BRITISH
MANDATE
USTRALIAN
MANDATE
W GUINEA

JAPAN'S ISLANDS OF MYSTERY

Books by WILLARD PRICE

JAPAN'S ISLANDS OF MYSTERY

JAPAN RIDES THE TIGER

BARBARIAN
(*A Novel*)

CHILDREN OF THE RISING SUN

PACIFIC ADVENTURE

ANCIENT PEOPLES AT NEW TASKS

THE NEGRO AROUND THE WORLD

AMERICAN INFLUENCE IN THE ORIENT

JAPAN'S ISLANDS OF MYSTERY

Willard Price

WITH PHOTOGRAPHS AND MAPS BY THE AUTHOR

THE JOHN DAY COMPANY

New York

Eighth Impression

Japan's Islands of Mystery is for the most part new, but incorporates brief sections of the author's earlier *Pacific Adventure*, revised to date.

Contents

Illustrations

PHOTOGRAPHS

MAPS

TO
MARY VIRGINIA PRICE

I:

Stepping Stones to Japan

IT IS significant that although in more than two years of war with Japan we have consistently decried "island hopping," this war has been a war of "island hopping."

There must be a reason for this contradiction.

The reason appears to be that "island hopping" has its merits.

Our impatience to strike directly at Japan is understandable. The Doolittle raid was just what the public wanted. We had no mind to nibble at the tips of the tentacles of the octopus. We wanted to smash the head and heart. This did not seem too difficult to persons with a preconception of American power and Japanese weakness.

But a long time has gone by without a repetition of the Doolittle raid. Even if it is repeated it will mean little—until it can be multiplied a thousandfold in force.

The truth is that there is no shortcut to Tokyo. There is no easy way to lick Japan.

Russian bases are not the answer. It is not at all certain that the Soviet will come to our aid immediately after the defeat of Germany. Russia will have earned a rest. She will need time to gather strength for a new and most difficult war in which men and supplies must be transported to a front six thousand miles from Moscow. Russia has not forgotten what happened the last time she came to grips with Japan. Nor will she forget the delay of the United Nations in establishing a second front in Europe, justifiable though the delay may have been.

It would be suicidal for Russia to give us Siberian bases until either we or the Russians are ready to defend them against Japan. Nippon's finest army is poised in Manchuria ready for just such an eventuality.

That Russia will attack Japan seems certain. Russia will *not* leave it to us to take Manchuria. She considers that her function. But the taking of Manchuria will be one of the last acts of the war. British and American troops are still far away and China's armies are fully engaged. So Russia can afford to wait.

The probability is that Russian action will be delayed until the Japanese enemy has been beaten to his knees. Then Russia will come in at the kill. This may be a trifle disappointing to us, but more than this we cannot expect of our Russian allies whose magnificent war upon Germany has saved us millions in men and money and years of time.

Therefore the early prospect of striking at Japan from Vladivostok or Kamchatka may be dismissed.

The possibility of full use of a liberated China as a springboard to Japan is also remote. The ultimate importance of China can hardly be exaggerated. "The key to the final victory over Japan lies in China," says Admiral King. Note, however, the word "final." China will not play her full role until just before the knockout. The reason lies in the fact that the Burma Road, when recovered, and the new roads from India, together with air transport, cannot soon equip China for a major assault upon her firmly entrenched enemy. The Himalayas forbid.

Only when help can be brought to China by the open and smooth road of the sea can the help begin to be adequate.

But the sea off the China coast is barricaded by Japanese islands.

And now we begin dimly to perceive the importance of "island hopping."

Let us get the situation clearly in mind. Our best though not earliest hope is to attack Japan from China. But we can never get adequate forces and supplies into China through and over Himalayan passes. We must be able to use the comparatively short and direct route from the American West Coast and Hawaii to the Chinese seaboard.

In the way of the execution of this plan there is just one obstacle— the vast island world of the Western Pacific now under the control of Japan.

So some rhyme and reason begin to appear out of the curious anomaly that while there has been general agreement that we do not wish to approach Japan "island by island," our hardheaded army and navy chiefs have been doing just that and probably will continue to do just that.

Our line of battle from Hawaii to Australia is separated from Japan by some ten thousand islands. There are 7,083 islands in the Philippines alone, 1,400 in Micronesia. It took us six months to master one island, Guadalcanal. There is dismay in the thought that even if we required only a single month for each island, it would take us 10,000 months, or 833 years, to reach Japan. This absurdity is at the bottom of our dislike of "island hopping."

But there have been indications that the "island hopping" may turn into a sort of leapfrog. Our Navy vaulted over Kiska to take Attu. Kiska, its line of supplies cut off, fell without a fight. Kolombangara was by-passed and Vella Lavella taken. The Japanese evacuated Kolombangara. There is every likelihood that as the United Nations forces become stronger and the enemy weaker, entire groups of islands will be skipped and neutralized by attacking only the principal bases. For example, it is conceivable that after a stiff fight on Mindanao, southernmost of the Philippines, the battle may shift to Luzon, the northernmost, leaving the rest of the 7,083 islands of the archipelago to fall of their own weight. Reducing the half dozen major bases of Micronesia may determine the destiny of 1,400 islands. Taking Chichijima would probably render impotent the 20 islands of the Bonins.

So, although there is no easy road to Tokyo, this one is not so difficult as it may at first appear.

And the essential fact is that it is the only road now open to us.

If there were no other reason for following it, the fact that it is the naval road should be enough. Because of the remoteness of the theater of action, our war against Japan has been and will be for a long time largely a naval war. And the best place for the navy to fight is on the ocean. Our great naval strength would go begging if the fight were transferred far inland.

Nothing would please the Japanese more. Japan's chief power lies in her army—not her navy or air force. We have nibbled away much of her navy, but her land forces are intact.

Fortunately we have "the choice of weapons." A duelist who has the choice of weapons would be foolish to choose the favorite weapon of his antagonist. We have overwhelming superiority in ships and planes. That means sea war, if we have anything to say about it. And since we hold the initiative, it is for us to say where the fighting shall take place.

Certainly there will later be some heavy fighting on land, and the reopening of the Burma Road is an essential preliminary. But skilful management may keep the land war to a minimum and raise the sea war to a maximum. If the sea war is carried relentlessly to its conclusion there may be much less land fighting than we now expect.

Applying still further the principle of leapfrog, it may be possible largely to bypass Japan's armies on the Asiatic continent. It is not necessarily true that we must clean all the Japanese out of China, Indo-China, Thailand and Malaya before attacking Japan itself. Nor will it be necessary first to take the Netherlands Indies.

The logical route to Japan is not around these Robin Hood's barns but straight from where we are to where we want to get. We are in Hawaii, the Aleutians and Australia. If we close in more or less directly upon Japan from these three points, our Aleutian path will lead down through the Kuriles and Hokkaido to the Japanese main island, Honshu, a distance of only 1,600 miles. This is our shortest, but worst, route. Execrable weather and rough terrain make it difficult for our best weapon, the airplane.

Our Hawaiian path will swing through Wake and the Marshalls, the Marianas and the Bonins to Japan. This natural Hawaii-to-Japan route "was, for a long time before the war," writes Hanson Baldwin, Military Editor of the *New York Times,* "the classical and traditional war college approach, but political considerations, which forced a dispersal of our strength in the Pacific, and lack of adequate naval-air strength in that ocean, have so far prevented the start of any such undertaking. But as our strength vis-a-vis Japan increases, it is likely that this traditional approach—aimed directly at the heart of the enemy—will supplant in importance the subsidiary operations."

The Australian route will pass through Rabaul and Truk to Palau which is only five hundred miles from the Philippines, which are less than two hundred miles from Formosa which, in turn, is but sixty

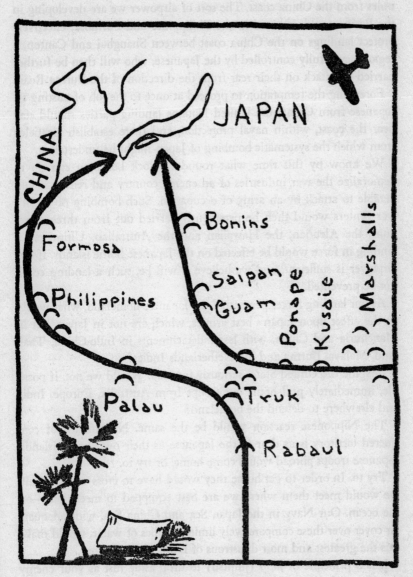

JAPAN

CHINA

Bonins

Formosa

Saipan

Guam

Ponape

Kusaie

Marshalls

Philippines

Truk

Palau

Rabaul

STEPPING STONES TO JAPAN

miles from the China coast. The sort of airpower we are developing in the Pacific could, if based in the Philippines and Formosa, effectively protect landings on the China coast between Shanghai and Canton, a region never fully controlled by the Japanese, who will then be further harried by attack on their rear from the direction of the Burma Road.

Foregoing the temptation to proceed at once to the job of ousting all Japanese from China, the United Nations landing parties should stay near the coast, within naval protection, and there establish air fields from which the systematic bombing of Japan might be undertaken.

We know by this time what round-the-clock bombing can do to demoralize the war industries of an enemy country and render it vulnerable to attack by an army of occupation. Such bombing of Japan's war centers would then be persistently carried out from three directions, the Aleutian, the Hawaiian and the Australian. Ultimately a landing in force would be effected on the Japanese home islands. If our airpower is sufficient, and we believe it will be, such a landing could not be prevented.

As our landing forces penetrated the Japanese homeland, what would be the effect upon Japan's best armies, which are not in Japan, but in Manchuria and China, with lesser detachments in Indo-China, Thailand, Malaya, Burma and the Netherlands Indies?

Imagine the United States seriously invaded. Would we not, if possible, immediately pull home our troops from Australia, Europe, India and elsewhere to defend the homeland?

The Nipponese reaction would be the same. No amount of conquered territory is as dear to the Japanese as their own home islands. Japanese troops abroad would come home, or try to.

Try to. In order to get home they would have to cross water. Again we would meet them where we are best equipped to meet them—on the ocean. Our Navy in the Japan Sea and China Sea, with adequate air cover over these comparatively limited bodies of water, would make this the greatest and most disastrous of Dunkirks in history.

It is a principle of *judo* (jiujitsu) to drop aside just as your enemy thrusts and let him dislocate a shoulder or break his own back. Better than a gigantic frontal attack upon Japan's magnificent armies in Asia

6

is to let them invite their own fate on the sea under the guns of our ships and planes. I have said that some heavy land fighting would also be necessary. Of course China must be completely liberated. But the task of United Nations armies on the continent would be made immeasurably easier by a voluntary exodus of Japanese to defend the homeland. It would be the business of our forces afloat and above to see to it that most of these homing pigeons should never arrive.

Let it be constantly kept in mind that we shall be at our best if we fight Japan's armies as little as possible with armies and as much as possible with ships, planes and strategy. That this is the view even of the United States Army is suggested in General Marshall's characterization of our Pacific war as "predominantly oceanic."

Moreover, placing reliance chiefly upon ship power and plane power instead of sheer slogging man power may, at a conservative estimate, save a million American lives. Is that an item worth considering?

The army is not precluded from this oceanic fight. In fact experience has proved that neither the ship nor the carrier-plane can excel the landbased army bomber in island-to-island warfare. It is the peculiar virtue of "island-hopping" that each island acquired furnishes another solid land base from which bombers may take off for the next objective. Thus the army air force is distinctly a sea weapon.

As for the infantry and mechanized units, they will get enough action to satisfy them when they invade the Japanese homeland. Why multiply the problem a hundred times by taking on all the Japanese-occupied continent as well?

The aftermath of a successful conquest of Japan would be the accelerated cleansing of China and Manchuria of the remnants of Japanese resistance and the isolation of southeastern Asia and the Indies from Japan. With the line of supplies between them cut—again a sea job, not a land job—marooned Japanese interests in the tail of Asia cannot survive the final mopping-up.

Keep most of our American forces to fight on the main Japanese island of Honshu.

Strike the kingpin squarely and the other nine will fall.

7

And the best, shortest and safest route to the kingpin is by sea, over the island stepping stones.

We have no need to apologize for "island hopping." Japan is an island. Our most direct approaches are paved with islands. This is an island war.

II:

The Key to the Pacific

OF THE three island-paved roads to Tokyo, the Aleutian is the poorest, because of wretched flying weather and lack of landing fields. No doubt this road will be used, but it will hardly rank in importance with the others.

The Hawaiian road is the best of the three. The Australian road was forced upon us by the necessity early in the war of defending Australia. Brilliantly exploited by General MacArthur and Admirals Nimitz and Halsey, this road has been proved thoroughly practicable.

But both of these good roads are temporarily blocked by the most mysterious and in many ways the most formidable group of islands on the surface of the globe today.

Micronesia is in the way. Once conquered, Micronesia will be a valuable part of both roads. Its stepping stones are necessary to the advance on Tokyo.

We cannot make the long leap to Tokyo across open sea. We must go by way of the islands. The reason is, of course, that advance units, whether ships or planes, must always have bases near at hand where they may be refueled or repaired. Fighter planes cannot fly vast distances. Bombing planes can, but only by loading so heavily with gasoline that few bombs can be carried.

Thus, when the great march along the Hawaiian road begins, it will probably halt first at the Marshalls (a part of Micronesia) where excellent bases may be captured and used. From these bases the next thrust may be projected to Ponape and Truk (both in Micronesia). From the magnificent base of Truk the war will step to once-American Guam (also in Micronesia), thence to the Japanese base of Chichijima (Father Island) in the Bonins, from which it is only two hours' flying time to Tokyo.

The Australian march has been delayed for many months in the Solomons and New Guinea. It is now moving on relentlessly to Rabaul and thence to Truk, the major base in Micronesia where the two roads meet—but only briefly, for it is quite probable that while one force moves on to Guam the other will deviate to Palau, a splendid Japanese base, still in Micronesia, from which a further drive upon the Philippines and up the China Sea to Japan may be launched.

Whether our advance will make these exact steps is of course speculative. But in general these routes cannot be avoided.

The only point for emphasis here is that Micronesia bars both roads.

Micronesia is, in the words of a Japanese admiral, "the key to the Pacific." It was Japan's key to unlock the treasures of the Philippines and the Indies. It will be our key to unlock Japan.

What is now our chief obstacle will become our chief advantage.

Japan did not fail to appreciate the value of the 1,400 islands of the Micronesian archipelago dotting the sea all the way from Japan to the equator. We should probably not be at war with Japan today if these islands had not been given to Japan as a mandate by the Versailles Conference at the close of World War I.

"The strategic importance of those islands in the eyes of the Japanese navy," writes Hugh Byas of the *London Times* and *New York Times* after two decades in Tokyo, "was the most potent of all the incentives to war which culminated at Pearl Harbor. Without these islands it is probable that Japan would not have embarked on the scheme of conquest which brought her into the World War as Hitler's ally. The possession of the islands made the scheme of conquest feasible and the attack on America hopeful. . . . Until the islands were acquired from Germany, Japan's naval strategy was essentially defensive. . . . With the islands charted and surveyed the strategists of the Naval General

Staff took their plans against the United States fleet out of the pigeon-holes and redrew them. As the strategists studied the possibilities of sea power plus island-based air power, they saw vast opportunities opening for the offensive in the South Seas of which they had long dreamed."

Micronesia extended the Japanese arm to the equator. It placed the Japanese fingers within easy reach of the Philippines, New Guinea, Borneo, Java and even Australia.

Three months before Pearl Harbor a young Australian was speaking of his country's fear of Japan.

"But I think it's foolish," he said. "Why, Japan is thousands of miles from Australia!"

"I think you are mistaken," I said. "Japan is closer to Australia than I am to you."

He smiled at what he took for an effort to be facetious.

"I'll go further than that," I added. "The Japanese world and the Australian world are as close together as the drops in that glass of water."

I got a map and showed him the Australian islands extending to the equator. He knew about them, but he was puzzled by the swarm of islands north of the equator.

"Are they really there?" he asked. "Most maps don't show them."

They bore such names as the Carolines, Marshalls, Marianas, and over the mass of them was lettered "Micronesia—Japanese Mandate."

The southern limit of the Japanese Mandate was shown to be the equator—and the northern limit of the Australian Mandate was also the equator. Along that line, for some 1,400 miles, Australian and Japanese sovereignty met.

Even the most detailed map of the Pacific could hardly show all of Japan's Micronesian islands, for there are 1,483 of them, in addition to many islets and reefs bringing the total to 2,550.

The ordinary map contents itself with indicating only the largest. But the largest are not necessarily the most important in the strategy of the Pacific.

The young Australian pored over the island labyrinth with growing excitement.

"Why," he said, "they're in the middle of everything, aren't they? Close to Hawaii, just a jump from Japan, slap up against Australian waters, right next to the Dutch Indies—and look at your Philippines, smothered by them!"

From bases in Micronesia, Japan has attacked Hawaii, the Philippines, the Netherlands Indies, and the island possessions of Australia.

The dream had been bigger than that. It had included Australia itself, a continent seventeen times the size of Japan and with one-twelfth the population. The Japanese were intensely interested in the theory of the redistribution of territory, once suggested by Colonel House and endorsed in principle by Sir Samuel Hoare. If the "have" nations were to share their open spaces with the "have not" nations, the Japanese could think of no better place to begin than in Australia.

Only second to Australia were the great wealthy islands of New Guinea, Borneo and the Philippines, all of them containing territory that had not as yet even been explored and wild tribes not subdued. Hardly a month went by without word of negotiation with one or another of the Western absentee landlords of these rich estates to allow Japanese to come in and assist in economic development. Late in 1935 the Japanese South Seas Development Company succeeded in leasing 147,000 acres on the northern coast of Dutch New Guinea for the purpose of raising "Sea Island Cotton"; and Japanese development of other uncivilized parts of New Guinea awaited only the permission of the Dutch authorities.

I asked a Hollander about it. "Why don't you Dutch develop those sections yourselves?"

"What!" he said, "that hell? Not while there's beer on ice in Batavia!"

It seemed only fair to the Japanese that what the Dutch were not willing to do themselves they should let others do.

So the dynamic energy of a pent-up race flowed south. Between Hawaii with its 150,000 Japanese and the Philippines with its 25,000, and as far south as Yampi Sound, Western Australia, where the Japan

Mining Company aspired to develop 22,000,000 tons of iron, there was not an island of value in the western Pacific that had not been touched by the influence of the Island Empire.

But there were too many obstacles in the way of Nippon's economic expansion. Japan was not content with doing it the hard way. Her admirals and generals began to offer easy conquest of the fabulously rich under-world. The term, "the southward advance," which had been used as a slogan for business men, began to take on military significance. Micronesia made a military southward advance possible.

"These islands are made to order for Japan," said Admiral Suetsugu. "In fact, the Pacific equilibrium can be maintained only when Japan holds them."

He was right only to the extent that it is true that the equilibrium of the Pacific centers in this archipelago.

When the islands were deeded to Japan, President Wilson was not unaware of their importance, but he could do nothing in the face of secret treaties formerly concluded between Japan and other Allied powers. He remarked, in personal conversation, as reported by the member of the American delegation to whom he spoke, "that these islands lie athwart the path from Hawaii to the Philippines and that they are nearer to Hawaii than the Pacific Coast is, and that they could be fortified and made naval bases by Japan."

There was but one loophole through the great wall. That was Guam. But the Guam loophole could, of course, be blocked by Japan at any moment. To get around the Japanese world, it would then be necessary to go either by way of Alaska and the Aleutians, or south of the equator!

Calling attention to the vulnerability of America's trade routes to the Far East, Captain Dudley Knox, U.S.N., in the Proceedings of the United States Naval Institute, urged the purchase of the Marquesas and Solomon Islands as stepping stones across the Southern Pacific to supplement the American refueling base at Tutuila. The suggestion was fantastic but was born of desperation. A glance at the map is enlightening. So roundabout a route more than doubles the distance from San

Francisco to Shanghai. It is quite like going from New York to London by way of Brazil.

"The line connecting the Bonins, Mariana Islands and Palau," wrote Captain Taketomi of the Imperial Navy, "is the country's southern defense line. When this line is protected Japan will be able perfectly to control the North Pacific. While we hold this control no economic blockade is possible. Furthermore, this line cuts in two the line of the United States footholds in the Pacific running from San Francisco to Hawaii, Guam, the Philippines and China."

As war neared and rhetoric waxed, the islands were sloganized as Japan's "life line to the south" and Japan's "first line of defense." Behind this line of defense, Japan attacked China. America could bluster in vain. She was shut off from the scene of conflict by an island breakwater which together with the Japanese home islands barricaded the entire front of the Asiatic continent against interference from the West.

The continent is still so barricaded. We are subjected to the colossal absurdity of sending help to China by the back way over a route more than 13,000 miles long instead of the front way from Hawaii straight to the China coast, a distance of only 4,940 miles.

We are even allowing ourselves sometimes to think of attacking Japan by way of the Atlantic, the Mediterranean, India, Burma, China and thence by bombing plane to Japan, most of the way around the world, a total distance of 15,000 wriggling miles, instead of from Hawaii along the curve of the Pacific islands, less than 6,000 miles.

How long will Japan force us to go 15,000 instead of 6,000 miles to get at her?

Just so long as Japan holds Micronesia.

III:

What Is Micronesia?

WHEN the question, "What is Micronesia?" was asked on a quiz program, the answers ranged all the way from "a disease like amnesia," to "something to do with microscopes."

Micronesia is the blind spot of the Pacific. It comprises the Mariana islands, the Carolines and the Marshalls. It is bordered on the south by well-known Melanesia and on the southeast by still better-known Polynesia of which Tahiti is the center.

All three "nesias" are based upon the Greek word for island, *nesos*. Polynesia means "Many Islands," Melanesia, "Black Islands," and Micronesia, "Small Islands."

Any one of these archipelagoes extends over a greater area than the United States.

Pacific distances are fabulous. The world's greatest ocean occupies more space than all the land on the globe. It would hold two Atlantics and still have room for a few Mediterraneans. Better than half of all the world's water is in the Pacific. Its greatest north-south dimension is 9,300 miles and its greatest width, 10,300. The sun takes ten hours to cross it, nearly half of its circle around the globe. No other ocean plumbs such depths. Its floor is a third deeper on the average than the Atlantic. But there are curious trenches or canyons that drop farther below sea level than the world's highest mountain rises above it. Off Guam the United States telegraph ship *Nero* found a depth of 31,500 feet. This was supposed to be the most profound of ocean depths until in 1927 the German cruiser *Emden* measured a chasm off the Philippine east coast and reached a depth of more than 35,000 feet. Everest is 29,000 feet high.

It is small wonder that in so vast an ocean little Micronesia, only as large as the United States, should have been overlooked.

The Pacific islands may or may not once have been a continent as the romancers of the lost "Mu" would have us believe. It is true that they have been sinking for many centuries and are still subsiding. But we know that there was never a land bridge between the islands and Asia, at least not since the development of mammals. The fauna of the continent is not duplicated on the islands.

Man was more enterprising than his fellow-mammals and long before the dawn of history he migrated to the islands, or continent if there was one, and established a civilization somewhat like that of the Incas of Peru. Ancient stone buildings, pedestals and images found on Tinian, Ponape, Kusaie, and, outside of Micronesia, on Easter and other islands, suggest that a prehistoric race of considerable culture once lived here. It left enduring monuments but no written records.

And the Polynesians who came later also wrote nothing down. Their descendants do not know when or how they came.

But research shows that it was about the beginning of the Christian Era when they began to pack up and move from their old home, the Malay Archipelago. They were pushed out by the incoming Malays advancing from Asia.

It was the eternal story of force—of better machines of war triumphing over inferior machines. The Malays had weapons of metal; the old-timers, weapons of stone. The Stone Age gave way before the Iron Age. Fleets of canoes sailed eastward to the multitudinous islands of the Pacific. That was the great Polynesian migration.

During the centuries that followed, the people of certain islands remained as pure as when they had first arrived, untouched by other races. Their islands were too remote from the Asiatic mainland to be easily affected.

Not so with Micronesia. Its position, so important today, began to show its importance then. It was close to everything that mattered. Japan on the north, China and the Philippines on the west, the great rich lands of Borneo, Celebes and New Guinea on the southwest, the Melanesian island labyrinth on the south, pure Polynesia on the southeast, all began to pour racial elements into the pot.

Bloods were mixed. And out of the pot came a man, still brown, but

15

inclined to a Mongoloid yellow, muddied by tinges of Melanesian black, looking at you through a slightly slanted eye and speaking a language that was a jigsaw puzzle of roots from ancestral Polynesian, Malay, Chinese, Japanese, various Philippine tongues, and many others, including Hindustani. Nothing could illustrate more graphically the relationship of Micronesia to the Asiatic world.

Then came Magellan. In 1521 he discovered what are now called the Marianas. A century later Spanish Jesuit missionaries settled on the islands.

Thanks to the adventurous spirit of Spanish buccaneers, the Pacific became more or less a Spanish ocean.

Spain held it very loosely. England might have had it; and Sir George Grey was not the only Englishman to dream of a federation of all the isles of the South Pacific under the British flag. But nothing was done.

And now, with Japan dominant, an Englishman who likes to do his lamenting in the Latin he learned at Oxford remarks to me sadly, "Tarde venientibus ossa." Those who come late to dinner get only bones.

Germany put in an early bid. She contested Spain's claim to the Carolines (so named in honor of Charles II of Spain). The Pope was called upon to decide the issue. He awarded the islands to Spain, but stipulated free trading rights for Germany. So Spaniards ruled the islands and Germans did the business. The Germans were not content with this arrangement, as we shall see.

The Marshall Islands were explored by the British captains Marshall and Gilbert. Britain did not consolidate their findings and the group was annexed by Germany in 1885. Germany now looked with still more cupidity upon the neighboring Carolines and Marianas.

But the coveted islands fell into the lap of someone who did not want them—but now perhaps wishes very much that he had kept them. Uncle Sam took the Carolines and Marianas from Spain during the Spanish-American War. Germany, of course, had no part in the war, yet she hoped to profit by it.

"His Majesty the Emperor," stated a dispatch from Berlin to the

German ambassador in Washington, "deems it a principal object of German policy to leave unused no opportunity which may arise from the Spanish-American War to obtain maritime fulcra in East Asia."

Germany contrived a secret agreement with the Spaniards by which she was granted an option upon any Spanish lands in the Pacific that could be kept out of the hands of America.

When wind of these intrigues got to John Hay, the American ambassador in London, he wrote in a personal letter to Senator Lodge:

"They want the Philippines, the Carolines, and Samoa. They want to get into our markets and keep us out of theirs. They have been flirting and intriguing with Spain ever since the war began and now they are trying to put the Devil into the head of Aguinaldo. I do not think they want to fight. In fact they frankly tell us they can't. Hatzfeldt said the other day, 'We cannot remove our fleet from German waters.' But they want, by pressure, by threats, and by sulking and wheedling in turn to get something out of us and Spain. There is, to the German mind, something monstrous in the thought that a war should take place anywhere and they not profit by it. This is awfully indiscreet, but I get sick of discretion once in a while. Don't file me."

Since senators are paid by the public for their speech, not their silence, this information promptly became public knowledge. American public opinion had been seriously divided over the question of taking on new commitments in the Far East. The idea that Germany would get what they did not take put a rather new face on the situation. We did not want a close German neighbor in the Pacific. Britain also feared a German Pacific. Hay cabled the Secretary of State, "The British Government prefers to have us retain the Philippine Islands, or failing that, insist upon option in case of future sale."

Japan was not yet strong enough to dare to speak her mind. She pretended to welcome American sovereignty in the Pacific, but she did venture to convey the confidential suggestion that if the United States hesitated to undertake full responsibility in the Philippines Japan was willing to help through a joint or tripartite protectorate.

This raised a new ghost. A Japanese Pacific was no more palatable than a German Pacific and it was a desire to avert another calamity

17

rather than any wish to acquire more territory that led to the reluctant American acceptance of the Philippines.

Guam in Micronesia was also accepted because it was a stepping stone to the Philippines.

The rest of conquered Micronesia was magnanimously turned back to Spain. Spain promptly sold it to Germany for $4,500,000.

America had gone too far, or not far enough. Present events clearly teach that she should have stayed out of the Orient unless prepared to maintain her position there.

It is now painfully clear that no power can hope to hold the Philippines and Guam unless it holds also the enveloping archipelago of Micronesia. Any strong nation with bases in the Carolines which approach to within 500 miles of the Philippines, or the Marianas of which the nearest to Guam is less than fifty miles distant, can take both of these objectives within the first few weeks of war.

We took the lock, the Philippines and Guam, but would not accept the key, Micronesia.

So the matter uneasily rested until World War I. Germany was more active in the islands than Spain had ever been. The Spanish period had been largely a regime of priests who forced their religion upon the islanders with the bloody assistance of Spanish soldiers. Rebellions were frequent and disruptive. The Germans were strong enough to hold their own with only an occasional exception when a German governor was assassinated. They did not worry so much about religion. The natives could stew in paganism for all they cared so long as they raised plenty of copra. The Germans were born traders, not evangelists, and the island industries were developed as a government monopoly. The seat of administration was in German-held New Guinea. Germany also possessed the Bismarck Archipelago, later to become an Australian mandate. She had her feet solidly planted in China.

All this irked Japan, who was beginning to conceive of herself as the proper leader of Asia.

When the World War broke in 1914 Japan saw her opportunity. During the first few days of the war Japanese ships sailed south and occupied the German islands. British ships were also sailing on the same mission but did not get there in time. British authorities were much mortified but could only congratulate their ally, Japan, on her promptness.

Since the Japanese had taken all German islands north of the equator, the British took what was left, the German islands to the south of that line. Of course the final disposition of the islands would be decided by the peace conference at the end of the war. But the Japanese were not disposed to wait until then for an understanding. They made their views plain to the British ambassador in Tokyo in a secret conference on January 27, 1917. On February 16 the ambassador addressed to the Japanese Foreign Minister the following confidential communication:

"His Majesty's Government accedes with pleasure to the request of the Japanese Government for an assurance that they will support Japan's claims in regard to the disposal of Germany's rights in Shantung and possessions in Islands North of the Equator on the occasion of Peace Conference, it being understood that the Japanese Government will, in eventual peace settlement, treat in same spirit Great Britain's claims to German Islands South of Equator."

The Japanese agreed to Britain's counter-claim.

Japan next addressed the French government on the subject. France agreed, the *quid pro quo* in this case being that Japan would bend her efforts to bringing China into the war on the side of the Allies. Japan consented.

The Russian government, similarly approached, agreed, and forgot to ask for anything in return.

America had nothing to say about it since she was not yet in the war. The entire deal was put through with Nipponese dispatch during February and March of 1917 so that, when America joined the Allies in April, the destiny of the Pacific islands was already sealed.

I do not suggest that this secret diplomacy without benefit of America was underhanded. If America had been moved to fight for democracy when Germany first flung down the challenge in 1914 instead of after three years' delay, she might have prevented the rising of many ghosts which haunted President Wilson at the peace table.

Only American vacillation and lack of a clear-cut Pacific policy were to blame when we assumed territorial commitments in the Western Pacific with the express purpose of forestalling the Germans and Japanese, and then permitted the key to those commitments to fall into the hands first of the Germans and then of the Japanese.

IV:

The Mandate Farce

BEFORE we describe the mandate farce as it was acted out in Micronesia let us acknowledge that the mandate system, properly applied, holds the greatest hope for the administration of territories whose people are not yet able to organize and maintain their own government.

But such a mandate should be exercised not by one power as its own special prerogative, but by an international body representing all powers.

This principle finds its solid basis in the rights of man. Mankind has a right to rule mankind, but no national group is justified in dictation of the conduct of any other group.

A mandate under the control of a single power is likely to be used for the benefit of that power with slight regard for the benefit of the inhabitants.

When World War I ended, the former German colonies in Africa, the Near East and the Pacific were in Allied hands. What should be done with them? Should they be annexed by the various victorious powers?

Those who had fought the war to make the world safe for democracy were a little ashamed of annexation. The Wilsonian current was running strong. "Self-determination" was in the air. The Fourteen Points still rang in men's ears. The Russian Revolutionists had declared themselves for "no annexations." Labor organizations in some countries were opposed to exploitation of backward peoples.

The mandate system was much nobler as at first conceived than as finally adopted. The suggestion came from many quarters that former German colonies should be placed under international control.

Those who opposed this "Utopian" idea had good arguments ready to hand. International administration had not worked well where tried, for example in Samoa. Australia and New Zealand feared to be exposed to the consequences of a wishy-washy administration of the former German islands south of the equator. They felt that the only way to be sure that the job was done thoroughly was to do it themselves. The Australian troops who had occupied New Guinea expected it to remain Australian. New Zealand had raised the flag in German Samoa and had no intention of taking it down. The Union of South Africa had spread northward at the expense of German possessions. France wanted part of the Cameroons. Japan, on the strength of her secret treaties, expected control of Micronesia with no strings attached.

So idealism stepped down from its perch and soiled its feathers in the mud of reality.

General Smuts of South Africa proposed that a League of Nations should allot mandates to single powers but should hold the right, in case of violation of the mandate, to withdraw it and grant it to another power.

Even this proposal was too advanced. The mandates were allocated by the Allied powers rather than by the League. Annual reports were to be submitted to the League which it could discuss ad infinitum but if it didn't like them there was nothing it could do about them. If the supervising nation was violating its pledges the League had no clear authority to withdraw the mandate. And of course the original idea of a League "to enforce peace" had already been shorn of any means of enforcement.

So Japan could smile politely when peace conference hypocrisy substituted the locution "mandate" for "annexation." Japan accepted this pleasantry as in no wise affecting her proprietorship over the islands.

Japan's maneuvering was completely successful. "The thing which more than any other contributed to this success," wrote E. T. Williams who as a member of the American Foreign Service was intimately informed of every phase of the Peace Conference, "was Japan's indifference to membership in the League of Nations and an intimation that, if her claims were not allowed she would not enter the League. President Wilson had his heart set upon the formation of such a League as a means to prevent war and the fear that Japan might refuse to enter such an organization weighed heavily no doubt in his decision to yield to Japan's desire."

Japan asked for a declaration of the principle of racial equality. The request should have been granted. Because it was not, it was all the more necessary to mollify Japan with concessions in the Pacific to save her for the League. Quoting again from Mr. Williams, writing in the *American Journal of International Law,* July, 1933,

"The Japanese newspapers . . . were represented as demanding an amendment to the Covenant of the League, abolishing race discrimination among the members of the League. The press urged that Japan hold aloof until that demand had been satisfied. The matter was voted upon by the members of the League, but inasmuch as unanimity was required, and there were votes against the recognition of racial equality, the chair ruled that the proposal had been defeated. Theoretically race equality should be admitted but the unwillingness to do so was due to the fear that restrictions upon immigration of Orientals into the United States, Canada and Australia might be called into question."

The terms of the mandate granted to Japan and under which she has governed Micronesia now for two and a half decades are of historical interest:

Article 1.—The islands over which a mandate is conferred upon his Majesty, the Emperor of Japan (hereinafter called the Mandatory), comprise all the former German islands situated in the Pacific Ocean and lying north of the Equator.

Article 2.—The Mandatory shall have full power of administration and legislation over the territory subject to the present Mandate as an integral portion of the Empire of Japan, and may apply the laws of the Empire of Japan to the territory, subject to such local modifications as circumstances may require. The Mandatory shall promote to the utmost the material and moral well-being and the social progress of the inhabitants of the territory subject to the present Mandate.

Article 3.—The Mandatory shall see that the slave trade is prohibited and that no forced labor is permitted, except for essential public works and services, and then only for adequate remuneration.

The Mandatory shall see that the traffic in arms and ammunition is controlled in accordance with principles analogous to those laid down in the Convention relating to the control of the arms traffic, signed on September 10, 1919, or in any convention amending same.

The supply of intoxicating spirits and beverages to the natives shall be prohibited.

Article 4.—The military training of the natives, otherwise than for purposes of internal police and the local defense of the territory, shall be prohibited. Furthermore, no military or naval bases shall be established, or fortifications erected in the territory.

Article 5.—Subject to the provisions of any local law for the maintenance of public order and public morals, the Mandatory shall insure in the territory freedom of conscience and the free exercise of all forms of worship, and shall allow all missionaries, nationals of any State Member of the League of Nations, to enter into, travel, and reside in the territory for the purpose of prosecuting their calling.

Article 6.—The Mandatory shall make to the Council of the League of Nations an annual report to the satisfaction of the Council, containing full information with regard to the territory, and indicating the measures taken to carry out the obligations assumed under Articles 2, 3, 4, and 5.

Article 7.—The consent of the Council of the League of Nations is required for any modification of the terms of the present Mandate.

The Mandatory agrees that, if any dispute whatever should arise between the Mandatory and another member of the League of Nations relating to the interpretation or the application of the provisions of the Mandate, such dispute, if it cannot be settled by negotiation, shall be submitted to the Permanent Court of International Justice provided for by Article 14 of the Covenant of the League of Nations.

This is the particular mandate to Japan. Back of it stands the basic definition of the whole mandate system as contained in Article 22 of the Covenant. The first two paragraphs are of most significance. In them we get a clear statement of the mandate idea:

"1. To those colonies and territories which as a consequence of the late war have ceased to be under the sovereignty of the States which formerly governed them and which are inhabited by peoples not yet able to stand by themselves under the strenuous conditions of the modern world, there should be applied the principle that the well-being and development of such peoples form a sacred trust of civilization and that securities for the performance of this trust should be embodied in this Covenant.

"2. The best method of giving practical effect to this principle is that the tutelage of such peoples should be intrusted to advanced nations who, by reason of their resources, their experience or their geographical position, can best undertake this responsibility, and who are willing to accept it, and that this tutelage should be exercised by them as Mandatories on behalf of the League."

So Japan settled down to the performance of her "sacred trust of civilization."

She played the role of the League's docile agent and servant in managing a charge placed in her hands by the League. The sham was kept up that real authority over the mandate belonged to the League. Japan as a League member was merely delegated to handle a League responsibility.

The full piquancy of the farce came out in 1936 when Japan resigned from the League and yet held onto her privilege of membership so far as the mandate was concerned. The play-acting was now over. The pretense that real sovereignty rested in the League and not in Japan was abandoned. Japan announced her intention of holding the islands by force if necessary.

No one dared call her bluff. The League was dumb. The British and American press protested, but British and American officialdom had nothing to say, being only too well aware of the wobbly juridical position of the League and of the whole mandate structure. Japan tore up the document of mandate and defiantly integrated the islands as part of her Empire.

But all this came later. At the beginning Japan was a model of meekness. She dutifully made an annual report to the League, each report consisting of a large printed book of several hundred pages telling everything except what the League wanted to know. Along with the report she sent a representative to Geneva to explain it. When pointed questions were asked, he would amiably explain that he did not have personal knowledge on the point mentioned, but would inquire of his government and be prepared to answer the question in the next annual conference. So the easy-going officials of the League's Mandates Commission were put off from year to year.

In each report the Commission noted with some uneasiness that expenditures on the islands were far out of line with the requirements of commercial development. It was suspected that Japan was violating her pledge to establish no military or naval bases in the islands.

But it was difficult to prove anything. The members of the Mandates Commission, comfortably leather-chaired in Geneva, could hardly contemplate a journey of investigation to the South Seas. Nor did they wish so deliberately to cast suspicion upon a member in good standing of the League. They noted with disquiet that the gates of the mandate had swung shut. No non-Japanese ships were allowed in Micronesian seas. As for the Japanese ships, white men had great difficulty in booking passage on them. To those who ran up against the polite stone wall of resistance in the Nippon Yusen Kaisha ticket offices, the situation breathed a strange air of expectancy. Were great things preparing in the islands? Was there to be war in the Pacific?

V:

"So Sorry—Full Up"

I HAD made many visits to the Far East, writing for British and American publications. Some of the visits were brief. One was five years long. During these sojourns I had traveled through all of Japan's territories and spheres of influence—except Micronesia.

My attempts to secure passage to the *Nanyo,* as the Japanese call their Micronesian dependency, were gently rebuffed.

From 1914 when Japan took the islands no American journalist had been allowed to stop ashore in the *Nanyo.*

A very few American and British travelers had succeeded in securing passage and had usually been hurried through the archipelago, never permitted to stop over on any island from one boat to the next.

One exception was the British Major Bodley. The Japanese ship on which he was traveling was wrecked on the reef of Yap. Even the ingenious Japanese could think of no way to avoid taking shipwrecked passengers ashore. But he spent only three days on the island before a ship arrived to whisk him away.

Another exception, a pretty grim one, was Colonel Earl Ellis of the United States Marines who penetrated Palau, looked about, and then died. The Japanese reported that he had drunk himself to death.

Two United States naval officers managed to slip ashore on Ponape. Nothing more was heard of them until Japan informed the United States that they had lost their lives in an unfortunate accident. A request that the bodies be returned to the United States was refused.

Major Bodley, bitter over Japanese refusal to let him see any island except so long as the ship lay in port, wrote me in 1935:

"Unless you have strings which you can pull with strength, I think you will find difficulties in getting a passage—much less stopovers."

26

After years in Japan, I had strings, but pulling them seemed to avail nothing.

More successful was Alexander Hume Ford, Director of the Pan Pacific Union. Because of the hands-across-the-seas nature of his organization, he was accredited with being a "true friend" of Japan and was allowed a through ticket.

Upon his return, I met him in the place where one always meets anyone—the lobby of Tokyo's Imperial Hotel.

The captain of the Japanese ship on which he had traveled had been very co-operative, he told me, and had given him much information about the islands.

"But did you get off the ship and stay in the islands?"

He looked at me with some alarm.

"My dear man," he said, "that isn't done."

I wrote to Ernst Lang, head of the Liebenzeller Mission which supervised some German missionaries left over from the German regime. He replied warily, not knowing whether he dared have anything to do with me.

"The Japanese who are now in possession of the islands are very suspicious, therefore you must not be surprised if they examine you and observe wherever you go. They are doing so with every foreigner. For that reason we do not like to have much connection with foreigners visiting the islands, but if you are going as missionaries, that will be another thing I hope."

We could not pretend to be going as missionaries, therefore had to bear up under the suspicion that we were going as spies.

Foreigners could not be absolutely barred, because the mandate stipulated free access to the islands. But they could be, and were, artfully discouraged.

"Full up" was the first excuse of the Tokyo steamship office. When I insisted upon seeing the passenger list and found that the ship was anything but full up, there were other excuses.

It was a very dangerous voyage, I was told, the shipping lanes were full of treacherous reefs, typhoons were frequent, tropical diseases were prevalent, and the natives were savage head-hunters.

Moreover the ships, all being Japanese, served nothing but Japanese food. My wife and I might grow weary of rice, bean-curd, raw fish, and octopus tentacles.

And there was no place to stay on the islands. There were no hotels.

"We can live in Japanese inns."

"On most islands there are none."

"We have an 'Explorer's Tent.' It can be set up under any palm tree."

"But each piece of land belongs to some native."

"Perhaps he will rent it. Or take us into his house. He may be glad to have paying guests."

The passenger agent looked pained.

"Live with the natives!"

"Why not?" And I tried to make clear how valuable such contacts would be for the purpose of securing certain ethnological material wanted by the National Geographic Society and the American Museum of Natural History.

But considerate officialdom continued to be solicitous of our comfort. And suspicious of our motives.

An officer of the *Kempeitai*, Japanese Gestapo, came to our house in Hayama. He had a notebook. He smilingly asked our ages, our fathers' names, mothers' names, grandfathers' names, grandmothers' names, names of all places we had ever lived in or visited. Finally he asked,

"What do you wish to see in the islands?"

I could hardly say "Fortifications." So I shrugged it off with, "Fauna and flora."

He wrote that down. Then he asked,

"Are they friends of yours?"

Amused, I answered, "Yes."

"How old are they?"

"Well, Fauna may be ten million years old, and Flora considerably older."

It is not prudent to joke with the *Kempeitai*. Mrs. Price unknowingly saved the situation by coming in at that moment from the kitchen with a plate of hot American doughnuts. The officer put away his notebook.

For months we were put off with objections and excuses.

Meanwhile, in Geneva, the Mandates Commission was asking very pointed questions. Why, they inquired of Japan's representative, had an American ship of scientists bent on viewing an eclipse of the sun been refused entry to mandate waters? Why were foreign ships not allowed in the harbors? Why were the island airports not accessible to all nations?

The Commission knew of my attempts, and the attempts of others in the past, to enter the forbidden islands. They charged Japan with barring foreigners. Japan's delegate at Geneva heatedly denied that foreigners were barred. The controversy was published in the European and American press. The discussion was doing Japan no good.

One morning when the cables were particularly hot with criticism of Nippon for her suspected militarization of the mandate, I was received with smiles at the government South Seas Bureau. Tickets for my wife and myself were pressed into my hands.

"Japan is being unjustly accused," the official said. "We have decided that you should go and see for yourself."

I paid for the tickets and demanded a paper authorizing us to land on any island and go where we pleased. Grudgingly, it was provided.

Our troubles were over.

But I soon found that the document was worthless. The Japanese captains of the ships on which we traveled had instructions to prevent us from leaving the ship at any port.

Our troubles had only begun.

VI:

Into Forbidden Seas

I DO NOT know the sensation of stepping off the edge of the world but I believe it must be something like that of embarking for little-known Micronesia. As soon as the ship has pulled away from the dock you are a month from Japan. That is, if you should change your mind as to the lure of potluck with the natives, it would take you one month to get back to that wharf—by the first return steamer at the nearest port of call.

"Why are there so few ships on this run?" you ask a Japanese companion at the rail as the last paper streamer connecting the ship with the shore breaks and falls into the bay.

"Wrecks! Two ships have been lost in a year. Reefs, you know—coral reefs—those waters are full of them. Get between two of them—then along comes a sudden squall, or a typhoon—and the ship just naturally goes on the coral. One of the most dangerous steamship routes in the world. Yes," he adds, looking over our venerable *Yokohama Maru* appraisingly, "it's fortunate they put only their oldest ships on this run—so it doesn't matter much if they do smash up."

That slightly forlorn feeling is accentuated by the fact that we are the only foreigners on board. The Japanese are pleasant enough and it is hard to imagine anything sinister behind their polite indrawn breath. But we cannot forget that we are going to a destination where we are not wanted and from which certain of our compatriots failed to come back.

Gradually we make friends and the feeling of strain vanishes, for a time.

Our ship carries twenty first-class passengers, sixty intermediate and two hundred steerage. The steerage passengers are going to Saipan to work in the sugar factory. An agent in Japan contracted them for periods varying from five to fifteen years. He paid each of them an advance of about twenty yen and bought their steamship tickets. They will get one yen a day (about 25 cents). The day will be ten hours long. Some of them tell us that they didn't want to come. When they signed up they didn't know it was to be for so long, or so far away. The sugar company is so heavily subsidized as to be practically an arm of the government.

If the Japanese abuse their own people in this fashion, we wonder a little what treatment is accorded the Kanaka natives of the islands.

Southward. Past the suicide island, Oshima, in whose volcano every year more than eight hundred of the disillusioned seek sulphurous oblivion. Past Lot's Wife. Into translucent waters. The overcoat is still comforting.

Two days out and the ship's officers all appear in white. It happens to be a raw winter day. That makes no difference. It's a rule of the company. White two days out. But heavy red flannel underwear may be seen peeping from under the captains white cuff!

We pass among the brawny islands called the Bonins or Ogasawara. We are following in reverse the path United Nations forces will take to Tokyo. For those coming along this particular route, the Bonins will be the last stepping stone before the Japanese homeland. They lie 550 miles from the Japanese coast.

The Bonins are now Japanese, but they were once white mans territory. The American flag waved over them; before that, the British. Their earliest recorded discovery was by the Spanish explorer Villalobos in 1543. Later the Japanese found them and named them Munin meaning "empty of men," of which name Bonin appears to be a corruption. Their strategic importance was emphasized by the Japanese patriot, Hayashi Shihei, in 1783. He narrowly escaped death for his pains, for this was during Japan's era of seclusion when no Japanese was permitted to leave the country, contact with the outside world was forbidden, and any man suggesting Japanese expansion in the Pacific or Asia was considered a traitor.

How greatly has Japan changed.

American whalers put in at "Empty of Men" for water and fresh fruits.

In 1827 the British captain Frederick William Beechey took possession of them for George IV. But the boss of the islands was for many years an American. His name was Nathaniel Savory. He came from Hawaii, bringing with him a Dane, an Englishman, a Genoese and 25 Hawaiian natives. Savory ruled the little colony.

In 1853 the man who opened Japan dropped in at the Bonins on his way. Commodore Perry dreamed of coaling stations at intervals across the Pacific for the convenience of American ships.

Why wouldn't the Bonins make a good coaling station? But they belonged to Britain—or did they?

Perry decided that they didn't, raised the American flag, formulated an American code of government, and persuaded the colonists to elect Savory chief magistrate. He also established a base for his squadron in the near-by Loochoo Islands. He believed that American presence in islands so close to Japan would persuade that country to listen to American demands.

He too realized the high strategic importance of the islands. He could hardly foresee the time some ninety years later when American presence in these islands would indeed persuade Japan to listen to American demands.

Perry's mission was to open a road to China. He was commissioned to open Japan not so much for the purpose of trade with Japan as of utilizing Japan as a coaling station on the way to the richer East. He believed that the Bonins under an American flag would not merely be a foot inside the Japanese door, but a way-station to China.

"Every day of observation strengthens the opinion," he wrote to Washington, "that the large and increasing commerce of the United States with this part of the world makes it not only desirable, but indispensable, that ports of refuge should be established at which vessels in distress may find shelter."

"Some other power," he warned, "less scrupulous, may slip in and seize upon the advantages which should justly belong to us."

And when his government continued indifferent, he wrote again:

"It is self-evident that the course of coming events will ere long make it necessary for the United States to extend its jurisdiction beyond the limits of the western continent, and I assume the responsibility of urging the expediency of establishing a foothold in this quarter of the globe, as a measure of positive necessity to the sustainment of our maritime rights in the east."

But American policy still stood on Jefferson's principle that "nothing should ever be accepted that would require a navy to defend it."

America's action in flinging open the gates of Japan without preparing to defend American interests against the powerful Japan that was to be the outcome of such action, was another case of going too far or not going far enough.

The opening of Japan was as Foster Rhea Dulles says in his excellent *America in the Pacific* "an ironic outcome to Perry's own ambitions in the Far East. He hoped to plant the seeds of American power in the western Pacific and launch the United States upon a career of colonial expansion. And he did promote our commercial interests in Asia and raise American prestige to new heights. Yet at the same time the most significant result of his expedition was the impetus it gave to the rise of another Pacific Power which was in time to become our most formidable rival for control of the Western Ocean. If it had been possible in 1853 to foresee Japan's future role, Perry's program might have been viewed at Washington in a far different light."

Perry's proposal to extend over the Loochoos "the vivifying influence and protection of a government like our own" and to make the Bonins, and Formosa as well, American outposts, was declined by his government.

Only seven years after Perry had made Japan world-conscious, the Japanese took the responsibility that Perry had failed to persuade his own government to accept. They dispatched two high officials and forty colonists to hold the Bonins for Japan. They renamed the islands Ogasawara and based their sovereignty on the claim that the islands had really first been discovered by a Japanese, Sadayori, Prince of Ogasawara, in 1593.

"The Bonins thus became to Japan," writes Professor Paul Clyde, who knows well this part of the world, "what Pearl Harbor was to be to the United States—an advanced naval outpost in the Pacific."

Japan annexed the Loochoos in 1879, calling them Ryukyu and Formosa in 1895, renaming it Taiwan.

Our ship was not scheduled to call at the Bonins, but our captain put in on a special errand for his government. We entered the harbor of the island known as Peel in pre-Japanese days, now Chichi Jima (Father Island). The ten largest of the Bonins have been rather fantastically renamed after the various members of the family, as follows, from south to north:

> Ani Jima (Elder Sister Island)
> Mei Jima (Niece Island)
> Haha Jima (Mother Island)
> Chichi Jima (Father Island)
> Ani Shima (Elder Brother Island)
> Ototo Jima (Younger Brother Island)

At the northern end are Yome Shima (Bride Island) and Muko Shima (Bridegroom Island), separated or perhaps we should say joined by Nakadachi Shima (Go-Between Island). The go-between who finds a mate for your daughter or son is regarded almost as a member of the family in Japan.

There are twenty islands altogether in the Bonins although, if one includes islets, as many as 97 may be found. Strangely enough, the number varies from time to time. This part of the Pacific floor is in a state of volcanic commotion and small islands appear and disappear. Several earthquakes a day are recorded. Submarine disturbances may pile the ocean high along the island shores on one day and on the next suck it so low that boats are beached on the rocks.

The harbor of Peel Island (we may as well turn back to the old name for it may soon be restored) is a minor Japanese naval base. It is comparable to Pearl Harbor only in its strategic position, not in strength. The harbor is too small for a major naval establishment. Looking from the ship's deck—our stop in port was too brief for shore-going, even if that had been allowed—we saw a circular harbor, actually the crater of an ancient volcano, a mile and a half wide. Rugged, craggy hills nearly surrounded the port. Tucked between them and the water was a small town of Japanese colonists, and multi-colored natives who came out to our anchorage in small boats. Doubtless there was some American blood in these folk, but so well mixed with the blood of the other early inhabitants, Hawaiian, British, Genoese and Danish, as to be indistinguishable. Confusing the issue further, the American sailors had

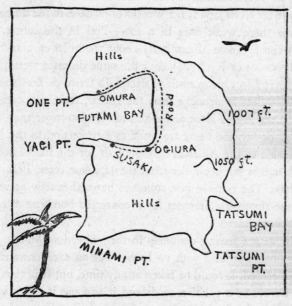

CHICHI JIMA OR PEEL ISLAND

imported dark wives from the South Seas. Probably there was one blood not to be found in the mixture—Japanese. Only rarely do the Sons of Heaven deign to adulterate their pure strain with that of "inferior" races.

Certain hilltops had a peculiar truncated appearance that one associates with hidden gun emplacements. I have no doubt that we were looking into the muzzles of unseen shore batteries. Japan was still bound by her pledge made at the Washington Conference in 1922 not to fortify the Bonins. But foreigners were strictly barred from the islands. An Anglican bishop who had made a yearly trip from Japan to the Bonins to visit his churches there was told in 1935 that further visits would not be advisable. He was the last man of alien blood to step ashore.

But the naval base of Peel Island need cause no tremor to the lads of the United Nations advancing from the south. They will already have overcome far more difficult hazards than this. Indeed, Japan's stronger outposts are far from Japan; her weaker ones, close to the home islands.

Here are three weak ones in a row—Peel in the center, Marcus (called by the Japanese Minamitori) about 700 miles east, and Amami (in the Loochoos or Ryukyu) about the same distance west.

These three bases mean nothing except in terms of fleet strength. If the Japanese fleet is stronger than the Allied, these outposts are formidable. If the Allied force above and afloat is stronger than Japanese air and sea power, the bases are futile as a protection to the Japanese, but invaluable to the Allies as springboards for the final assault upon Japan. Marcus is but 900 miles from the Japanese coast, Peel, 550, and Amami, 200. The trio are best suited to be used exactly as we would wish to use them—as air bases for a concerted bombing attack upon Japanese cities.

Already we are feeling definitely in their direction. Marcus, a small island five miles around with no harbor but an excellent airfield, has twice been raided. It could be taken at any time, but doubtless will not be until we are in a position to defend it and use it along with Peel and Amami in the final roundup.

So it is quite possible that the Bonins will soon return to American or British control—who cares which? Perry's dream will belatedly come true. They will be a small but attractive acquisition. The archipelago is rich in pineapples and palms, cedar, boxwood, ironwood, rosewood, sandal and white oak. There are sugar plantations on all the important islands. The climate is ideal. The temperature, winter and summer alike, hovers around 75 degrees. The beaches are lovely coral strands. The islets are enticing as sites for homes but he who buys one and builds a house on it is apt to wake up some fine morning and find both house and lot disappearing beneath the waves.

This volcanic uncertainty persists in the islands we pass as we sail on to the south. On the captain's chart is the legend: "An island [Lindsay] reported hereabouts unsuccessfully searched for by U.S.S. *Alert* 1881." The captain remarks that an island is missing now that was here a year ago. Names on the chart suggest the ominous forces at work beneath: "Disappointment Island," "Submarine Volcano," "Sulphur Island," "Volcano Island."

Then we enter mysterious Micronesia through a portal guarded by a fire-breathing Cerberus. The flaming island-volcano, Uracas, is the counterpart of Stromboli off the Italian coast. It erupts frequently and violently, its white-hot coat of flowing lava illuminating the night, its reverberations shaking the passing ship, and its ashes strewing the decks.

"We pass it at two in the morning," said the captain. "Do you wish to be awakened?"

"*If* it erupts," was the cautious answer.

It was Uracas's night off. We were not awakened. But on the return voyage we were to see and photograph it by daylight—a truly imposing cinder-black cone 1,046 feet high with perfect toboggan-slopes kept smooth and straight by the frequent flows of lava and ashes. It is crowned with white sulphur, deceptively like snow. Dense clouds of yellowish smoke belch from its crater. Forever it grumbles under its sulphurous breath. Of course not a sprig of green has the temerity to grow on this savage island.

We are now among the islands of Micronesia, a world by itself with its 1,400 islands spread over a sea measuring 1,300 miles north and south and nearly 3,000 miles east and west, reaching within 2,000 miles of Hawaii on the east, 500 miles of the Philippines on the west, and running farther south than Singapore. It is halted, in fact, only by the equator.

The first islands we pass are those of the necklace-like string of the Marianas. They are picturesque volcanic islands sometimes a thousand feet high. From north to south they are named Supply Reef, Maug, Asuncion, Agrihan, Pagan, Alamagan, Guguan, Sariguan, Anatahan and Medinilla. Most of them are uninhabited and unvisited except by fishermen. They seem of small military value.

But the southern islands of the Mariana chain are quite different. They are larger, broader, better fitted to bear airdromes on their backs. Saipan, Tinian, Agiguan and Rota are not volcanic but built of coralline limestone.

We reached beautiful Saipan on a bright winter morning. The ship anchored outside the reef, two miles off the west shore, in a translucent jade green sea mottled with dark brown patches where seaweed floated just beneath the surface. The green island rose from the shore in gentle slopes and level terraces, ideal for either sugar plantations or airfields.

We had been on shipboard for five days and were eager to feel solid ground beneath our feet.

VII:

Saipan, Sugar-Coated Bomb

"You will not wish to go ashore here." The captain had come up behind us as we stood at the rail.

I reminded him that we had a permit from the Tokyo authorities.

"Ah, so," he said. "But they left it to me to arrange details. I fear you would not be comfortable on this island. There are many flies."

I tried not to smile. You must never be amused at a Japanese if you hope to get around him. And you must agree with him.

"Indeed!" I said gravely. "In that case, we would be much better off on board."

A lighter drawn by a tug came up on the starboard side to take off passengers. The captain was busy on the port side, watching the cargo barges. Just as the tug was beginning to pull the passenger lighter away, we ran down the companionway and hopped in.

There was a shout above us. The captain was glaring down from the bridge. Mary smiled her most engaging smile and held up something she had brought from our cabin. It was a fly swatter.

The captain's face was a study. Never were a smile and a scowl more perfectly combined in one expression.

On the dock was the ubiquitous Japanese policeman.

"You are the Americans, yes?" he accused us. "I heard about you. But I understood you would remain on board."

"So sorry," I said in the best Japanese manner. "Slight mistake."

I produced the paper. He waved it aside.

"I shall have to take you to the governor," he announced sternly.

This was all that could be desired, for the path to the governor's bungalow led for two miles through town and countryside, affording an excellent idea of Saipan. And when the squat, jovial little governor saw us and found us harmless, he not only permitted us to roam at will over his precious island, but at our request radioed governors of other islands, suggesting that they receive us.

The captain was right—there are flies on Saipan. The formerly unproductive Marianas are now plantations of sugar cane. In the Saipan sugar factory, whose manager trained in an American mill in Cuba, train-loads of cane come in at one end and sugar comes out at the other. The pressed and crushed cane is used as fuel for the boilers.

A sweet smell not only hangs over the roaring factory but pervades the entire island, and seems to have attracted all the flies of the Pacific.

In a small wayside fruit shop we had lunch, fighting the flies for every bite. Our Japanese policeman ordered bean soup. When it was set before him it contained six flies. We watched with curiosity. Would he send it back? Would he pick out the flies with his chopsticks?

He raised the bowl to his mouth, locked his long upper teeth over the edge to form a sieve, and drank the soup. The six flies remained in the bowl.

He smiled. "We get used to them," he said.

The fly is not without honor in Saipan. A fly saved the island. A certain insect was ruining the sugar cane. The sugar experts imported a parasitic tachinid fly from New Guinea, *Microceromasia sphenophori*

Vill. by name. It laid its eggs in the pupa of the harmful insect, and when its larvae hatched they fed upon the pupa, thus destroying it.

Therefore flies, at least those of this particular family, are enshrined in the affections of Saipan sugar folk. They must never be killed. And since it is difficult at a glance to distinguish them from other varieties, all flies gain immunity.

Saipan, when one can see it through the flies, is a lovely isle of billowing cane fields edged with coconut palms, breadfruit, banana, flame trees and tree ferns. The oleander and scarlet hibiscus spread riots of color. Also flowering gorgeously is the crape myrtle called by the Japanese *sarusuberi* (monkey slide) because the trunk is so slippery that a monkey cannot climb it. There are also odd "sleeping plants" which close their leaves at sunset and open them at sunrise. They are indeed so sensitive to light that they will fold when a dark cloud obscures the sun and open when it passes. We recognize the small tree known to science as the *Barringtonia asiatica,* the poisonous fruit of which is crushed and dropped into pools. It has a narcotic effect upon the fish which, stupefied, float belly-up to the surface and are readily scooped in with a hand net. The poison does not affect the edibility of the fish.

Fruit is abundant. We sample papayas, bananas, custard apples and guavas. The most delicious fruit is not yet ripe—the mango. The tree on which it grows is one of nature's most magnificent, with a glossy broad head casting so dense a shade that "sleeping plants" beneath it would never wake.

The male rose-crowned fruit dove announces to us with its loud colors that we are now in the latitude of tropical birds. Its colors are rose, green, yellow, orange and purple. How could any female of its species resist it when it perches in the sunlight, presses its bill against its breast while erecting the bright feathers at the back of its neck, and booms its low call?

A comic bird is the megapode which flies as sluggishly as a cargo plane and waddles when it walks. It is useful in the garden, for it industriously scrapes up the decayed leaves and rubbish into a mound in which it lays its eggs. It is half domesticated and will come running if you knock two stones together.

40

A black object flew close over our heads flapping slowly like a crow, and an unpleasant odor like that of dirty wet rags floated down. A boy brought the thing to earth with a slingshot. It was a flying fox, three feet broad from tip to tip. Its face was foxlike with pinched nose, small pointed ears and large eyes. The flesh is eaten by the natives. It is said to be good though a bit tough, and has no odor after the skin is removed. But we did not try it.

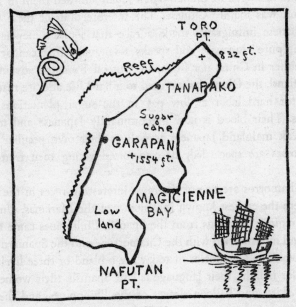

SAIPAN

Saipan is hotter, for some reason, than islands nearer the equator. The overcoat that felt so good in Japan is parked at the N.Y.K. office to be picked up on the return voyage and we buy sun helmets in a little Japanese store. Some idea of the difference between British and Japanese economy may be had from the fact that the same sort of pith helmet that would have cost five dollars in India may be had here for fifty cents.

Saipan, with all its exotic natural charm, is not quite the perfect

South Sea isle. There are too many people in coats and pants. The brown, bare and picturesque Kanakas are few. Scurrying everywhere are busy Japanese. Their number has been swelled today by the 200 sugar slaves who came on our ship. There are 40,000 Japanese here, 4,000 Chamorros and 1,000 Kanakas. Seventy per cent of the Japanese are Okinawas; that is, they come from the Okinawa (Loochoo or Ryukyu) Islands. The Loochoos, like so many territories Japan possesses, once belonged to China. When Japan annexed them in 1879 the population was mainly Chinese. The interbreeding of these Chinese with Japanese immigrants made a race that looks somewhat better than the "pure" Japanese and speaks a language that can be understood neither in China nor in Japan. Cut off from the advantages of the mainland, the Okinawas are used to a hard life and are readily impressed for hard labor at low pay in the sugar plantations of the Marianas. Their blood is now predominantly Japanese and many of them speak mainland Japanese as well as their own peculiar dialect. Their bosses are spectacled, staccato-voiced young men from Japan proper.

The Chamorros are one of the most interesting races in the Pacific. They were the earliest known inhabitants of the Marianas. Under the Spanish regime, Tagalogs from the Spanish Philippines came to these islands and intermarried with the Chamorros—and the Spaniards added their quota. The Chamorros of today are a blend of three lively races. Their color is light, their language is half Spanish, their women wear the long skirts and balloon sleeves of the Philippines, and their men play guitars.

While our ship lay at anchor we stayed at the balconied, tropical-Spanish hacienda of Concepcion Reyes. The home of this handsome widow was always overflowing with relatives, friends, and perfect strangers, for if you hear the sound of music in a Chamorro house, you just walk in. There is none of the exclusiveness of the Japanese home.

Music there was, day and night, and dancing on the floor of polished wood—bouncing dances that made the colored pictures of saints and angels tremble on the walls. But not on Sundays. Then guitars were laid aside, the men put on embroidered coats, the women placed high combs in their hair and mantillas over their shoulders, and all went to the Spanish mission.

∴

A grimmer reality of Saipan was its development as a military base. What we learned of the preparations, throughout the whole Micronesian archipelago, for the war that has now come, proved of interest to our Navy Department and State Department. Shorn of details, the situation in Saipan is as follows.

The area of the island is 72 square miles. It is fifteen miles long, north and south, and about four miles wide. There are no high mountains, the chief elevations from north to south being 832 feet, 947, 1,554, 479 and 294. Between these mild elevations are flat areas ideally suited for the several airfields that have been built on Saipan. The southern end of the island is low and flat.

The only town, Garapan, lies on the west side. The whole western shore is bordered by a lagoon edged by a coral reef. Outside this reef our ship anchored and a lighter brought passengers through a break in the reef across the lagoon to the town docks.

Since the loading of cargoes of sugar into a ship lying two miles off shore and more than often rolling in a heavy sea was difficult and expensive, the Japanese began to cut a deep channel 90 meters wide and 1,600 long through the reef and to dredge the lagoon so that ships might come up to a pier in a quiet harbor, the reef serving as a sea wall.

They were hard at work on this project when we visited the island. The pier, made of a demolished hill, was almost completed. The coral floor of Tanapako Bay, for so the man-made harbor was called, was being dredged away. The new harbor would be about a thousand yards in diameter. It would accommodate, at the very most, four ships of not more than 3,000 tons.

The absurdity of League of Nations fears that Tanapako Bay was being developed as a naval base was apparent to anyone who would sit swinging his legs over the edge of the new pier. He could look across the lagoon, over the low reef, and across the sea for miles. Likewise a battleship miles away could look into and shoot into the lagoon. It was entirely exposed. A reef scarcely high enough to make the waves comb was its only protection. There was no bay guarded by headlands or high islands. The shore line was practically straight. Behind it there were no cliffs or crags that would serve as a shelter for guns. The land sloped upward gradually for a distance of two or three miles inland and every point on that slope would make an ideal target for an enemy ship. If Japanese strategists were designing a trap in which to commit naval hara-kiri they could devise nothing better than Tanapako Bay.

But on the other side of the island is a bay worthy of the name. It is Magicienne Bay. It lies between two short peninsulas and is roughly two miles square. Here too the hills bordering the harbor are low, averaging less than 400 feet. But this harbor will undoubtedly be used by the Japanese as a minor naval base. It is quite possible that some of the large expenditures that distressed the League of Nations went not where the Japanese claimed they went, into the sugar port, but into the improvement of Magicienne Bay for the purposes of war.

The chief value of Saipan lies not in her harbors but in her usefulness as an airdrome. Even short-range fighter planes, by making stops on the intervening islands, can easily cover the 1,300 miles from the Japanese mainland and will find plenty of parking space. For Nippon's heavy land-based bombers it is an ideal springboard—and will be just as ideal for our own when we are ready to make use of it. Even before the capture of the Bonins splits the distance, long-range bombers based on Saipan can reach any center in Japan.

It is a pity that the Japanese who have so capably developed the commercial possibilities of the islands have by aggression forfeited the right to enjoy the fruits of their labor. Saipan in peace time exports sugar to the value of more than $6,000,000 annually. Tapioca has also been intensively cultivated and has yielded a rich return. The fishing industry of the island is scientifically organized.

The boom town, Garapan, is a place of contrasts. The streets are choked with charcoal-burning automobiles and primitive oxcarts. The buildings include thatched huts of the Kanakas, substantial stone houses left from the German regime—looking as if they had been built for a land of storm and snow—and modern Japanese stores. An old Spanish mission contrasts sharply with near-by radio towers, dried-bonito factories, and a half-mile of geisha houses. There were in 1937 nearly 13,000 vehicles in Saipan, 171 miles of road and 93 miles of railroad.

Brisk little Japanese boys attend modern schools. Attendance is compulsory—for them, but not for the Chamorros or Kanakas. No one cares much if they remain ignorant. Anyhow they will disappear in time. The modern tempo is too fast for them. They are being squeezed out. They must lease their land to a Jap at the Jap's own figure—and if he does not pay, nothing can be done about it. By this smooth process most of the land has passed into Japanese hands. The Japanese trade only with each other. The Chamorro and his Catholic faith are derided. When a Chamorro lad had the courage to say to a taunting Jap, "Please respect our God as we respect your Emperor," he was thrown in jail and never seen again—for it was the most grave of offenses to speak in the same breath of the Japanese Emperor and the Christian God.

"I hope you had a pleasant time on shore," said the captain when we came aboard. "I am glad I was able to arrange it for you."

"We appreciate your kindness very much."

Bows and inhalations.

VIII:

Tinian, Paradise Lost

So close together are these "anchored aircraft carriers" that only four miles of sea separate Saipan from the next island, Tinian.

Coasting down the shore of Tinian toward the anchorage at the southern end we saw another great natural airdrome, for Tinian is an almost level coral flat thirteen miles long, six wide, with a total area of 38 square miles. It has elevations only at the northern and southern ends and these average not more than five hundred feet. The country is open and parklike, groves of big trees alternating with sugar plantations.

Tinian has no bay for the protection of ships. The *Yokohama Maru* anchored a mile off the southwestern shore. A tug came puffing out towing a lighter. No objections were made when we stepped with others into the lighter, and presently we were invited to come up higher and sit in state behind the wheel of the tug. Passing through a break in the coral reef which is dangerous because invisible, we drew up alongside a cement pier.

As we disembarked, the inevitable young man stepped up. "I will guide you."

But it was not a policeman this time. Tada was the local superintendent of the *Nanyo Kohatsu Kabushiki Kaisha* (South Seas Development Company) a gargantuan concern under direct government control and operating on government subsidies. It is responsible for the entire industrial development of all Japanese Micronesia. *Kohatsu* is a magic word in the South Seas, a word of dread to some, of opportunity to others. The *Kohatsu* has broken many a man and made many a man rich. It regards the dark islanders merely as so many labor units and has power to impress them, and pay them as and if it pleases.

But in Tinian it could not mistreat the natives, for there were none. They had been deported long ago to other islands by the Spaniards who loved this island so well that they wanted it as their private estate.

The business of the *Kohatsu* on Tinian is sugar. A large sugar factory stood just north of the pier.

As we left the pier we passed under a triumphal arch which workmen were decorating with gaudy paper streamers and sprays of foliage.

"Big celebration tomorrow," Tada explained. "In honor of completion of the sugar factory."

It was worth celebrating if one could judge from the Grand-Central-like proportions of the quarter-mile long, cement-walled factory.

46

"How long did it take to build?"

"Five years."

The Japanese had come to mandated Tinian with the intention of staying.

We crossed twelve tracks converging from the plantations to the sugar factory—a veritable Chicago railroad yards, but in miniature, the tracks two-foot gauge, the locomotives small with falsetto whistles.

Although we had been resting on board, hospitality required that we first go to the *Kohatsu Club* to "rest." Shoes off, we padded through an inn-like building, upstairs, to a *tatami*-floored room overlooking a lovely garden with pool and flowering trees. We sat and drank cider. Tada told us of Tinian's present and we told him of its past—for we had been reading of the thrilling visit of that adventurous Englishman, Anson, to Tinian in 1742.

England was then at war with Spain. Commodore Anson was sent to attack Spanish possessions in the Pacific. The Pacific is a big ocean, and was bigger in the days of sail. Going for months without finding land where fresh meat and vegetables could be obtained, the crew succumbed to scurvy. No day passed without the burial of eight or ten men, sometimes twelve. The captain and three-fourths of the men were near death.

So it is small wonder that Tinian looked like paradise itself when it was sighted on the morning of August 27. Careless of the chance that the island might be strongly garrisoned by Spaniards, Anson anchored, and headed an expedition to shore in the pinnace and cutter. He encountered only a Spanish sergeant and a few dark helpers who had been jerking beef. For the island was used at that time as a cattle range to supply beef for the Spanish colony on Guam.

Imagine a crew of starving sailors set down amid an unlimited supply of fresh beef. According to the diary of the ship's chaplain,

"The Spanish sergeant assured us that there was plenty of very good water; that there was an incredible number of cattle, hogs, and poultry running wild on the island, all of them excellent in their kind; that the woods afforded sweet and sour oranges, limes, lemons, and coconuts

47

in great abundance, besides a fruit peculiar to these islands, which served instead of bread."

Twenty-one men were buried on the first and second day. Then the surviving invalids began to recover. They remained for two months on the island. The chaplain's description of Tinian still holds good:

"The soil is everywhere dry and healthy, and being withal somewhat sandy, it is thereby the less disposed to a rank and overluxuriant vegetation; and hence the meadows and bottoms of the woods are much

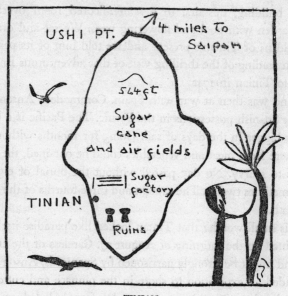

TINIAN

neater and smoother than is customary in hot climates . . . These vallies and the gradual swellings of the ground which their different combinations gave rise to were most beautifully diversified by the mutual encroachments of woods and lawns, which coasted each other and traversed the island in large tracts. . . . Hence arose a number of the most entertaining prospects."

And he waxed even more enthusiastic as he described the thousands of fat cattle, "lords of this happy soil," the myriads of poultry laying fabulously large eggs, the pigs that God made for roasting, the coconuts "with the cabbages growing on the same trees" by which he doubtless referred to the new leaf-shoots from the palm heart which resemble cabbages and are a favorite South Sea dish.

This Heaven-favored isle was now, by conquest, a British possession. But Anson had no means to enforce his claim. To do so it would be necessary to conquer nearby Guam, the seat of the Spanish government. But he had only one ship and he looked in vain for other vessels of his scattered fleet to come to his support.

Regretfully he sailed away and lost Tinian to the Spanish who in turn were to lose it to the Germans and they to the Japanese.

"And a good thing," said Tada. "Europeans don't belong here. They had the *Nanyo* for three hundred years. We have done more to develop the *Nanyo* in twenty years than they did in three hundred."

Which could not be denied.

"So long as Japan does not use the islands for military purposes," I suggested, "I'm sure everybody is quite willing that they should be left to Japan to develop."

Tada's face tightened. "It is not for others to dictate Japan's conduct. If the Emperor chooses to use the *Nanyo* for military purposes, his will supersedes the rules of any League of Nations."

Mary smelled a fight. "Shall we go out and see the island?"

We descended to slip on our shoes and walk through fragrant lanes hedged with flowers. Purple bougainvillea embowered the attractive cottages of the Japanese colonists. These homes were not fenced away from public view as in Japan, nor were the gardens artificial miniatures with dwarf pines, stone lanterns and arched bridges. Instead, the yards were full of flowers, allowed to grow as Nature meant them to. Palms cast their long-fingered shade. Papaya trees were heavy with "the melons that grow on trees." Lemons, limes, oranges, guavas, ripened in the warm sun. And the sun was not too warm. The island evidently had sufficient but not excessive rainfall. Beyond the houses stretched fields of sugar cane and pleasant green groves. The only dust rose from the airfield. The inhabitants of this village depended upon rain for

49

drinking water, and every yard contained a large tank, a pipe running to it from the roof.

"Do you get lonesome for Japan?" I asked.

I had never met a Japanese away from home who was not homesick.

"Not at all," said Tada. He went on as if to justify this apparent lack of patriotism. "You see, this is really Japan too. We get all the radio programs direct from Tokyo. And the latest samurai movies. And the weather here is better. We don't have the *nyubai* [Japan's suffocating rainy season]. Instead of being too chilly in winter and too hot in summer, it's just about right all the time. And the swimming is good."

We were now passing through the business section of the little port town. The buildings were typical Japanese structures, light and thin, looking as if they had been thrown up in an afternoon. They stood elbow to elbow down the street with no space between—Japanese stores, school, hair dressing parlor, cinema, phonograph shop, hardware shop, fishmonger's stall, Shinto temple and Buddhist temple. The narrow strip of town was wedged in between a sugar plantation and the lovely coral beach. On the beach rested outrigger canoes of the Loochoo type brought by Okinawas from their old home. The Loochoo canoe is extremely high and so narrow that no one without slim hips could hope to wedge himself into it. Half of the Japanese of Tinian are from the Loochoos.

Then we passed into another world. Contrasting oddly with the tinkling life of the flimsy Japanese town is the majesty of the ruins just outside. A prehistoric race has left behind what appear to have been the foundations of their buildings. Twelve stone columns five feet in diameter and fifteen feet high are topped with great stone hemispheres, flat on top as if they might at one time have supported the floor of an important building, possibly a temple. The natives of Spanish times called these ruins *Houses of the Ancients*. But they knew no better than we what their purpose may have been. For a time it was supposed that they were tombs. One was called *The House of Taga* and there was a tradition that Taga's daughter was buried in the lofty capital. Sure enough, the Spaniards found bones in the cuplike stone hemisphere. But they were unable to judge whether the bones were the remains of an aborigine or of a much more recent islander. No scientific measurements were recorded.

The pillars are of coral rubble solidified by a mortar made of burnt coral lime and sand. If the Chamorros ever knew such a technique they have long since forgotten it. Nor would the Chamorros of today have any idea of how to raise the great half-balls weighing several tons each to the tops of the pillars.

The probability is that the pedestals are the work of the same unknown people who raised gigantic structures and images in Yap, Ponape and Easter during the centuries when Egypt was building the pyramids. But they left no inscriptions on their buildings, as the Egyptians did, to tell their story to later generations.

It is a bit eerie among these ghostlike columns and even the Japanese as well as any Chamorros who visit the island give the *Houses of the Ancients* a wide berth. No one will touch the stones or cultivate the ground near them. Strange apparitions are said to appear—and we began to believe it when, in the gathering dusk, we distinctly saw a face peer out over the edge of one of the bowllike capitals.

"It's only a cat," I said.

The thing made a low moaning "hoooo" the like of which could never come from the throat of a cat.

We looked around for Tada. He was walking away rapidly toward the village, beckoning to us to follow.

"Not that I'm afraid of it at all," he explained when we caught up to him, "but I just don't like it. It's one of the short-eared owls; we have a lot of them on Tinian; they have big eyes and a cat's face, and they catch lizards. But,"—and then the primitive animism that still haunts the mind of the Japanese Shintoist came to the surface—"who knows what it was before it was an owl!"

Perhaps it was Taga's daughter.

IX:

Guam Without Regrets

ONLY six miles from Tinian we pass another "anchored aircraft carrier," Agiguan, a four-by-two mile tableland—small, but some thousands of times more adequate than a floating carrier, and within bombing distance of Japan.

Then comes Rota, a high tableland about nine miles long and four wide, its level sugar plantations easily replaceable and in some cases already replaced by airfields.

Then we see America.

It is hard to believe that peacetime America and Japan lie within forty-nine miles of each other.

We think of South American countries as our close neighbors and seek to develop a "good neighbor policy" and "hemispheric solidarity." That is all very well, except that it leads us into the false notion that Europe is relatively far away and Asia positively remote.

Counting the Canal Zone as our southermost outpost we are still 2,400 miles from Argentina, our most important Latin neighbor, and more than 3,000 miles from Uruguay.

Russia across the Bering Sea is only 52 miles from United States territory.

And Japan lies three miles closer.

From our ship's deck we can see at the same time Japanese Rota and American Guam, 49 miles apart.

This fact has high significance. It was probably one of the causes of the war. The envelopment of Guam by Japanese bases, the closeness of other islands of Japanese Micronesia to the Philippines, the Indies and Hawaii, tempted Japan with the promise of easy initial conquests.

Not that propinquity in itself is a bad thing. The separation of the

United States and the British Empire by nothing more than the unfortified Canadian border spells no danger if the neighbors have made up their minds to be neighborly—and if each is strong enough to assert its rights. But in the Western Pacific a Japan definitely hostile to white sovereignty was faced by weak American outposts thousands of miles from home bases.

In the Washington Disarmament Conference of 1922 the United States agreed not to increase the fortification of the Philippines or Guam. Fulfilling the spirit as well as the letter of this agreement, the United States removed the heavy guns that had been laboriously and expensively installed on Guam's promontories during World War I.

But in 1936 the Washington Treaty expired. Japan refused to renew it.

The way was now open for the fortification of Guam, if desired. In 1939 the Navy asked Congress for $5,000,000 to improve the harbor and airport. The request was refused. The next session of Congress repeated the refusal.

But early in 1941 Congress relented sufficiently to pass an appropriation of $4,700,000 of which more than four million was to be used for harbor improvements including the construction of a breakwater and the balance for "passive defense" facilities such as bomb shelters, communication centers and power plants.

The reluctance of Congress discouraged the Navy from asking for what it really wanted, the sum of $200,000,000 to make Guam an advanced fleet base. Even $75,000,000, the Navy pointed out, would equip Guam as a first-rate air and submarine base. The relatively piffling grant for "passive defense" was grudgingly accepted.

Congress was and still is roundly criticized for refusing to fortify Guam. The criticism of Congress is our most popular indoor sport. I have often joined in it. But sometimes Congress shows a glint of profound wisdom. I believe it was so in this case.

Suppose we had thoroughly fortified Guam. What then?

Turn the picture around. Imagine the Japanese in possession of Catalina Island off the California coast. Suppose that Japan spent $200,000,000 or, for that matter, a billion, or ten billion, in the fortification of Catalina. What would prevent the United States fleet from sailing out of nearby San Diego harbor and taking over Catalina, valuable fortifications and all, within forty-eight hours? The net result would be our enrichment by whatever amount Japan had expended on the island.

An isolated Japanese base within sight of our shores would be helpless and futile. Just as futile and helpless would be Guam, even if armed to the teeth, thousands of miles from home, but in the very heart of the enemy stronghold.

The threat to put America's head in the Japanese jaws was received in Japan with mingled amazement and amusement. That we could be so ignorant of the vulnerability of Guam was incredible. We had forgotten or refused to take seriously the statement of a man who really knew, namely our own "Fighting Bob" Admiral Evans, who said of Guam:

"Anyone who wants it can take it in an hour."

The expenditure of $200,000,000 on Guam would merely have meant a princely gift to Japan from American taxpayers.

Britain spent $600,000,000 on the fortification of Singapore. Japan reaped the benefit.

Fortunately we did not have the time to spend even the appropriation of $4,700,000 in Guam before Japan took the island on the third day of war.

The point is that our position in Guam was untenable from first to last. It would have been tenable if we had occupied not only Guam but all the islands of Micronesia at the close of the Spanish-American War. The alternative was to stay out of the Far East altogether. Either course would have made some sense. A fortified but isolated Guam made no sense.

We need have no regrets for failure to fortify Guam. Thank Heaven and Congress that we did not.

X:

Guam Has Possibilities

WHEN all the islands of these seas are United Nations property, then will be the time to think about pouring money into Guam. For then Guam can take it and pay dividends, industrially, commercially and strategically. It has already proved a valuable way-station for our China clippers. It is on the direct route from California to Hawaii, Manila and Canton. It is an ideal police station for the Western Pacific, 1,500 miles from Tokyo (bombers with that range are already well past the mockup stage), 1,500 from Manila, 1,500 from Australia, 1,500 from Wake. It is the halfway post between Pearl Harbor and Singapore. Most important, it is close to the geographical center of the key archipelago of Micronesia.

What the Navy's Hepburn report in 1938 claimed an isolated base on Guam would do, a base properly supported by other bases in the surrounding 1,400 Micronesian islands actually would do:

"1. Assure practical immunity of the Philippines against hostile attacks;

"2. Impede, if not actually deny, extensive hostile naval operations to the southward;

"3. Reduce to its simplest possible terms the defense of Hawaii and the continental coast of the United States; and

"4. Enable the fleet to operate with greater freedom in meeting emergency conditions that might arise in the Atlantic."

Guam seems to have been intended by nature to serve as a gigantic airdrome. Its entire northern half is one continuous plateau from 200 to 500 feet above the sea. It corresponds roughly to the deck space of 28,000 aircraft carriers. Moreover this plateau is lower in the middle than along the edges, forming a sheltered shallow saucer. It terminates in a precipice which drops sharply to the sea. Viewed from our ship the island reminded one of Gibraltar, except that the cliffs of Guam are more abrupt and formidable. No wonder the early Navy engineers sent to Guam came back with glowing accounts of its possibilities as an "American Gibraltar." That was before the day of the plane, and it is as a landplane base that Guam is most promising.

The engineers saw its potentialities as a fleet base. Those potentialities have never been developed. Apra Harbor on the west side of the island is about three and a half miles wide and four to twenty-seven fathoms deep. It is divided by a peninsula and an island into an inner and an outer basin. It is guarded by a coral reef, which almost completely surrounds the island. However, so far as Port Apra is concerned, this reef is not quite where it should be, but bobs up in the form of dangerous coral heads in the harbor. The two basins would need to be dredged to a uniform depth and a breakwater constructed to keep out the sea and to make the harbor torpedo-proof.

The clippers which flew on a weekly schedule covering the distance from Alameda, California to Guam in four days came down on the surface of Apra Harbor. These clippers were at first twelve-passenger planes, but by 1941 they had grown to be seventy-four-passenger machines weighing forty tons. After the war they will be larger still. A large seaplane needs plenty of room for landings and take-offs. The present cleared space, and the small ramps built in 1917, will be entirely inadequate for the expected trans-Pacific air service of the future.

Guam also has possibilities as a rich, tropical farm and garden. It has exported 2,000 tons of copra yearly. However the officers of the naval station which has governed Guam have not been particularly interested in agriculture. Guam's resources are untapped. While Guam's exports have been about $100,000 annually, those of Saipan, half its size, have been under Japanese management four times as much.

"A pity!" says a Japanese sugar man at the ship's rail as we pass the blue cliffs of hermit Guam. "The largest and most fertile of all these islands. And not used." Guam could produce more and better sugar than Saipan and is also well suited to coffee, cacao, tobacco, cotton, pineapples and, in the rich lowlands, maize and rice. There is fine

Micronesian canoe, with outrigger. The sail is not cloth, but is
made of interlaced leaves of the pandanus.

Spearing fish requires more than a strong arm. Nice calculation is necessary to make allowance for the refraction of the water and the speed of the prey.

timber in the hills of the southern end. The northern plateau, or those parts of it not needed for airfields, could readily be laid out for sugar cane or coconut plantations. There are no better fishing grounds in the Pacific than the waters around Guam.

The *Yokohama Maru* would have been no more welcome at Guam than an American ship at a Japanese island. The exclusion policy

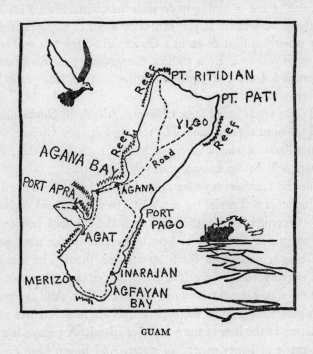

GUAM

worked both ways. So we did not land on Guam; but later acquaintance with the island yielded these items which may be of interest to the Yanks and Aussies who will one day be landing on its few beaches or parachuting down in the interior.

The first thing to note is that the natives are friendly. And, by the way, I do not in this book at any time use the word "native" in a derogatory sense. It merely indicates a member of a people indigenous to the island as contrasted with a newcomer, and there is no more odium

57

inherent in it than in saying that you are a native of Canada or a native New Yorker.

The natives of Guam have been treated so squarely by the U.S. naval station that they have none of the antipathy for the Westerner so common in parts of the Far East where the white man has not been white. In fact the Chamorros carry their enthusiasm to extremes. Anything "states-side" (that is, having to do with the United States) is ideal and devoutly to be wished. If you can draw a tin of sardines from your pocket when you float down in a Chamorro village you will receive a tumultuous welcome. Even without the sardines you will be cared for and guarded from the Japanese at the cost of Chamorro lives if necessary.

And there are 21,000 of these Chamorro friends on Guam, ninety per cent of the normal population. The rest are Filipinos, Chinese, Negroes and miscellaneous whites. Of course how many Japanese there are now on Guam will not be known until you get there.

While the Chamorros prefer canned goods from the United States, their liberators will prefer the marvelous fresh fruits and vegetables of Guam. Coconuts are plentiful, and it is the pleasant custom of the island to permit passers-by to help themselves to the nuts, provided they are agile enough to climb up and get them. The mangoes of Guam are excelled nowhere. The sweet, sun-ripened pineapple puts to shame the sour canned travesty of this noble fruit. And the great yellowing globes hanging on the papaya trees are in themselves sufficient explanation of the lure of the South Sea islands. A papaya is a watermelon made of honey instead of water. And if you have ever eaten papaya and decided that you didn't like it, suspend judgment until you try the Guam variety. Then there is the custard apple or sweetsop. The native won't understand either name, so ask for *atis*. And breadfruit, bananas, oranges, yams, taro . . . but no spinach. Boys who enlisted to get away from spinach will like Guam.

If one is stranded in some uninhabited and waterless area it is well to know that one can get a drink by cutting the *guiji* vine, to be found anywhere in the jungle. If a piece of vine about three feet long is cut off, sap will flow in a lively stream from the cut portion. It is not as good as a coke, but it will slake thirst.

It is not necessary to get out either a sun helmet or ear muffs on Guam. The summer heat is not as great as in many regions farther north, and there is never a frost. The thermometer hovers about the 81-degree mark all the year round. Earthquakes are frequent, but mild. Storms on the other hand are rare, but violent. Guam is in the typhoon belt. The worst typhoon in forty years struck Guam Nov. 3, 1940 with a 110-mile-per-hour wind that made three-fourths of the natives homeless, wrecked the Pan American Airways hotel and damaged the Navy hangar.

City joys are modestly represented by the attractions of Guam's capital town, Agaña. The demands of American officers and men have resulted in more entertainment facilities than can be found in any island town short of Pago Pago or Papeete. Agaña is a city of 11,000 friendly people. It has, or had before the Jap occupation, three cinema theatres, several pool halls, numerous bars and restaurants, good club-houses of the Elks and Masons, an American Legion post, respectable but friendly Spanish-Chamorro girls of considerable beauty, and more English spoken than anywhere else within fifteen hundred miles. As evening approaches it is pleasant to stroll under the coconut palms in the wide green Plaza de España before the governor's palace of Spanish days, later used by Americans as Government House. This park is at the center of the city and is a restful place for convalescents, a rendezvous for lovers and the scene of band concerts and entertainments.

The cheerful people of Guam have had a none too cheerful history. Magellan when he discovered the island in 1521 named it and the other islands of the group The Isles of the Lateen Sails. But he felt less romantic when a few toughs stole one of his small boats. He landed with fifty men, burned down the entire village and killed as many natives as he could find. The Chamorros that day were introduced to the "flying death." When pierced by an arrow they would "stand in astonishment . . . and draw it out by either end, staring at it until they died."

Magellan thoroughly looted the homes and lands of his victims and returned to his ship with heavily loaded boats. He rubbed the picturesque name Isles of the Lateen Sails out of his logbook and christened them instead Ladrones, Islands of Thieves. What the natives christened him has not been recorded.

When the story came back to Spain the Islands of Thieves appealed to the priests of the Inquisition as a needy field for their evangelistic labors. Yet it was not until 1668 that Jesuit missionaries came to the island and erected the Sweet Name of Mary church in Agaña. The missionaries were accompanied by soldiers. Conversions were made at the point of the sword. Drums beat in the hills and the natives rose in bloody riots. The Spaniards fortified the Sweet Name of Mary, turned their capital city Agaña into an armed camp and made war upon the stubborn unbelievers. Slaughter of innocents on a Hitlerian scale followed. Those who could, escaped from the island. The native population, about 55,000 when the Spaniards came, dwindled to 100 in only eighteen years. After the religious wars had burned out there was a slow increase, but when the United States took over Guam in 1898 there were only 9,000 natives, one sixth of the original population.

But under American rule for four decades the population has more than doubled. The population of Guam on July 1, 1941, was 23,394 of which 21,994 were Chamorros.

Smallpox and Asiatic cholera have been wiped out. Guam has become one of the cleanest and most wholesome spots in the tropics. The peonage common under the old regime has been replaced by a wage economy.

The Spanish government discouraged education of the Chamorros on the ground that it would "render them unfit for future usefulness." The first teachers were United States marines. Later native teachers took their places. Attendance was compulsory, not optional or indifferent as in the Japan-held islands. All teaching was in English. Now it is doubtless in Japanese. That will do no harm. Guam will not forget its English in three or four years, and in the postwar Pacific a knowledge of Japanese will be useful. The Japanese are an irrepressible people and although their military aggression will be halted, their genius for making and trading cheap articles of daily use will be felt throughout Asia. The day of the Jap is not ending, it is just about to begin. It will dawn more brightly when Japan's warmongers are in their graves.

Guam has twice been easily captured. What will happen the third time?

When the Spanish-American War broke, the *U.S.S. Charleston* sailed into Guam's Apra harbor and fired on the fort. There was no reply. Presently a boat came out from the fort bearing Spanish officials. They climbed on board and apologized for not having replied to what they had supposed was a salute. They explained that they had no ammunition. If they could purchase some they would take it to the fort and do their visitors proper honor.

They were astonished to learn that there was a war on, and that they were prisoners. Guam was taken without a shot, except those fired in "salute."

The conquest of Guam by the Japanese was not quite so swift, but it was accomplished in three days. It had been slyly prepared for. Some months previously a Japanese ship was wrecked, we now believe by intent, on the Guam coast. The shipwrecked sailors were of course taken ashore and seemed to be much interested in the defenses of the island. Japan was notified of the wreck and offered to send another ship to pick up her sailors. Guam countered with an offer to send them on an American ship to the nearest Japanese island. This offer was rejected. Finally a rendezvous was arranged and the sailors were transferred from an American to a Japanese ship on the high seas.

Whether they had learned much on Guam is doubtful for trickery was suspected and they were closely guarded.

On the morning of Pearl Harbor, Guam was attacked from all sides by large naval forces. Its defenders were only 555 U.S. sailors and marines. Their rifles could hardly hold off bombing planes and ships' guns, but they did delay the inevitable landing for nearly three days.

The lesson of this action, as of many others, is that naval and air superiority can take any "Gibraltar" no matter how well protected by cliffs, reefs or other natural advantages. That superiority we now have and will increase. The gentle Chamorros of Guam will soon see the Stars and Stripes flying again over Government House. Their taste of Japanese rule will not have dulled their appreciation for everything "states-side."

XI:

Yap Is Unique

Yap is unique. There is nothing else like it in the seven seas. It is a relic of a forgotten age, the only spot on earth where stone coins up to twelve feet in diameter are used as money.

We were determined to shake off our ship and spend a month on Yap.

The prospect was not bright.

"An American professor came through last year," the captain told us. "He wanted to stay on Yap. He had a letter from the Gaimusho [Foreign Office]. But he could speak no Japanese and the governor of Yap could speak no English. The governor couldn't find any place for him to stay. He had to go on with the ship. After all," he continued cheerfully, "that's the best thing to do—make the ship your hotel. It's more pleasant on board than on shore. Dengue fever, you know. And the food is bad. No vegetables. No meats. You have to live out of cans."

But to have to live out of cans did not seem so terrible after nine days of slimy *tofu*, tough *yuba*, sour bean soup, and octopus tentacles of the consistence of rubber bands, in the swaying dining saloon of the *Yokohama Maru*. This is not a wholesale diatribe against Japanese food. It can be good. More often it is not. The national psychology forbids coddling the stomach. The comfortable Chinese believe in happiness, gastronomic and otherwise, and are master cooks. The ascetic Japanese regard happiness as a cheap and incidental virtue, if a virtue at all, and endure their frequent stomach-aches as opportunities to show their fortitude.

We sailed into Yap harbor and dropped anchor. Governor Mizuno came aboard. I asked him if he had received a radiogram from the governor of Saipan. No, he said, he had not. I showed him our Tokyo document, authorizing us to land. He sucked his teeth and bowed.

"You are most welcome," he said, "but unfortunately there is no hotel on Yap."

"Can we make arrangements to stay at some private home?"

"There are few Japanese on the island and they have no provision for guests."

"It would not need to be a Japanese home."

The governor stared. I went on quickly. "Have we your permission to live with the Kanakas if we can make our own arrangements?"

He smiled incredulously. "Most certainly." The Japanese, in their self-importance born of an inferiority complex, hold themselves strictly aloof from the Polynesians and cannot conceive of white persons living in a native hut. The governor bowed and strolled away, doubtless feeling that he had diplomatically disposed of the matter.

During the voyage we had made the acquaintance of a deck passenger, a handsome lad whose father was one of the twelve kings of Yap.

His canoe had been brought alongside by the bumboatmen. We took the governor at his word. Slipping into the canoe with our brown host we got away unnoticed under cover of the general confusion.

In a craft like those of a century ago, hewn out of a single log, stabilized by an outrigger and fitted with a sail made of pandanus leaves, we skimmed over the lagoon toward the island of Rumung.

Tol had worn clothes on shipboard. Now they were neatly stowed away in his palm-leaf basket. His bare feet clutched the gunwales. Pole in hand, he poised aloft, bronze against the blue sky. A crimson loin cloth, a red coral necklace, some blue tattooing, a hunting knife, and a long comb projecting from his thick mop comprised his make-up.

He was a cheerful soul. His smile would have been flashing if his teeth had been white. But being a young man of fashion, his teeth were a gleaming ebony. This effect had been achieved not merely by the stains of betel-chewing but by a special blackening process, using a paste of groundsel and other herbs applied to the teeth every day for five days.

"Too bad," said Tol. "Makes very sick. But it gives good black, yes?" And he displayed his teeth from ear to ear.

He spoke a little English, for he had lived in Guam. He had successfully avoided any other contamination of civilization.

"Your things good for you," he philosophized. "Our things good for us. Mix—no good!"

Truly the Kanaka seems so different a man from the white Westerner that he can perhaps justly lay claim to a different mode of life. "Kanaka" is an indefinite word to describe this reddish-brown, black-haired, deep-eyed, wide-nosed and large-mouthed race, but we have no better word. According to the dictionary, "Kanaka" means "loosely, any South Sea islander." Therefore the significance of the word differs in different parts of the Pacific. In Micronesia "Kanaka" is a convenient nickname for one who would be more accurately but too burdensomely called "a man of Polynesian-Melanesian-Paquan-Mongol blood coming in the main from a Malay race which probably had Dravidian antecedents."

Although the Kanaka is a kaleidoscope of all racial colors, black, brown, red, yellow and even white, he blends into a brown and has the characteristics of the brown race. That is, he is a sea-rover, a bold navigator, a fisherman, not given to grubbing in the soil nor to the ways of trade and business. In school, arithmetic is his hardest subject. But he can always tell you where the fish are biting. And Tol was so much at home in a boat that he seemed a part of it. The Micronesians have always been fearless sailors. Those who had large trees on their islands made dugouts. Others tied strips of coconut wood together with coconut fiber to form canoes. In them they ventured sometimes five hundred miles away from home. A sea captain, coming upon a canoe of natives three hundred miles from their island, beating their way home against a head wind, invited them on board his ship for a rest. He presented them with a compass and taught them how to use it.

But one of them pointed to an old chief and said, "His head all same compass."

Yap consists of a main island with the islands of Map and Rumung and a fling of islets. All are gemmed in a lovely lagoon thirty-five miles long and five miles wide, girdled by a coral reef. One must pass Map to get to Rumung, but since Map is too attractive to be skipped, it seemed a better idea to land and walk the length of the island while a Kanaka boy took the canoe around.

No sooner had we gotten ashore than Tol had his eye on some betel nuts. They hung in a cluster, thirty feet up, just under the leaves of a betel or areca palm, which has a trunk too large to climb hand over hand and too small to grip with the legs. How was he to reach those nuts? Tol knew. He would use the Kanaka elevator. Beside the path was a large shrub, the Indian mallow. Its bark is the native's substitute for cord. Tol stripped off about five feet of bark and tied it in a loop big enough to fit over his ankles. Thus hobbled, he could tightly grip the trunk of the areca between his insteps. A series of quick jumps and grips and he was up among the nuts. He cut loose a cluster—then slid down almost as fast as it fell.

He cut one of the nuts in halves, laid one half on a leaf of piper methysticum of which there was an abundance at hand, dusted in a little lime from a bamboo tube which is part of the equipment of every Kanaka, folded up the quid and popped it into his mouth. His jaws began to revolve. Presently a vivid carmine juice stained his lips and a look of perfect contentment covered his features.

What was this magic? We tried the ingredients, not in combination, fearing the effect might be too much like a bolt from the blue, but seriatim. The nut caused an astringent, persimmon-like pucker. The leaf was as hot and spicy as cinnamon. And the lime lifted the roof of the mouth clear off and removed it to another county. Our first lesson ended in complete failure. There was never a second.

The coconuts were more to our liking. Tol sped up a coconut palm, scorning the hobble, for the trunk was large enough to be gripped by arms and legs. My wife, not to be outdone, went up another. And I up a third; but somehow lost enthusiasm for the ascent when an enormous

65

black fruit-bat, three feet from tip to tip, swooped from the fronds and circled within a few inches of my head. At such a moment one does not take time to analyze coolly the stories one has heard about the bloodsucking propensities of these evil-looking winged beasts. Although there are many suspicions and superstitions, the Yap bat seems to be in the main vegetarian and has a special fondness for the young coconut.

He has two rivals. The huge red-and-blue *birgus latro,* or robber crab, has claws a foot long. He tears off the husks and shells of ripe coconuts and devours the kernel. The natives fear him for he can tear open a skull as easily as a coconut. But he will not attack unless cornered. One caught and confined in a stout box made of three-quarter-inch boards broke his way out and escaped.

The other rival is the rat. Some islands are overrun with these voracious rodents. They do great damage to the coconut crop by eating the buds and flowering stems. This diet appears to agree with them for they attain the size of hedgehogs. A full-grown rat in the middle of a moonlit path is enough to turn one against the tropics for life.

On one of the small islands of the Uleai group, dominated by huge rats, someone had the brilliant idea of landing a shipload of three hundred cats. It was some months before the ship paid a return visit to the island. The king paddled out in his canoe and came on board.

"Well," said the captain, "how about it?"

"All dead," replied the king.

"Wonderful! Now you'll be at peace. No more rats."

"No more cats," corrected the king. "The rats killed them all."

On our way up the beautiful, palm-shaded shore-path of Map we came upon another example of the contest between man and the animals for possession of the fruits of the forest. We saw a small boy chewing gum as if his life depended upon it. Now and then he would draw it out in a long white ribbon, then flip it back into his mouth and chew more vigorously.

"Where does he get the gum?" I asked, scenting the trail of the trader. But I was mistaken.

"From the breadfruit tree," said Tol.

66

He drew his knife and slashed the trunk of a nearby breadfruit. Out trickled a white juice. This juice, he explained, is allowed to ooze for a day and solidify. Then it must be chewed to make it soft and adhesive. While we waited, the boy completed this important operation—then he clambered up onto his father's shoulders, fixed a stick hori-

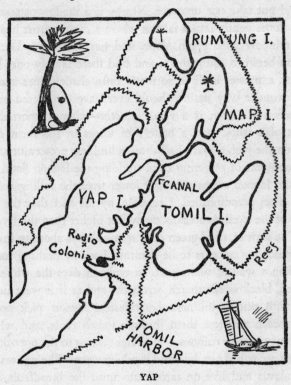

YAP

zontally like a perch just below some luscious papaya, and wrapped the gum around the stick.

"Birds come for fruit," said Tol. "Light on stick. Can't quite reach papaya. Can't get away from stick. Boy come—kill. Or take for pet."

And we entered for a moment the boy's house where eighteen birds in bamboo cages shrieked their testimony to the efficacy of that gum. Having added an iguana and a vampire to his collection, the boy had

67

made a very respectable start on a Yap zoo. Incidentally the family had moved out under the trees.

Map, the loveliest of the Yap group, is the tropic isle of one's dreams. The path winds through a grove of stately coconut trees, heavily loaded —and it is best to dream with eyes uplifted lest the fifty-foot fall of a two-pound nut take one unaware. Nearby is a shadow-patterned sand beach. It slopes gently into a lagoon where a master artist has tried to make a rainbow with green alone, and has succeeded. Dazzled by colors, you begin to count them, and find there is only one. But that one, green, expresses itself in so many tints, shades, hues and moods that you wonder why nature should ever have considered any other colors necessary. Green is a versatile actor—when supported by the stagecraft of a tropic sun, a battery of kliegs in the form of white breakers on the reef, a black backdrop, a limitless proscenium, and the million footlights of reflecting coral studding the lagoon floor.

The calm lagoon seems curiously lower than the rolling ocean outside—an effect accomplished, I suppose, by the fact that the level of the crests of the swells is actually many feet higher than the level of the lagoon. The sinister, dead-green deep seems always about to invade the place of peace but appears to be dammed back by nothing more substantial than a wall of white surf. In typhoon days the white wall is demolished, black swells march across the reef as if it were not there, blot out with octopus-inkiness the iridescent lagoon, pick up canoes from the beach and toss them through thatch roofs, and where the island is low, rip their ruinous way straight across to the opposite shore. Plantations are wiped out, by wind if not by waves. The natives tighten their lava-lavas and live on taro-potato until the breadfruit, banana, orange and coconut trees begin to bear once more.

On our chart of Map, villages are indicated by large circles such as a map of Europe might use to mark Paris, Berlin and Rome. But in the coconut forest it is difficult to know when one is in a village. The houses are scattered and well concealed in the woods, apart from the trunk-line path. Very rarely does a village have a Main Street. The Kanaka makes full use of the privacy which the jungle affords. The man particularly wants privacy—for his wife. She should be too busy,

68

he thinks, to spend her time in idle chatter with other women. Chatter is man's prerogative. The only conspicuous building of each village is the All Men House, a clubhouse for male gossip of an evening while the women stay at home dry-cleaning the dinner dishes with leaves and putting the babies to bed on the bamboo slats. The All Men House is generally perched on a promontory or platform projecting into the lagoon.

At one place we came upon a large aggregation of Kanaka men sitting on the stones before an All Men House, chewing betel nuts. They were there to put on a new thatch, the old roof having been destroyed by last year's typhoon. There were no signs of imminent toil. The work had not gotten beyond the stage of discussion, mastication and expectoration. Stones all about were blood-red with evidences of deep thought. If betel is a stimulant, surely they must have been stimulated to build to heaven.

Apparent bloodstains mark all the frequented trails of Yap. Most of these trails are not dirt paths, but stone causeways upon which any such mark is clearly revealed and easily studied. By the freshness of the stain, the good betel-juice reader can tell you how recently within a few minutes someone has passed that way. He can also tell you many other things about the spitter, basing his conclusions upon such considerations as volume, chemical strength, frequency of discharge, relative location, angle of deflection and so on. Knowing the particular betel habits of individuals he can often tell exactly who has passed, as well as whether he was in a hurry, tired or brisk, calm or excited, traveling light or under a load, in company or alone, talking or silent, where he stopped to rest, where to chat, where he interrupted his betel-chewing to eat, what he ate as betrayed by the juice of the new quid, and many other considerations more recondite. What the American redskin could tell from a footprint the redmouth can deduce from a betel stain. There are, of course, certain men who are experts in this lore. They are sometimes the *machamach,* or medicine men, who find it advantageous to bolster up their reputation for wizardry by some of the arts of the detective. A writer of detective novels, weary of fingerprints, might well get new material for a deduction plot from a study of the jungle-dweller's methods of analyzing the story of the betel stain.

This art of detection is not a local phenomenon. The traveler will come upon it among the Battaks of Sumatra and the Bagobos of Mindanao. Nor is it confined to southern Asia. The Aymara Indians, descendants of the Incas of Peru, practice it; and I recall seeing an irate Indian on the shore of Titicaca, after someone had secretly been using his balsa, solving the guilty man's identity by the betel print on the logs.

At the end of Map we found the canoe and paddled across a rough stretch toward palm-plumed Rumung. A break in the reef let old ocean come roaring in. A sudden squall made matters worse. Sea and sky darkened. The translucent greens were gone. There was another green now—a savage, lurid one. The coconut-shell bailer was kept more than busy. Waves, tangled in the outrigger, flew into a rage and showered into the boat. On the reef lay the great hulk of the wrecked *Shizuoka Maru.*

"I did that," said Ocean. "Now what can I do for you?"

We were soon soaked to the skin, but too busy to notice. The sail could not be used since we were going into the teeth of the trade wind, but even had we been going with it the gale was too violent for a sail of pandanus leaves. Our narrow, sharp-pointed paddles had to be used with quick, flashing stabs—not with the slow, powerful stroke of the American Indian's broad blade. Sometimes they went deep into a crest. Sometimes their points only scratched the surface of a trough.

The canoe pirouetted on its nose.

"Hang on!" advised Tol, grinning his great black grin. "Plenty sharks here."

A last great puff, and the wind dropped. The sun burst forth. Of such spasms is Yap weather made. There may be a dozen squalls in a day, no one of them more than five minutes long.

We landed, dripping, at the village of Fal. A hot sun dried the tropic-thin clothing as we walked.

"My home!" announced Tol. Before us stood a high-gabled thatch house among swaying coconut palms. Out came Tol's father and mother, king and queen of Rumung.

There are twelve native kings in the Yap Islands. Some of their old glory is departed, but they are still respected and obeyed by their people and are recognized by the Japanese government (provided they recognize it!).

Our king looked like his fellow Kanakas except more so. His comb was longer, his earrings finer, his tattooing represented a greater variety of fish and birds, and his teeth were a more successful black. His royal robes were summed up in a lava-lava, not of the simple domestic make, but imported from Mokomok where the most skillful gee-string artists of Micronesia are purveyors to Yap royalty. Do not get the impression that he was any caricature of a king. Tall, straight and fine, he possessed dignity in his own right, and inspired instant respect and liking. A sojourn of some years in Guam, before he took over authority upon the death of his father, had provided him with acceptable English.

The queen was a sweet little lady who wore a flower in her hair and dripped spiders and centipedes from the jungle fastnesses of her grass skirt. Although not warned of our coming, she accepted us immediately as if the entertainment of American guests were a common occurrence in her household. But she told us later that she had never before even seen an American.

Tol's sister came out with a pink pig in her arms, the favorite pet of Kanaka maidens. So long as she kept her mouth closed so that her betel-black teeth and scarlet tongue were not visible, she was pretty. She wore the neck-cord which indicates that the bearer is of marriageable age and ready to listen. Her name was Rtep, and she had much of the charm of her namesake, the *rtep*, loveliest of Yap's orchids.

The king's home—and ours for the time being—had breadfruit pillars, pandanus-thatch roof, reed walls, and floor of round bamboo poles. It consisted of but one room. There was nothing that resembled a door; it was necessary to climb in through the windows, the sills of which were about three feet above the ground and level with the floor of the house. That is, from the outside these apertures looked like windows, and from the inside they passed as doors. Each was provided with a thatch shutter, hinged at the top, and propped open with a paddle. This shutter, projecting like an awning over the door-window, prevented even a moderate storm from entering the house. In a real storm the shutters were closed. Then the interior was as dark as a pocket. Of course there was no glass.

Nor was there a nail in the structure. The house was tied together. Even the heavy framework of typhoon-resisting pillars and beams was lashed in place with cords made of fiber obtained from the outside husk of the coconut.

There was no ceiling. One looked up through a maze of beams into the gloom of the high peak where lizards rustled in the thatch.

The interior was innocent of furniture—except that, because his wife favored it, the king had put in a wash-cabinet, retrieved from the wreck of the *Shizuoka Maru*. No one used it. He had taken nothing else from the wreck, deeming such articles inappropriate in a pure Kanaka house. Mats, now rolled against the wall, could be laid out at bedtime. At one end of the room the flooring was omitted and the stone-and-dirt foundation served as a fireplace. Upon it a few large stones were arranged to hold pots. The fire was an open fire of dry coconut leaves or coconut shells. This fireplace was used only in bad weather, cooking ordinarily being done in the large stone-paved court.

Well displayed outside the house was the king's wealth in the form of large discs of stone money. The house stood under coconut palms on the shore of the kaleidoscopic lagoon. A half mile away the Pacific roared on the reef and sent up towers of spray around the hull of the wrecked liner.

The civilization of the outside world suggested by that ship was in odd contrast to our surroundings. We seemed to have moved back a good thousand years.

He who wishes to see the South Sea islands of the past before modernity took the color out of them should visit Yap.

"Yap" means *The Land*. To the Yap native it is the only land, the center of the world.

He rejects with high scorn the tomfooleries of civilization. For it is firmly believed that any copying of alien customs will anger the deities

72

Where you will sleep on Yap. The All Men House is set out into the lagoon on a rough stone platform. (See Chapter XII).

In Yap's port town, the Kanaka youth wears a necklace and a
bicycle. In the jungle, no bicycle.

of Yap and bring disease or death to the culprit. Perhaps this is in part a heritage from early times when too close association with malady-bringing foreign sailors did mean just that—disease and death. Therefore the Yap native has, as firmly as his overlords will let him, withdrawn from all contact with the outside world.

So this is the best spot, not only in Micronesia, but in the entire Pacific, to study the traditional and unchanged customs of the Kanaka; thus providing a background against which to view the swift changes taking place on other islands.

Three more girls appeared and busied themselves about the yard. We were not introduced to them.

"Your sisters too?" I asked Tol.

My mistake. He looked shocked.

"They are slaves," he said.

They set up two new fireplaces in the yard. There were already three. Evidently out of matches, they skilfully made fire by friction in one fireplace, then carried it to the others. A pot was placed on each. Soon five dinners were boiling. The girls were running frantically back and forth across the yard from pot to pot.

I asked Tol, Why five fires instead of one? Why five big pots when one would contain all the stew of taro, yam and pork that was being cooked?

"Taboo," he said. "Each person, one pot. Girl no matter, she can eat from mother's pot. Man cannot eat from woman's pot."

"What would happen if he did?"

"No longer be head of house. Be slave of woman."

So by this odd superstition, the work of the woman is multiplied many times. It is all very well at the king's home where there are slaves. But in the ordinary home there are none. We were later to see in the grounds of one dwelling as many as seven fireplaces, each covered by a thatch roof—seven kitchens to one house—and all tended by one woman!

Dinner was extraordinarily curious. Instead of all gathering at one board, each went off in a corner by himself with his pot, scooping out the food with his fingers. Every man crouched protectively over his pot, guarding it against the baleful influence of the women. Only the mother and daughter dipped their fingers into the same pot.

The stew was good. Vaguely we expected a dessert of tropical fruits. Instead, the meal was topped off with sardines, one tin for each person.

Sunset colors were beginning to play across the lagoon.

Perhaps Tol sensed the apprehensive question that was asking itself in our minds.

"Sleep my house no good," he said. "Too small. Too much woman. Sleep in All Men House."

XII:

Where You Will Sleep On Yap

WHY a house full of men is a more appropriate place for a married couple to spend the night than a house of "too much woman" was not clear. But one does not cross-examine a host.

We went to the All Men House. It was a large building, nine-tenths roof. Its steep, lofty thatch, descending so low over the door-windows that they were mere holes, gave the effect of an enormous fur hat over a small, squat face. Apart from the village, set out into the lagoon on a stone platform and bathed in the trade wind, it was an ideal place to get away from mosquitoes and women.

The All Men House is for all men and men only. Exception was made in the case of a foreign woman. Evidently the honored status of guest superseded the despised status of woman. It was a mark of special courtesy and respect—this permitting a woman to sleep with the men. Perhaps it was a gasp of appreciation that escaped Mary as we peered into the tomb-dark interior. There was a mingled odor of dried fish, fermented coconut, and Kanaka—together with what seemed like a dash of morgue, although we did not know then a dead chief lay in state at one end of the great room.

74

"You like?" asked Tol. "Very clean, this house!"

In that case there was nothing to do but be thankful that we were not to sleep in a dirty one.

The All Men House is always the chief pride of a village. Every village has one. The descriptive English name, "All Men House," was applied by white traders in the days when English and American buccaneers sailed these waters. It stuck. The Kanakas themselves use it, but have also their native name, *Febai,* often corrupted to *Pebai. Fe* means "money," and *bai,* "house." The "Money House" is so called because any stone money that belongs to the village rather than to individuals is stacked up about this town hall.

Distinction should be made between the *Febai* and the *Falu.* A rich village will have both. They look alike. Foreigners, including the Japanese, apply the name, All Men House, to both. Their functions, however, are different. The *Febai* is a solemn place, for village councils. No levity is allowed. Strangers are excluded. The *Falu* is a gayer rendezvous, a clubhouse for the men of the village, a hotel where passing strangers are entertained, a place of dancing and feasting. The *Febai* commonly stands in the heart of the village, the *Falu* on the shore.

Confusion may be due to the fact that a poor village, unable to erect both, will make one building serve as *Febai* and *Falu.* It was so in this case. But the Kanaka thinks of the house differently according to the use that is made of it. On council nights it is invested with all the dignity of a royal council chamber and the wayfarer must cool his heels outside until the deliberations are over. On other nights it is a *Falu,* a place of gossip, rest and revelry. Tonight it played that role.

An old chief welcomed us on the stone platform with the usual potation of cool, sweet coconut juice served in the original container. There is no drink more refreshing. Nor is there any you will remember longer, for to drink without dripping is impossible and the stains are permanent souvenirs.

Then he drew an ugly fifteen-inch knife with which, according to later reminiscence, he had split open seven heads in the old war days; and he split the nuts. He chipped from each husk a piece to serve as a spoon. We scooped out the soft, white meat.

75

Sunset, with a fanfare of colors. The shadows of the forest come out and take the lagoon. Tol, having heard that there is a lantern somewhere in the village, goes to search for it.

May he take his time. Until he returns there will be no necessity of going inside. It is pleasant, sitting on the stone platform with discs of stone money as back-rests. Above the trees rides the faint old moon in a silver caravel of new moon. The palms brandish their silhouetted arms in the persistent trade wind. The forest rustles like thousands of Kanaka grass skirts. Lagoon wavelets slap the shore. Beneath all, always, is the boom of the surf on the reef a half mile away.

No, there is something more persistent than the trade wind or the surf—the molar movement of the brown shadows that crouch beside us.

Tol comes back with a lantern, a ship's lantern from the wreck, that fount of all good things. An old man makes fire with flint. But it soon appears that there is no oil in the lantern. Oh, well!

"What do you usually do?" I ask.

"We burn fires." But they had thought that the effete foreigners would need a lantern.

We crawl inside and presently brisk fires of coconut leaves and shells are burning on two square spots left unfloored for this purpose. The interior flickers on and off like a pre-Hollywood cinema. Brown bodies, crimson or blue lava-lavas, black curly hair, cream-colored combs, red coral necklaces, flash on and off. Giant pillars and beams grotesquely leap forward and retire into the gloom, all without moving a muscle. No pillar has been shaped by a tool. It twists and bulges here with the same individuality it possessed in the forest.

In this hall twenty feet wide by sixty feet long there are no less than thirty-four pillars. Many of them are three feet in diameter. Naturally they somewhat obstruct the view. But the supports must be strong, for typhoons are frequent in Yap. These columns are matured coconut trees; young ones are weak. Above us are six slightly arched transverse beams, also four great beams running the length of the house. Above these again are the rafters climbing steeply into a singing blackness where the high peak cuts into the trade wind.

The dark space above the beams is greater than the space allotted to humans below them. In this lofty cavern a few fishing nets have been hung to dry. The rafters are of a wood the Spaniards called *palomaria* and the natives call *dauk*. Upon the rafters is a lattice of bamboo, and to this lattice is sewed a thatch of coconut leaves. To judge by the uproar aloft, every leaflet has a loose outside tag whirring in the breeze.

One unique feature of this building is that it always leans forward into the wind, just as a man should when walking against a heavy gale. Each end is pointed like a ship's bow, and each gable projects far beyond the base. The rafters within slant, half of them toward one end of the building, half toward the other end. Thus the structure is buttressed against possible trouble coming from either of two directions.

Why only two directions? Because the trade wind of winter bears down from the northeast and the summer trade from the southwest. Storms and typhoons come with most force in the path of the trades. Therefore a building which, Janus-like, turns two defiant faces toward the opposite dangers, is likely to stand.

The betel nut floor is partitioned off by logs into sleeping compartments six by eight feet in size. The wall, formed by the log, is only six inches high, yet the sleeper will be as safe against intrusion between his logs as in a locked room in a metropolitan hotel. One half the floor is thus divided into sleeping compartments. The other half is left open for dancing, except that it is punctuated by three fireplaces.

The clans are gathering. Men slip in through the low windows, crouching like animals or gliding like snakes. Some have already had too much toddy. Each carries a long knife in his lava-lava. Each also carries a disarming vermilion-and-black smile.

It is surprising to see a *yukata,* or summer kimono, come in through the window. It is worn by a Japanese—the only one hereabouts. He is a trader in copra. He buys nuts from the natives, dries the copra and sells it in Colonia, the Japanese settlement on the main island, for shipment to Japan. He lives here alone in a little, dark, native house. He has no Japanese wife. Several Kanaka women console him. We are to see one of them tomorrow smoking a Japanese pipe at his front door.

He sits in blue-and-white *yukata* among the brown bodies, smokes a

77

cigarette, says nothing, lights a piece of coconut husk at the fire to serve as a torch, and goes home.

A punk made of a piece of glowing coconut husk serves as the Kanaka candle. It is sufficient to light the path. Since it smolders only, without flaming, it is of no use for any close work.

A people without light enough to read by during the leisure of the evening is bound to be backward. Edison was the foremost educator in history. But Edison would be baffled in Yap. For even if every house were ablaze with electric encouragement there would be no reading done. Because there is nothing printed in the Yap language. Life without books, magazines, newspapers, seems incredible. Yet here it is. There is no library in the All Men House. No newsstand in the lobby where the world may be bought. In Yap the world is a distant unreality, like Mars.

In fact Martians have visited this All Men House as often as Americans. That is, it has never before accommodated either. Yet there is surprisingly little staring. We are accustomed to the open-mouthed wonder of the back-country Japanese village where the entire population slowly revolves on its heels from the moment the strangers appear at one end of town until they go out at the other. But the Kanaka does not gape. For one thing, constant chewing precludes gaping. But the reason is that the world means nothing to him. The Japanese is inquisitive because he is acquisitive. He is interested in the world and intends to make it his own. The Kanaka is content to let the world go by. He will not bother it if it will not bother him.

True, callers at the king's house would sit on their heels for hours and smile at us. But they were shy of trying on any of our outlandish garments. Anything foreign is to the Kanaka an object of amusement —not of imitation. The Japanese looks to learn. The Kanaka looks to laugh.

A rather debonair old man dressed in a trim Vandyke beard comes to speak to us.

"He great artist," says Tol. "You wish to see something?"

An opportunity to examine native art! We accept with alacrity.

Vandyke kindles a dry stem at the fire and leads us into the mysterious blackness at the far end of the room. We come upon a long bundle wrapped in nipa mats. Sculpture in wood, perhaps, of the sort sometimes used to adorn a boathouse—for it seems about the size of a human figure. The nipa mats are laid aside. It is a human figure, but not in wood.

"He was one of my father's best chiefs," says Tol.

But Vandyke's interest is not so much in the greatness of the dead as in the work of art which he, Vandyke, has produced with the corpse as a canvas. Intricate convolutions in yellow paint cover the body. The saffron has been mixed with coconut oil to give it gloss and the effect is luminous and ghostly in the flickering light. There is a yellow bar across the forehead, a yellow circle on each cheek and another on the chin. Three great circles adorn the chest and abdomen. Bars seem to elongate the arms and legs. There is an abundance of minor decoration . . . fish, crabs, canoes, and other blobs rather too futuristic to be interpreted. Evidently the artist gave his fancy free play. What a pity that his canvas was so perishable! Already the brown skin is beginning to shrink back from the bony frame.

"When did he die?"

"Seven days ago."

"When will he be buried?"

"Perhaps two weeks. Perhaps three weeks. Long time, because he great man. Many villages come to honor with dance. Every night another village. Tonight one village come. You see dance."

A cough in the dark. We can now make out two slaves standing on guard at the head of the dead, two more at the feet. The vigil lasts day and night, Tol explains. When one man tires, another takes his place.

The artist shows us his brush made of fine, soft fibers of coconut husk, and brings out a coconut shell containing the remains of his paint, which had been made from the saffron-plant. Then he explains some of his designs, tracing them out over the leathery skin with his finger, tickling the ribs of the dead.

79

We leave the art lecture flat and return to the fire. Vandyke follows, voluble.

"He wishes to know," says Tol, "did you like?"

How could we be so remiss! "It was beautiful. Tell him we enjoyed it very much."

"He wishes to know," pursued Tol, "do artists in your country do anything like that?"

"Nothing like that!" we assure him. Vandyke glows.

The village that is to have the honor of honoring the dead tonight has arrived—that is, the male contingent of it. Now there is only the king to wait for. He comes presently. Those who are standing hastily sit down. In Kanaka lands that is the position of respect. For example, men who stand poling a canoe must be seated when the canoe passes a *Febai* or *Falu*. The story runs that in German times a canoe containing a German and several Kanaka chiefs, all drunk because it was the Kaiser's birthday, passed the All Men House at Balabat. The tipsy revelers made much noise and did not sit down. This was lese majesty to the Balabatese, who paddled out, pulled the offenders out of their canoe and threw them into the sea. The German sputtered vows of vengeance. He complained to the German governor, who summoned the king of Balabat.

The king, upon entering the governor's office, hastily sat down in the nearest chair which happened to be the governor's, leaving the official standing. The governor roared with laughter. He had intended to punish Balabat, but he felt more amusement now than annoyance.

"Well, that just shows how different our customs are," he said. "We rise to show respect and you sit down for the same purpose. Can't you see that our people can never remember which to do when they pass your Houses—get up or get down? So you'll have to allow that, either way, we mean respect."

It was so ordered. And since that time allowance has been made for the remiss manners of officials, doctors and missionaries. But the natives are especially friendly to those who remember to sit and make their pole-men sit.

However, when another petty kingdom sends an official message to the village, the royal messenger is expected to stand.

A pedestrian carrying something that belongs to the village may keep it on his shoulder as he passes the All Men House. Any private burden must come down, unless it is stone money which, although privately held, is regarded as belonging to the realm; or unless it is a handful of bananas, since the lowly banana has been exalted to semi-sacred status by its use in all ceremonies.

These nuances are explained to us later. But, at the moment, I fear it is only through a lucky impoliteness that we remain politely seated when the king enters.

He greets the old men of the visiting village while the young men prepare for the dance. They have oiled their bodies until they gleam like living waves. Vandyke is doing a little impromptu but inspired art work on the stomach of the leader. Some have twisted palm-leaflets into hornlike shapes and stuck them into their fuzzy *chevelure* along with their *roai,* or mangrove combs. They wear flowers behind their ears, chaplets around their heads, chains of flowers over one shoulder and under the other arm. The tame masculine gee-string is covered by a shimmering grass skirt more spectacular than the woman's—the garb of the ancient Yap warrior.

Now they line up before the king. They first give an ear-splitting yell; its purpose is to silence all inane chatter. For the dancers must be heard as well as seen. What they say is more important than their movements. And the literary genius who writes—not on paper but in his mind and theirs—the script for such an occasion is no less an artist in his field than Vandyke in his. The dance itself consists of little more than a shuffling of feet, clapping of hands, and slapping of thighs and chests with reports like pistol-shots. But all this is merely punctuation. In between claps and slaps unfolds the story . . . in this case, an account of the dead chief's exploits and a lament for his death.

It runs on for half an hour.

XIII:
Yap Ways Are Odd

A MIGHTY shout, and the dance is finished. Then all sit down and join in a mournful, hushed death chant, in which the phrases are separated by long silences. It is simple and impressive. When it is over, the visitors silently light torches at the fire and slip out. A spell seems to be over everyone.

Tol came to us whispering, "I have mosquito net for you."

The mosquito net, when unfolded, betrayed its lack of strings with which to tie it to the pillars. The lack was easily supplied. Over a beam hung strands similar to those Tol had used to hobble his feet when he scaled the areca palm. This material is the inner bark of the abutilon, or Indian mallow, known to the Japanese as *ichibi* and to the native as *puksi*. The withes were as thin as paper and only a quarter-inch wide, yet I could not break one with my hands. They were amply strong to hold up a heavy canopy.

Because of their durable character these strips are also used as clothing. They make up the supposedly decorative rag-tag that loosely covers the close-fitting gee-string. Sometimes this shaggy festoon is dyed a brilliant color. The foreigner is hard put to see anything beautiful about it, but the Kanaka is inordinately proud of it. Sometimes it spells his undoing. The police cannot very well clutch and hold an oiled body, but can easily get a firm grip upon the tough *puksi*. And if handcuffs are needed, a strand from the prisoner's garment can be knifed off and used to bind his wrists.

Our mosquito net was a relic of native handicraft. It was made of loosely woven threads of bark obtained from the Ponapean nim tree.

Within this wooden tent, a wooden bed was laid and wooden pillows. The bed consisted of two rough mats made from the leaves of the pandanus tree. They hardly mitigated the rigor of the floor of betel palm trunks laid side by side. These trunks were about three inches in diameter. Of course they left a well-defined pattern of creases and ridges on the form of the sleeper. Nor did they lie evenly on the stone foundation. Some bulged higher than others. So the night was to be one of semi-conscious search to find cracks into which the bones would fit. Oh, for the plasticity of a sea-pudding that can ooze itself into conformity with any bed!

The pillow was better. It too was of wood, but soft, spongy driftwood like cork. Compared with the uncompromising block of pine provided to the wayfarer in a Korean monastery, it was softest down. The coast is watched for logs that have been lightened and softened by long immersion in the sea, drifting to these shores perhaps from the Philippines. When these are not available, pillows are made from the trunk of the tree-fern or the pandanus. The effete use a rolled-up mat. Today Japanese pillows are being offered. But the natives prefer their logs and mats to the Nipponese head-rest for men which has all the sleep-wooing qualities of a sack of oats, and the thinly upholstered wooden neck-rest for women which has both the design and effect of a guillotine. The softest pillow I saw on Yap was a feather-filled affair left behind by a German. But even it seemed hardly practical for any ordinary human being who has not been cross-bred with a giraffe; for, since the pillow is three feet square, one must have a neck at least two feet long to be comfortable on it. Thinking back across a career of pillows, the best I remember was an Italian cemetery grave-mound made soft by a hundred-mile stint on a bicycle. Which would indicate that pillow-comfort is relative after all and depends upon the contents, not of the pillow but of the day.

Certainly we sank gratefully into the bed of tree-trunks and driftwood after so full a day. We could hardly spare attention to Tol who was giving us an inopportune lesson in Yap language.

"*Quefel a nep—mol*. That is what we say. It means, 'Good is the night—sleep!'"

"Good night," I murmured. "I suppose you are going home now?"

"Oh, no," he said. "I stay here. All these young men stay!"

Curious . . . perhaps worth while waking up to understand this.

"But they all have homes?"

"Oh, yes. But many people home . . . parents, sisters, much woman. Only one room. Very bad, young man stay home. Perhaps do wrong with sister. Very bad. So live here."

"At what age do they come here?"

"Age fifteen."

"And how long do they stay?"

"Until get married."

Thus the *Falu* is a bachelors' hall for the segregation of budding manhood. A necessity in a land of tropic passions and one-room houses.

The hall seemed full of men moving stealthily about in the dying firelight.

"Are all these bachelors?"

"What?"

"Bachelors. A man, not married, is a bachelor."

Tol absorbed the word as best he could. "Betsula, betsula. Very good. So I am betsula. No," he explained, "many men here to go fishing, early morning, when tide comes. At home, never know. Here, someone wakes them when tide in, all go together."

So the *Falu* was also a fishing lodge.

And a hotel. "Are there many strangers here tonight?"

"Five, six. Two of them second class men. But we allow. Too far for them go to second class village."

Class divisions are sharp in Yap. Each village is confined to one class —that is, there will not be first, second and third class people mixed together in one village. This was a first class village. Inferiors might come to work in it in the daytime, but, unless assigned to night duty, they would go back to their own village at night. A low class man may not stop in the *Falu* of a high class village, except by special permission if a village of his own class is too remote. But a high class man may stop in a *Falu* of any class.

"Do the guests pay anything?"

"Pay? You mean money? To stay here? Certainly not!" Tol was

evidently shocked by the idea. A hotel that would charge its guests! Ridiculous!

Men with their hair down looked like hags silhouetted against the embers. Many of the oldsters still effect a topknot, and since it can be a most uncomfortable lump between the head and a pillow, the hair is released at night. The windows were full for a moment as the men voided their cherished quids into the outer darkness. Then, with sighs, coughs and grunts, they sought repose on the slats. Only the four guards remained erect and chewing. The betel would solace them during the long hours as they stood at the head and feet of death.

One more visit from Tol. He passed me a small root.

"If anything bite, rub this on."

"Bite? What will bite?"

"Tick perhaps. Flea. Spider. Not much because this very clean house. What you call, scorpion, sometimes. Centipede maybe. That's all."

Various sleepy protests from my wife.

"But no worry," was Tol's assurance. "No bite much this week."

"Why not this week?" Mary wanted to know. "Is it their vacation?"

"Dead chief," said Tol, pointing not to the end of the room but up into the beams as if his spirit floated aloft.

"What has the dead chief to do with the bugs?" I inquired.

"Ghost. Take care of everybody. Not let any harm come. Good man . . . good ghost."

A sensible theory, that. The Kanaka, although he has many more superstitions than the civilized man, is more placid about them. We have so few ghosts that we find one terrifying. The savage feels himself continually surrounded by spirits and gets used to them. And why, indeed, should all ghosts be malicious? Naturally, the ghost of a good chief would be a good ghost and would let no evil betide his friends or guests.

Logically convinced if not emotionally reassured, we slept.

Sleep was fitful. The presence of the dead chief near us was vaguely disturbing. With the first hint of dawn the fishermen awoke and began to bustle their nets, tackle, spars, poles and paddles out from the low

85

door-windows onto the stone platform. We went out to watch the preparations.

The canoes were fitted out. Then came a lull during which the betel-chewing process was tuned up for the day. Still they did not go. Why did they wait?

Across the lagoon came a canoe with a single occupant. He had been sent out a half hour early and came back with his mission fulfilled, for he brought with him one fish. The fish was promptly cut into eighteen pieces—for eighteen men were to go fishing—and each man took a piece. Then the eighteen fishermen stood in a row on the end of the platform. At a word, they solemnly threw their bits of fish far out into the water. That done, they took to the boats and were off.

The idea? An offering to the god of the sea. If the first fish caught is eaten, the deity will say that men are selfish and do not deserve a plentiful yield. If they give back to the god what is his, he will give them more.

The analogy to the doctrine of bread cast upon the waters is obvious. Also the analogy to the miracle of the division and multiplication of fishes. Some students have seen a connection between the custom and missionary influence. But inquiries among the oldest grandfathers who remember the beliefs of their grandfathers reveal that the custom antedates Spanish missions in the islands.

One is frequently brought up short before a supposedly Christian, or sometimes Buddhist, doctrine found among savages who never heard of Christ or Buddha. Thus reminding us that the larger part, although not necessarily the better part, of the great religious systems was derived from man's common heritage of belief. Christianity and Buddhism owe much to paganism.

We watched the canoes cross the lagoon, pass out through a break in the reef, and climb up upon the rollers.

Beside me, Vandyke was whispering to Tol. Tol relayed his message. "He going to paint another one this morning. You like go watch?"

I looked at Mary.

"Tell him we have a previous engagement to attend a murder," she said.

XIV:

Land of Stone Money

CIVILIZED man is a thinly veneered barbarian; and we found that it did not take many days for us to become accustomed to most aspects of the primitive life of Yap.

But we never ceased to marvel at the money. Surely it is the strangest in the world. And the largest.

If a stroller on Broadway, instead of jingling the coins in his pocket, were to come down the street rolling a coin as tall as himself, he should achieve a sensation. But such coins are common in Yap. In fact some are twice this size. Place one such on edge, and a tall man must stand on a tall man's head to reach the top.

In the center of each coin is a round hole. In an important coin, this is as large as a manhole. When the coin is to be paid, a tree is thrust through the hole and a crew of perhaps one hundred men, half of them at each end, partly lift and partly drag the coin over the ancient stone-paved jungle trails to the creditor. There are no wheeled vehicles on Yap except one or two ox-carts in the port-town, and there, of course, Japanese money is current. In the outlying islands Japanese money is rarely seen.

Even with coins only two or three feet in size, "going shopping" is no slight matter.

"I must pay the trader," said our hostess, the queen. She did not sally forth with a pocketbook. She went down the shore path under the palms followed by two husky slaves sweating under the weight of two three-foot stone discs supported on the shoulders by bamboo poles thrust through the holes.

The trader accepts such currency cheerfully. Of course he cannot exchange it for foreign goods. No bank in Tokyo, London or New York would recognize his slab of rock as collateral. But he can pay it to some other native for copra.

A chief's daughter admired one of my wife's dresses.

"May I have it? I shall pay for it."

"Please take it . . . as a gift."

The girl would have none of that. She paid, and paid handsomely. Four slaves groaned into our courtyard with a pretty penny measuring four feet and weighing about two hundred pounds.

Our bewilderment as to what to do with it was soon relieved. The next day the chief took it back and returned the dress.

The girl, walking about in the garment, had scandalized and horrified the good people of the village. If a foreign woman chose to wear such a thing they could not help it . . . but a daughter of Rumung! For one thing, it revealed the contour of the thighs, and that the bulky straw-stack worn by the Kanaka belle assuredly does not do. On the other hand, it concealed the breasts, as if they were something to be ashamed of. No respectable Kanaka woman would cover her bosom. That would insult the gods who made it. Thus the proprieties were quite different above and below the waist. But perhaps one does not need to go to Yap to find human reason meeting itself coming back when it tries to decide the illusive question as to just what constitutes modesty.

How did Yap get such an unwieldy coinage? The tradition is that a thousand years ago one of the more disreputable gods thought to cause dissension among men. They were at peace because they had nothing to war over. He would give them something to war over. Money.

He whispered to a king of Tomil a plan to make him great and powerful. Obedient to the heavenly vision, the king sailed south over unknown waters to islands of the Palau group. There he found shining rock (calcite) which the malicious deity instructed him to have his men hew out with their shell axes into flat pieces rounded like the orb of the full moon. These were loaded into the canoe and brought to Yap, not without many perils. The god cast a spell over the people that caused every man of them to desire nothing so much as one of these

88

heaven-sent stones. To obtain them, they paid to the king of Tomil great riches in the form of coconuts, canoes and houses. So the wheels became a medium of exchange for goods.

And those who tell the legend go on to say that there has been no peace in Yap since then. The golden (or stone) apple of discord disruptured the island paradise. Formerly there had been no covetousness, for there was nothing to covet. No man desired his neighbor's coconuts for he had his own. There was food enough for everyone and no one wanted clothing. Greed was born when money came in. There was quarreling among relatives as to who should inherit which rock. Feuds between neighbors. Wars between villages. The elders of Yap, ignorant of the fact that the Bible agrees with them, have their own bitter reasons to believe that the love of money is the root of all evil.

"Nine quarrels out of ten are over money," one told me.

How the god must have laughed!

There was only enough of the first money to be tantalizing. Expeditions set out to get more. They went not only to Palau but to Guam where an even finer stone could be obtained. But it is four hundred miles to Guam and the seas are stormy. Many canoes were lost, particularly on the return voyage when loaded to the danger point with great stone wheels. It was not uncommon for twenty canoes to set out for Guam and only one return.

Of course the difficulty and danger in securing the stone kept up its value. There could be no counterfeiting, for there was no similar stone to be found in Yap. It is a calcite or crystallized carbonate of lime which forms in veins filling the cracks in limestone or other rock. There is nothing inherently precious about it. It has value to the Yap native only because it is hard to get and because it is the accepted medium of exchange.

These goings-on amused not only the god but an Irishman who was not named O'Brien. But that name will do until his *café-au-lait* children cease to be sensitive about the old rascal's exploits.

Buccaneer O'Brien cast anchor in Yap harbor during the Spanish rule (a rule that was largely characterized by the lack of any) and proceeded to look the natives over with a view to making what he could out of them. He soon found that they would give copra, fish, women, anything they possessed, for stone money.

Very well, stone money they should have. He had heard that large pieces were especially in demand. That was where he fitted in. On his schooner he could transport pieces many times as large as could be carried in canoes.

I found on the island of Palau a cross-eyed old native sailor with the shamrock tattooed on his brown skin who had sailed with Captain O'Brien for years. He told me the story.

"He came to Palau and went to the king. He asked for many men to help dig stone money.

"The king said, 'What will you give?'

"The captain gave rope. He gave paint to paint the bodies of the dead. Dye to color lava-lavas. And some guns. He promised to give more when the work was done.

"The men of Palau dug . . . many months, years. Small stones took little time. But it took two years to dig out a great wheel.

"We kept taking the wheels to Yap and selling them to the natives for copra.

"But the chiefs of Palau became angry because he paid no more and was cruel to the men. They looked for chance to punish him."

The opportunity came when Captain O'Brien was wrecked in the Palau group on the island of Babeldaob at Alklung. The natives seized all his goods. But this punishment was not enough.

"Now we'll give you what you gave us." They lashed him to a tree and brought out a cat-o'-nine-tails salvaged from his own ship. They flogged him.

After his release he lost no time in lodging complaint at Hongkong. A warship visited Palau and demanded an indemnity in the form of large quantities of copra and bêche de mer from the offending village of Alklung.

Time passed and the indemnity was not paid. Then came two warships, the *H.M.S. Lily* under Captain Evans and the *H.M.S. Comus* under Captain East. Their men landed and burned the village to the ground. The people fled to the interior. Captain Evans was in favor of pursuing and exterminating them. But Captain East, old and kindly, said, "They have run away. Let be."

Upon return to England, Captain Evans complained, "It was impossible to do anything on Palau, because of East."

So Captain East was considered too old and gentle to teach the savages of the South Seas due respect for the white man. He lost his command.

Captain O'Brien sowed trouble by supplying the natives with guns—but he was not the only trader to do that. For one gun he must have fifty five-gallon cans of turtle shell, or fifty rice bags of bêche de mer.

He married a native woman of Nauru. And since her younger sister didn't want to be left alone, he married her too. The two wives seemed to find it an ideal arrangement. They lived together happily on a charming islet of Yap, their joint spouse being most of the time away on one foray or another.

Several old chiefs of Yap and Palau recalled only too well how the doughty captain had taken a gang of natives to work on his island, Mapia, near New Guinea . . . and left them there. He said it was too much bother to bring them back. The survivors finally attracted the attention of a passing ship and were rescued.

"When he saw a girl he liked," said a reminiscing chief, "he would take. A pig—'Put it on board, I'll eat it.' No pay. Bad man. But when the Germans came they stopped his wild tricks."

Life lost its savor after that for the burly and jovial buccaneer. The Germans hedged him in with *verbotens*. One day he stocked his schooner for a long voyage, kissed his wives and a few other ladies good-by, and sailed away. He never came back. Some say that he went to an island known only to him, for he was an excellent navigator and knew the South Seas as few men did. Others suppose that he was lost at sea.

However that may be, he left behind him monuments that will stand to his memory for thousands of years. The largest coin of his minting that I saw measured twelve feet and was estimated to weigh about two tons. Flip that over the counter! But the greatest of all is said to lie at the bottom of Yap harbor. While being transferred from the schooners deck to a raft, it slid into the water. The old men who saw it swear that it was twenty feet wide . . . but that may be a fish-that-was-lost measurement.

The great museums naturally want some of these monoliths, unique in the history of the world's coinage. They have taken a few of the smaller ones; but have not yet undertaken to bargain with the natives for a giant stone, remove it without benefit of motor truck, and ship it to the other side of the world. The natives might well do without the stones, for they have brought them nothing but trouble. Lacking currency, they would step back to the stone-age system of barter.

Nor would it be a long step. In fact barter is used today in most Yap transactions. The clumsiness of the currency makes it easier to trade goods for goods.

There are standard terms understood by everybody. Two coconuts sell for one match. Ten nuts will buy one roll of bread of regulation size in Colonia. Ten nuts are the equivalent of one pack of Golden Bat cigarettes. The man who has brought his nuts from a great distance may demand and get one or two cigarettes extra. Ten leaves of tobacco buy twenty-five nuts. One cider-bottle of petroleum goes for twenty nuts and a beer-bottle of petroleum is paid for forty nuts.

The natives sell chickens, eggs, pigs, in the same way—for petroleum, phonographs, harmonicas, not for money. They do not understand money in the form of small silver and copper pieces, so insignificant compared with their majestic coins of stone. They cannot get the values through their heads. Too much mathematics involved. Besides, who knows how long this foreign money will be good? First Spanish money came. Then German money, and Spanish was no good. Then Japanese money, and German was no good. But Yap money is always good. It goes on forever.

The foreigner who regards these stones as of little value will be sharply disillusioned when he tries to buy one. He must pay goods to the value of about seventy-five U.S. dollars for a Guam wheel a foot in diameter! The Palau wheels cost less. A poor specimen, waist-high, is valued at four thousand coconuts, worth in the islands about twenty dollars. A stone man-high is worth many villages and plantations, and the stones two-men-high are considered to be beyond price.

The great stones, of course, will not be owned by individuals but by communities. They are displayed outside of the All Men House which thereby acquires the native name, *Febai* (Money House).

Private homes are flanked with smaller pieces, from two to five feet high. The Yap resident would think it as curious to take his money inside the house as we would to leave ours in the yard. How could anyone see your money if you kept it in the house? Moreover, there would scarcely be room left for the family.

However, the small pieces, six inches or so in diameter, are kept indoors. Not only because they would be too easily carried away if left outside, but because the householder would be ashamed to show them. It would be like displaying pennies. He would be thought a poor man.

Therefore large stones are in demand. Rather than accept small wheels, the creditor prefers to let the bill mount until he can be paid with a handsome wheel big enough to attract real attention as it leans against his house.

Such coins are rarely stolen. It is hard to slip away with half a ton of rock. Still it could be done while the people of the house are absent. But where could one take the booty? It would be futile to remove it to some island outside of the Yap group because, there, such currency is not used. If it is kept in the Yap Islands it will be traced. There are no inscriptions on these coins by which to identify them; but the details, strata and measurements of every wheel are memorized by the owner. He would recognize his wheel anywhere.

The larger wheels even have individual names and are known by name and appearance to everyone in the islands. They are even better known than people; for people come and go, are born and die, but these familiar faces remain from generation to generation. Every wheel has its story, and those several hundred years old are rich with legends.

Today the mint is idle; no more stone money is being "coined." This may be partly due to the growing competition of Japanese money. There is a greater reason. The population has shrunk to half its former size, but the supply of money has remained the same. So there is more than enough to go around. In other words, Yap's currency is inflated. Also the value of labor has risen. So it would cost more to go to Palau and dig out new wheels than the wheels would be worth.

Although the use of the wheels as currency is slightly decreasing, the hoarding spirit will long keep up the value of the old stones. As each family dies out its stones are quarrelsomely claimed by others, still giving delight to the malicious god aloft. As house after house is abandoned, the wheels pile up around the homes of the survivors. Perhaps even before Macaulay's New Zealander sits upon the ruins of London Bridge and contemplates what was once London, someone may perch upon a twelve-foot coin in a long-deserted Yap village and gaze about to see nothing but huge round monoliths walling in the spots where thatch homes once stood. Like tombstones to a vanished race.

Will there be nothing left in Yap but money?

XV:
Footprints of Spain

AFTER we had spent two weeks in the jungle, Governor Mizuno sent word that there was accommodation for us in the port town, Colonia.

It was an opportunity to see another side of Yap life—a side more comfortable but less agreeable.

Colonia seemed a metropolis after the jungle. For there are actually electric lights in Colonia, and a road smooth enough for bicycles. There are even a few bicycles. But I fear they are more for swank than for use, since the most languid rider can cover the distance from one extremity of the town to the other in forty seconds flat.

Colonia is on Yap's main island beside the harbor where Japanese ships cast anchor. From a distance it looks like a strip of white adhesive tape neatly stuck to the edge of the lagoon. It boasts four dozen resplendent sheet-iron roofs and is ashamed of half a dozen thatch roofs. The name Colonia has continued to fit during Spanish, German and Japanese times, since the one and only colony of foreigners has always been located here.

The Japanese government office is just where the Spanish office was, perched on a walled mound, suitable for defense in case of native rebellion. The jail is still called a calaboose. The sound of bells still comes down from the old Spanish mission where a black-bearded Spanish priest, weary of trudging from his house to the chapel every time there is ringing to be done, has stretched cords from the bells up the mountainside to his own veranda.

But the most striking reminders of old Spain are the natives who share Colonia with the Japanese. These natives are not Kanakas, but Chamorros, like the people of Guam. They look, act and speak like tropic-mellowed Spaniards.

Their names seem strangely out of place on these tropic isles.

We lived with Jesus Untalan. His wife was Mecaila. Their twelve children (for the Chamorros are more prolific than the vanishing Kanakas) were Vicentico, Manolo, Juanito, Maria, Teresa, Marcos, Tomasa, José, Filomena, Urzula, Joaquina and Felicida.

Their house was no thatch hut, but an old Spanish hacienda, white-walled, with two outdoor stairways going up the front of it like akimbo elbows to a second-floor veranda. The cooling trade struck it full blast. The lagoon shore was not fifty feet away. The view through the palms out over the sail-flecked lagoon was enchanting, if one could overlook the outhouse perched above the water at the end of a long and hazardous bridge of two logs.

Behind the veranda was a great room which served as living room, dining room and ballroom; for every night the room was cleared, the floor of excellent tamana wood was waxed, the girls turned on the phonograph, the boys took the guitars down from the walls, Jesus brought out his accordion, and there was music and dancing until the town's electric power was cut off at eleven. And sometimes a continuation by oil lamp and candle until after twelve.

95

Which did not prevent the whole family from going to early mass at six the next morning.

It would be hard to imagine an unchurchly Chamorro. "More than one hundred per cent Catholics," remarked the Governor.

The Chamorros take as much pride in putting on clothing as the Kanakas in laying it off. Church-going calls out the mantilla, the long, trailing, highly figured Philippine skirt, the diaphanous balloon sleeves. It puts the men in starched white and sombrero. Two-thirds of the chapel is filled with swirls of color and pools of white erect on wooden benches. The other third is occupied by dark-brown Kanakas seated on the cement floor, their grass skirts flipped under them. Ostrich-like, their slender bodies rise out of feathery masses of grass. Incense is swinging at the altar, but the overwhelming odor is that of grass. The chapel smells like a barn full of new hay.

"It's not right," says the padre. "My Chamorro parishioners complain. But what can I do? They would not be willing to pay for enough incense to drown out that smell . . . it would cost more than the mission is worth!"

Three centuries ago Spain took the islands. Imperial Spain . . . how magnificent was her outreach in those days! She equipped Columbus when his own people would not. She sent her conquistadors to take over the Americas. Her explorers looked upon the Pacific from both shores. Her navigators sailed down the coast of Africa, appropriating what pleased them, through the Indian Ocean, planted their flag in the Philippines, then lightly took over the islands to the north, even to the door of Japan. It is startling to find in these far Oriental lands the imprint of the mailed fingers of a small nation the thickness of the world away. Spain had a long arm in those days. And an itching palm. The world was none too large for her. But dreams of empire are like all dreams . . . morning comes.

After Spain's rude awakening Germany began dreaming where Spain had left off. The isles of the Orient and much else became German. Kultur should take the world. The dream faded in 1914-18.

Plagues brought by the Spaniards scourged the Marianas. On some islands the Chamorros were decimated. But, in the meantime, the

Spanish dons who had come, wifeless, to the islands had commandeered Chamorro women. Although in this they had no thought for the Chamorro people, they nevertheless inadvertently saved the race. For the half-caste children were a superior breed. The infusion of new blood revived the native race. Also the Spaniard transmitted to his children the white's measure of immunity to white diseases. So the mixed-blood Chamorros began to hold their own and to multiply.

It was not so with the Kanakas, for there was very little inter-marriage between Spaniard and Kanaka. All that the Kanaka got from the white man was his diseases.

Thus it happened that the Spaniards gave their strength to the Chamorros and their weaknesses to the Kanakas. The latter did not get the benefit of an infusion of Spanish blood which would offer resistance to Spanish ailments.

The Chamorros of today are a half-Spanish race. Their language too is half-Spanish. Many choppy Chamorro words have been fitted with perambulating suffixes so that they roll with Castilian smoothness, while many Spanish polysyllables that were nine-tenths flourish have been cut to a syllable or two for simple island use; and the whole is chanted in sing-song fashion with a plaintive questionlike rise at the end of each sentence. Tagalog words are also present and Tagalog strains in the blood, for the Spaniards brought Filipino soldiers to the Marianas.

The Chamorros are a good-looking people. In the Untalan tribe, Manolo, Vicentico and José were as stalwart and handsome as toreadors. Filomena who prepared delectable Spanish dishes for us, and Tomasa, who was a nurse in the hospital, would have graced a beauty contest.

In fact they did. A contest was organized by the little local paper to pick Yap's foremost Chamorro beauty. All applicants must have their photographs taken by Nobayashi, the photographer, and submitted to the paper. Doubtless young Nobayashi made every effort to employ his pictorial skill impartially . . . but first prize was awarded to his sweetheart, Tomasa, and second prize to her sister, Filomena.

Miss Yap received a mirror in which to study her golden-tan charms; and Filomena a parasol to protect hers.

We found life soft and urban in Colonia. To be sure, there was no such thing as a hot bath. And no ice. But what of that! There was always music, even in the springs of our iron bed. Caballeros everywhere twanged and hummed. My wife was in demand to play Yap's only piano, in the home of Dr. Yoshida. It had been retrieved from the wreck of the *Shizuoka Maru* but the salvagers had neglected to fish out a pianist along with it. The children of the Japanese school and the children of the native school sang, the latter more musically. And ever and anon there pressed against the trade the rich, searching notes of the mission bells . . . reminding us, as the padre did:

"All else comes and goes. This remains. You are the first Americans to live on Yap in more than twenty-five years. But soon, you will go. Nationalities come and go—English, American, German—the Germans ruled these islands but where will you find a trace of them today? But Spain! The Spanish government has gone but the essence of Spain, the spiritual aura of it, the incense of it, remains!"

Somewhat like, I irreverently thought, the grin of Alice-in-Wonderland's Cheshire cat which lingered on after the cat itself had disappeared.

But it's true, the Spanish aura remains. And it is especially evident on New Year's Day.

Spanish bells bring in the new year. The Untalan family (sans guests) go up to mass at six. There is so much suppressed excitement that breakfast burns. At ten the married sons come with their guitars, wives and children.

Mrs. Untalan is wearing a mantilla, a trailing large-flowered skirt and a puff-sleeved Filipino waist. Jesus has even put on a coat. The girls' skirts all sweep the floor. It is like a pageant of peacocks.

Down at the government office there is an official Japanese New Year's Banzai to the accompaniment of *saké*. But these will not go. They prefer their own way of celebrating. Besides, Mr. and Mrs. Untalan do not understand Japanese well. It's a task—this learning a new language every time the overlords change! Besides the Chamorro language and the Kanaka tongues they had to know Spanish in old Guam; then English when the Americans came in; then German to get along with the officials of Yap; and now it's Japanese.

The floor is cleared and waxed. The guitars strike up music of the lilting, swaying, hammocky sort. Jesus and Mecaila dance a very fast waltz slowly in jerky mincing steps. Four naked Kanakas come up on the veranda and look in.

At noon we sit down to a very Spanish dinner. The conversation is in the half-Spanish Chamorro with occasional lapses into a whining, steel-guitar sort of English for us or something like Japanese for the benefit of Mr. Nobayashi. He sits beside Miss Yap. He is flushed with the consciousness of how ravishing she is today.

In the afternoon, more dancing, to the phonograph. The waltz and the tango are popular, the fox trot unknown. Jesus plays the accordion and an old uncle does a sort of heavy-booted fandango that makes the floor shake. Mother Untalan retires from the scene to smoke a cigar. Mr. Nobayashi, with Nipponese perseverance, practices some steps the foreigners have brought from New York.

All the phonograph records are languid, tropical, like flowing mantillas. Aloha Oe and a dozen other Hawaiian melodies. Tangos and rumbas. The Peanut Vendor. Paloma, Manuela del Rio. Vuelta al Ruedo. The Hills of Tennessee. Singing in the Rain. My Song of the Nile. Oh, Susannah (with zither and guitar). Rose of My Heart. When I Looked in Your Wonderful Eyes. La Mulata (rumba). La Cachimba (rumba). Pangs of Love. Tango delle Rose. Drifting and Dreaming. Chiquita. I Kiss Your Hand, Madame. Io Te Amo. My Moonlight Madonna. And a couple of Rudy Vallées.

Harlem would despise this silken stuff as much as Yap would detest Harlem's broken glass.

The room is in character. At the front it opens through great double doors upon the spacious veranda among the palm-tops. Looking leftward, there is the phonograph in the corner with a guitar and banjo hanging above it. All the left side of the room is taken up by six colored religious pictures of pensive saints and anthropomorphic Jehovahs riding upon clouds in gilt frames against the whitewashed walls. Also

99

there is what appears to be a shrine, judging from Nobayashi-san's reverent expression when Tomasa goes through it to powder her nose—the door to the girls' bedroom.

In the back wall is another shrine, the door to the kitchen. Against this wall is a small organ. Also a sideboard upon which are two large pink shells, and two Santa Clauses in very hot-looking long red coats. In the corner is a huge, oval, gilt-framed portrait of a male relative with a mustache in full color . . . yes, the mustache. The likeness is brilliantly varnished. It bulges convexly like a medallion, or a ballooned shirt-front.

On the right wall is an oil painting of Mrs. Untalan with her crucifix. A sketch of the hacienda. Three more guitars. And two porcelain blue fish hanging on the wall mouths upward full of artificial flowers. There are doors to more bedrooms.

High in the walls are grilled windows into the next rooms. The ceiling is of blue and white boards in four different levels quite as in Spain or South America.

At four P.M. all go up to the Spanish mission again. And at seven, down to Juan Diaz's house for prayers. Meanwhile the Japanese carpenter who occupies one room is roaring drunk with New Year saké.

In accordance with Spanish custom, the evening starts late. At nine the married sons and daughters drift in, each coming first to kiss father Untalan's hand.

Governor Mizuno and his Chief Clerk Ikematsu, who has an encyclopedic knowledge of Yap as the result of eleven years' residence, grace the occasion. Also huge but light-footed Agapito Hondonero, who is stationed in this birthplace of typhoons by the Manila Weather Bureau so that the Philippine Islands may have due warning of trouble before it reaches them.

The guitars are at it again. Ask a young lady for a dance and she looks to her mother for a nod before she consents. At eleven the lights go out and so do the guests.

Candles are lit for bed-going. The family stands about for a few moments . . . too bad to end such a good day. The trade brings up the perfume of copra from the drying sheds.

No sound but the snores of the Japanese carpenter sleeping off his drunk in the next room. Mother Untalan's face warps into haughty disapproval. These pagans do not realize that New Year's was meant to be a holy day as well as a merry one.

She lights a nightcap cigar and goes to her room. Later we hear her praying at her open window, pausing now and then to smoke.

XVI:

President Wilson and Yap

WOODROW WILSON lived a quarter century before his time. He advocated an international organization to enforce peace. Congress disagreed with him. Now Congress agrees with him. He was opposed to handing over Micronesia to Japan. If he had had his way we should probably not be at war with Japan now. Lloyd George and Clemenceau overruled him. He wanted Yap internationalized. Perhaps now it will be. But much bloody water has flowed under the bridge since he made the proposal.

Wilson was a dreamer. We had no use for dreamers. We preferred to learn in the school of hard knocks. Very well, we are getting the hard knocks—may their lesson sink deep.

Although Wilson favored American withdrawal from the Philippines he did not wish to leave them exposed to the rapacity of Japan. For he was enough of a visionary to envision Japan's coming career of aggression. Yap is close to the Philippines. It is also close to Guam. Yap and Guam would have furnished a double door by which ships of all nations could have passed through the Japanese island-wall to the Philippines and China.

The most urgent reason for making an exception of Yap was that it was the seat of a cable station established by the Germans in 1904 as well as of a radio station put there in 1913. President Wilson was loath to see the cables pass into Japanese hands, since they offered an alternative connection with the Philippines and China if ever the American cable should be out of order. But the Japanese were equally conscious of the value of controlling Pacific cables. In the words of an American memorandum presented confidentially at the Peace Conference, "It is quite possible that Japanese eagerness for the former German islands north of the equator is partially stimulated by a desire for control of the German cable system."

The German cables were three: Yap to Guam; Yap to Shanghai; Yap to Celebes in the Netherlands Indies. Other lines completed the connection with the Philippines and many points in Asia. Yap was the nerve center of communications in the Western Pacific.

When the mandate was discussed in the Peace Conference Wilson rose to speak of Yap. Delegates scanned their charts, for the very existence of such an island was not known to most of them. The President stipulated, for his government, that a reservation be made in regard to Yap and that the question of the disposal of the island should be delayed for later consideration. He recommended that Yap be internationalized in order that control of its cables should not be monopolized by one power.

This suggestion was either forgotten or ignored, and Japan received mandate to all former German islands in the Pacific north of the equator.

Perhaps because of pressure of other matters the point was overlooked by the American delegation and no protest was made at the time. It was not until a year later that the question was revived. In 1920 the American government queried Japan as to plans for the international control of Yap. The Japanese government called attention to the fact that Yap had been included in the mandate to Japan. Another American note followed. It reviewed the reservations made by President Wilson and also by Secretary Lansing at the Peace Conference. Japan replied tartly that the Japanese delegate had been present at no session where such a reservation was made, and that if it had been made in his absence it was an act of bad faith.

This bluff was deflated by French delegates who clearly recalled the reservation having been made in the presence of the Japanese delegate, Baron Makino, who shared at the time in the informal discussion of the question.

Feeling as reflected by the press was very bitter both in Japan and the United States. For a year the controversy went on. It ended in victory for Japan. However, a treaty was signed to save America's face. In it the consent of the United States to the Japanese mandate was hurried over and stress laid upon minor concessions:

"The United States and its nationals shall have free access to the Island of Yap on a footing of entire equality with Japan or any other nation and their respective nationals in all that relates to the landing and operation of the existing Yap-Guam cable . . . Nationals of the United States shall have the unrestricted right to reside in the island . . . Nationals of the United States shall have complete freedom of entry and exit in the island for their persons and property."

These polite indulgences proved to be so much eyewash. Americans, however welcome according to the treaty, somehow never managed to stop over on Yap, much less set up housekeeping there. They were never forbidden, but only dissuaded, or diverted. The Japs are good at that. Everything they do is "for your best interest."

XVII:

When the Yanks Get to Yap

So FAR as I could judge, the Japanese had no intention of turning Yap into a stronghold. We may doubt that it will put up strong resistance.

True, the island must be approached with some caution. Yap has two jaws that will consume anyone who enters them. They are the two reefs flanking the tortuous entrance to Tomil harbor. It would be strange if guns were not now mounted on these reefs and if the twist-ing, two-mile passage were not mined.

The principal town, Colonia, is on this harbor. Doubtless the chief garrison of the island will be found in Colonia. However, our Navy may think best to ignore the trap-like harbor and reach the enemy by a different route.

Landings may be made elsewhere; although in this too there is some danger and difficulty. Yap's natural defenses are fairly good. The group of four main islands and a number of islets is protected by a coral reef thirty-five miles long separated from the shore by a lagoon about a mile wide. There is an occasional break to be found in the reef. But the lagoon is not deep enough for any but shallow-draft boats. Moreover, fast motorboats are very likely to come to grief on the fish weirs.

Some of these weirs are hundreds of years old, yet as solid as when built. The typical weir consists of a rectangular wall of coral blocks built on the floor of the lagoon and enclosing a space of some dozens of square feet. The wall of this pen is often three or four feet thick, offering a formidable obstacle to the prow of a fast boat. At high tide the wall is concealed under about a foot of water. As the tide goes down, fish are trapped in the pen. At low tide the top of the wall rises well above the surface, safely confining the fish until the fisherman comes with his net to scoop them out. Or the *yub* root is placed in the water, its narcotic poison stupefying the fish which float to the surface and are readily picked up with the fingers.

When the shore is reached there may be another obstacle—an almost impenetrable tangle of mangrove along the water's edge.

If it is necessary to step out into the lagoon to get the boat off the rocks or to wade ashore, anyone without thick-soled boots should walk warily. Lying on the floor of the lagoon is the sting ray.

There is no living thing, not even the shark, that the native fears more than the sting ray. It is a flat, pancake fish with a long tail like a riding whip. In fact the tail was commonly used by Spanish officers in the Philippines to quicken the movements of their native recruits.

Somehow the error has got into many valuable works that the sting ray carries its spine or barb on the end of its tail, and that, when

In the money! Mary demonstrates the size of one of Yap's largest
stone coins.

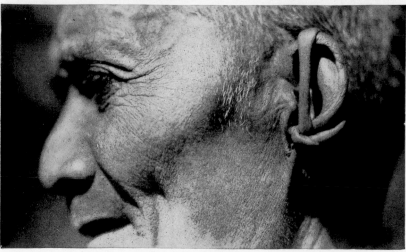

The extended ear lobe is useful for carrying packages. But it is in the way when there is work to be done and is then knotted neatly about the ear.

stepped upon in the muddy shallows, it flips up its tail in scorpion fashion, drives the barb deep into the flesh and leaves it there. Some even assert that the ray can fling its barb through space, just as a porcupine is supposed, also erroneously, to be able to shoot its quills.

Specimens brought ashore by our native friends carried their barbs, three to five in number, projecting upward from the body near the base of the tail. The fish loves to bask on the bottom in shallow water. The fisherman or bather who steps on one of the barbs is due for a painful death. The barb is sharply toothed along both edges. When an effort is made to pull it from the flesh, the teeth spread, making extraction without skilled surgical assistance impossible. Infection does the rest.

The barbs were formerly used for tipping spears, arrows and javelins. Assassins found them ideal for their purpose. Thrust into the chest or back, the sawlike bone was more deadly than a knife, for a knife can be drawn out.

"A favorite way of getting rid of your enemy," says an observer of conditions in Samoa, "was to set upright in the dried grass of the victim's sleeping mat a splintered spine of the sting ray. This, piercing the body during sleep, would do its deadly work. When embedded in the body there is no hope of life, for it is impossible to pull it out, and with each movement of the body the spine works its way into the vitals."

There are other unpleasant inhabitants of the lagoon—the barracuda with his sharp spear which he is not at all slow to use on intruders, the garfish similarly equipped, the pugnacious moray, the electric eel sometimes six feet long and packing a whale of a shock in his big battery, and the tiger fish whose tentacles violently burn the skin and whose squirted poison will cause loss of sight if it gets into the eyes.

Once on shore, there is not much to fear from Mother Nature. There are no snakes on Yap, nor any animal more dreadful than the mosquito, which is non-malarial. The big bat prefers fruit to human blood. The robber crab with his dangerous pincers a foot long will not fight unless attacked.

Moving through the jungle, it is well to avoid stepping on a green rock until one is sure that it is a green rock and not a *galuf*. This is a giant iguana four or five feet long. It does no harm unless annoyed, then inflicts a vicious bite. The natives dread it, not so much for its bite as for its supposed supernatural powers.

An excellent tree to avoid is the *chongot* or poison tree. Tall, with light bark and long leaves, it looks most respectable. But it is a villain at heart. Its acrid white juice causes terrible swellings and sores, often resulting in death. Arrows and spears are tipped with the poison.

Jungle roads are numerous. Some of them were paved with stones by the ancient inhabitants and the pavements are still in good repair. According to the *Japan Year Book* Yap in 1937 had 118 miles of road.

So there is not so much difficulty in getting about Yap after one lands as there is in making the landing.

Probably it will be found that the best way to land on Yap is from the air. Paratroopers may drop down upon the interior plateaus with very small likelihood of encountering any Japanese and may then come up in the rear of garrisons stationed at Colonia and other villages along the coast. These points will be vulnerable to air attack and also to sea bombardment. Since the island group is only sixteen miles long and four to seven miles wide, any point is within range of ships' guns outside the reef.

Assuming that Truk, 950 miles to the east, has been taken and is used as an air base, bombers may easily reach Yap. It is doubtful that fighter escort will be needed, but, if so, it can readily be provided either from carriers or from certain of the dozens of small islands that lie between Truk and Yap.

The fate of Yap will be even more decisive if Guam, only 500 miles distant, has been taken. And it may well be that this will happen first, since the hop from Truk to Guam is an easy one of 650 miles.

But the order to jump should not be given until it is certain that the plane is over a plateau and not a swamp. Yap's famous gluey bogs would seriously slow up paratroopers and make them clay pigeons for Jap snipers.

There are some 4,000 natives on Yap. They can be expected neither to help nor hinder. They do not love the Japs, but neither do they have pleasant memories of the white man as represented by the Spaniards and Germans and occasional roistering hell-raising American whalers. They will shelter the stranger in their All Men Houses with equal courtesy whether he be United Nations or Nipponese. They are a quiet, kindly people and hate no one. The Spanish priest made this comforting observation concerning them, "If they cut off your head it will not be because they hate you but merely because they want it as a souvenir." Actually they are too tired nowadays to cut off heads. Their number has diminished by half. Forty per cent of their women never bear. They are retiring into the shadows whence they came. They are content to sit on a piece of stone money and chew betel. They should be treated with sympathy and consideration. Under no circumstances should any hand be laid on their slender food supplies, which are barely sufficient to save them from starvation. Yap is fertile and can raise many kinds of fruit; but unfortunately it lies in the typhoon belt, and the typhoon destroys in an hour trees and crops that have been patiently nursed along for months. This adds to the apathy of the people. Heaven as well as the world seems against them.

Prize package of the men from the sky will be the cable and radio station. If they can take its defenders unawares and forestall its demolition by the Japanese, a valuable acquisition will have been made. And the heart of Japan's web of communications in the mandated islands will have been cut out.

The cable and radio station stands on a hill just back of the port town, Colonia.

Yap, in United Nations hands, will be a useful way station on the road to Palau, major Japanese naval base 300 miles to the southwest. Yap's harbor, a mile wide, is too small to serve as an important fleet base. But the plateaus of Yap are good potential airdromes. That on Tomil Island is about five miles long and a mile wide, 500 feet above the sea. At the southern end of the main island is a low plain which will also be found useful.

A final word. Preserve Yap for the archeologists. It has never been seriously studied. Its many stone ruins and its present inhabitants are both vestiges of a former age. With no written language, Yap has not yet caught up to the Egypt of hieroglyphics and papyrus three thousand years before Christ. Yap is one of the world's few remaining windows to the distant past, an invitation to learning if we are interested to know how our forebears may have lived before the days of recorded history.

XVIII:
You Will Hear About Palau

Before this war is over you will hear much about Palau. Now unknown, it may become as well known as Guadalcanal.

For Palau is the most important Japanese base in all Micronesia with the possible exception of Truk.

The importance of Palau is suggested by the fact that the Japanese made it the headquarters of their *Nanyo* government administering the entire mandate.

The visitor who sees no more than the harbor in which his passenger ship anchors would dismiss Palau as of no military value.

The *Yamashiro Maru,* though only three thousand tons, had to watch its p's and q's while wriggling through the tortuous two-mile-long passage connecting the open sea with the harbor. The deep blue channel between the jade green shoals was often only three times the ship's breadth. A strong wind together with a little miscalculation might easily pile the vessel on the reef.

Reaching the harbor, we found a six-thousand-ton vessel already at anchor. There was barely room to berth beside it. Three would be a crowd in Koror Harbor. Hence the comment in the book of a tourist who made the ship his hotel, "We do not need to worry about Palau as a naval base."

Certainly there was nothing here to suggest the existence on the other side of the island of a basin large enough to accommodate the entire Japanese fleet.

We were not hindered in disembarking at Palau, probably because it was considered that there were enough policemen on shore to take good care of us.

We stepped off not onto a pier but into a launch which proceeded to squirm through narrow canals between islands, with the bottom visible all the time, to tie up at last to Madelai pier on Koror, one of the 26 islands of Palau. About the pier the water was too shallow for any but small craft. However, a six-year plan had been laid out, to begin in 1936, by which the sum of nearly three million yen was to be spent in harbor improvements. The channels were to be deepened and straightened, and a causeway built from Madelai pier to the neighboring island of Arakabesan, where an airport was being built. If these changes were made, Koror Harbor is now of more use commercially. But no money could convert it into a really formidable fleet base.

As to the airdrome, that is another matter. We shall come to that later.

An amazing panorama lay before us as we stood on the pier. The rising slope of the island was covered with hundreds of half-finished houses on which carpenters were noisily at work. What looked like an entire town was being thrown up with mushroom speed. Trucks loaded with building materials roared through the newly-laid streets. Housing in a hurry must be provided for the flood of workers pouring in from Japan. For there was work at high wages in Palau. Although this was in 1935, Japan had already begun to prepare Palau as a spearhead for the attack upon the Philippines and the Netherlands Indies.

A few German missionaries were still left in Palau, relics of the German regime. I had written to one of them, Wilhelm Siemer, asking if he could take us into his home. He met us on the pier.

"We'll get a taxi," he said.

"But don't you live right here in the village?"

"Yes."

"Then, can't we walk?"

Mr. Siemer's trim black beard has an elfish way of pointing forward when he grins.

"You have been spoiled by Yap," he said. "In the first place, don't let anybody hear you call this a village! And in the second place, get into this car and let's go."

Taxi in the South Seas! It was all wrong. But we stepped into the car (from Detroit) and whirled up through a half mile of rising houses—attractive little homes they would be when finished, all in Japanese style, in plots roomy enough for plenty of shrubbery, and with a romantic view over the island-studded bay. Then through a fine old residential section (old in the boom-town sense, built three or four years ago). Past the extensive buildings of the South Seas government, for the central administrative offices of all the Japanese mandated islands are here. Past great radio towers. An airplane roared over them.

Then just as we expected the town to peter out into jungle, it only began to get serious. Schools, hospital, post office, steamship offices, a typical city park. Then stores, a mile of them, all Japanese, some of them department stores of considerable size. Here and there, as odd as a log cabin on Broadway, was a lone thatch hut with the elbows of Japanese shops in its ribs, or an All Men House with a photographic studio pushed under its overhanging forehead.

And what a furor! Gold-rush excitement. Five thousand people clattered busily about on *geta* where only a few years ago bare feet followed jungle trails. Everywhere crackled the Japanese staccato, sounding like machine-gun fire after the lazy Kanaka speech or the lilting Chamorro.

After a two-mile ride we reached Herr Siemer's home, and were still well within the town limits.

Here was a bit of Germany completely surrounded by Japan; like a sinking island, the waves every day lapping a little higher on its shores. For the Siemers fully expected the deluge in due time. There had been hints that they would not be needed. The Japanese could do everything, yes, even teach Christianity.

There is, of course, a strong native Christian church in Japan. This church sends out its own missionaries, Japanese, to carry the Cross to the islands of the South Seas. Japan is not so unreservedly Buddhist or Shinto as the Western world imagines. The supposedly "pagan" Japanese government subsidizes Japanese missions in the South Seas to the extent of 23,000 yen annually for the Protestant mission, 8,000 yen for the Catholic and 700 yen for the Buddhist. It is to be doubted that Japanese officials hold a prayer-meeting when sending their yen forth to evangelize the islands. In fact it is a sufficiently hard-boiled procedure activated by the conviction that religion, and especially Christianity, is "good for" the natives. It makes them "easy to govern."

Religion can more easily be made a tool of national policy if it is operated by representatives of the nation, not by aliens. So the day was near at hand when Japanese missionaries would take over the German work.

But there is one thing the Japanese can never take over, and that is the preparation of *obstkuchen* to compare with Frau Siemer's. Or *kartoffel-puffer*. Or *sauerbraten*. Frau Siemer had both the dimensions and disposition which make a perfect German *hausfrau*. She looked to us, who were half-starved after our sojourn on tin-can Yap, like an angel, slightly earthbound, as she came in from the kitchen bearing a halo in her hands, or was it a fruit pie? And Palau is a good provider. Fruits, vegetables and meats abound.

The Siemer house always appeared to be smacking its lips, for it was surrounded by an appetizing array of heavily fruited banana trees, coconut trees, breadfruit, papaya and soursop.

Red hibiscus blazed everywhere. In the nearby groves remained a few shaggy native houses, but crisp Japanese houses and stores were coming in. Only the inside of the missionary's house had successfully evaded Japanese influence. Bible texts in German adorned the walls. There were German pictures, hymns, books, newspapers, a German organ, German zither, German pillows, and a table that groaned three times daily in the best German tradition.

And yet these very German people were not primarily Germans, but missionaries. They sank their nationality in their work. They were there for the sake of the natives and the Japanese, not for the sake of Germany. They had not, as some hinted, been sent out as emissaries of the German government, nor were they subsidized by it.

Ludicrously the contrary. The Liebenzeller Mission which commissioned them had received orders from the Nazi government to quit sending money out of Germany. The Mission had been forced to notify these and other missionaries that they must no longer expect to receive funds from the homeland. If they could not support themselves locally they might leave missionary service and go into business. In other words, they were abandoned to their own devices.

But Herr Siemer had not become a missionary because he thought it would pay. Therefore he had no intention of quitting because it did not. His brown parishioners contributed a little. A museum in Germany paid him to make phonograph records of the speech and songs of the natives and to collect certain fauna, particularly rats! Therefore he might be pardoned if, on his errands of mercy, he was drawn to homes of the sort that might supply him with a specimen or two. At any rate, that kept him among the lowly.

The modest sum we paid for board was a godsend to the stranded missionaries. They gave us their best. We were forced to accept their bedroom while they went to sleep on the floor of the church.

Our early morning dreams were colored by the tones of the mission bell and the hymns of natives just beyond the thin partition at the head of our bed. The church and house were under the same roof; in fact there was a door from the bedroom into the church. And the bathroom opened into the pulpit . . . cleanliness next to godliness. Mrs. Siemer played the organ in the living room and an open door admitted its music to the church.

Upon the matted floor of the church sit fifty Kanakas, not barbarians like the people of Yap, but all clothed in cotton prints from Japan and righteousness from Germany. The women are on one side, the men on the other. Between them is the old white-bearded king. Every newcomer dips his bare feet into a tub of water at the door and scuffs them on a rag before entering upon the mats. The reverent air of the place would do credit to a cathedral.

But the natives of Palau in general seem more hushed and suppressed than those of Yap. They move like shadows. Perhaps it is because they see the tidal wave coming.

"Two hundred Japanese came on that ship," said one Palau veteran, nodding toward the liner from Yokohama that rode at anchor in the harbor. "On every ship they come. And those who are here have many children. It is the beginning of the end for the native."

"Why shouldn't the native and the Japanese live side by side?" I asked.

"Because these islands are small. Their resources are few. Not enough for a large population. What little there is will be taken by the most energetic. I mean the Japanese. They are used to going after what they want; we are used to having nature bring us what we want. Ours is the better philosophy, but theirs will win. The Kanaka's day is done."

The Japanese have complete contempt for the native and prefer not to remember that their own blood is partly Micronesian. One of the racial currents making up the people now publicized as the sons of heaven came from Malay and Polynesian lands up through the Micronesian melting pot to Japan, there to blend with the Mongoloid element from Asia. Many traces of this pilgrimage may be found in Japan. For example, the legends of the Japanese have it that their god, Izanagi, wore a "multitudinous and close-toothed comb in the right bunch of his hair." Exactly such a comb has been worn immemorially by the natives of Yap, whence the custom was probably brought north and practiced by the early barbarians of Japan. The Japanese only a century ago blacked their teeth and, in fact, the mistress of a *machiai* or waiting house for geisha still does, as a matter of fashion. The Mongols never did this. It is distinctly a Micronesian and Malayan habit. Japanese houses of the early period resembled those of the islands. The influence is still felt and the flimsy Japanese house of today is not nearly so well suited to the rigors of a Japanese winter as to the seasonless climate of the South Seas.

Old Japan followed the odd custom of confining a woman every month and particularly at childbirth in a "parturition house," a one-roomed, windowless hut situated in the forest well away from the villages. Exactly the same custom is practiced to this day in Yap. The *dopal* is the house of childbirth, also the prison of the girl who has just reached puberty and must remain in the *dopal* for some months until she is fully mature. Every woman must spend a few days of each month in the *dopal*. But it is not in any sense a clubhouse for women as the All Men House is for men. It is the most dreary and dilapidated retreat imaginable, a place of penance, often placed on an islet in a reeking swamp so that men may not easily get to it or women escape from it. When anyone has a right to come or go, boards are placed across the waters of the swamp, and later withdrawn, like the draw-bridge over a castle moat.

Adolescent girls were regularly violated in old Japan. A youth associated intimately with many young girls until he had finally made his choice. The identical custom persists in Yap. A man would not think of marrying a woman without first testing their congeniality by means of premarital relations. Girls are tested long before puberty—hence the necessity of the *dopal* so that they may for at least a few months while maturing be undisturbed.

Cannibalism was not practiced in Micronesia but head-hunting was; and in feudal Japan head chopping was a privilege of the samurai.

Also one is struck by the fact that the ancient gods of Japan and the South Seas are very similar.

Observing the attitude of the Japanese toward the islander, one would never imagine that they were brothers under the skin.

Currents flowed both ways. Black and brown influence came north, yellow went south. There is more than a trace of Mongol blood in Micronesia and it probably came from Japan.

The Japanese, before their era of seclusion, were great sea-rovers and pirates. There have been many authenticated cases of Japanese junks being wrecked in the islands. It is believed that the island of Lele at Kusaie was settled by Japanese. When a Japanese training ship visited Kusaie in 1884 the king told the visitors that his people were descendants of the Japanese race. There are frequent traces of the Japanese languages in the dialects of the islands. There are many similarities in culture.

Long before Japan formally took over the islands, James M. Alexander noted the Japanese strain in Micronesia. He wrote in 1895:

"The Micronesians are a mixed race, part Polynesian and part Japanese with traces of Papuan. The Japanese element is accounted for by the fact that Japanese voyagers have occasionally been storm-driven to great distances over the ocean through the belt of Micronesian islands. In 1814 the British brig, *Forester,* met with a Japanese junk off the coast of California with three living men and fourteen dead bodies on board. In December 1832 a Japanese junk arrived at Hawaii with four of her crew living. The Micronesians are darker and of smaller stature than the Polynesians, but in the western Micronesians they are of lighter complexion and more like the Japanese."

Just as the sailors of shipwrecked junks found the islands congenial, so the Japanese of today, ordinarily quite unwilling to emigrate, find themselves quite at home in these balmy tropics. Not that it is all beer and skittles—or *saké* and *sashimi.* Glowing accounts in Japanese papers have led many emigrants to expect a paradise. It is no paradise. Anyone who goes must have the pioneer spirit. He must take along a plentiful supply of courage. And a can-opener—if he goes to islands that have not already been made to produce by Japanese enterprise.

The cost of living is almost double that of Japan. Typhoons are frequent. There are scorpions on land and sharks in the sea and dengue fever in the air.

But the islands have their good points too. If living costs are high, so are wages. There is more room than in Japan. Your house is not wedged between others; it stands alone in a lovely garden in which flowers are always blooming.

Summer is eternal. The heat is actually less than that of summer in Japan. All the year round the temperature wavers between seventy and eighty-five degrees Fahrenheit. Thanks to the sun and the sea, the air is warm and cool at one and the same time.

Doctors agree that the climate is healthful. But too many Japanese, even in the islands where food is plentiful, make the mistake of depending too much upon canned foods from Japan. They would do better to eat also the fresh native foods, breadfruit, taro, yam, arrowroot, vegetables if any, chicken, pork, fish, coconut, bananas, pineapple and papaya, to insure good health.

As for recreation, there is good swimming and boating inside the protecting reefs, and even mountain-climbing on some islands.

As for work, the immigrant must bend his own back to it, but he can also employ native help cheaply. Moreover, the government is kind. It always stands ready to aid the Japanese in their fishing or farming enterprises.

XIX:

Japanese Flood

THE drastic change in the population of Micronesia has had a profoundly disturbing effect. For a century the population stood almost still at about 50,000. Then a few Japanese began to filter in. Several hundred were already there when Japan took the islands in 1914. By the time her mandate was confirmed in 1919 the number had risen to 3,000. It went on up to 19,835 in 1930, 32,214 in 1933. In 1936 the census recorded 56,496 Japanese, the native population still resting at 50,000. Thus in twenty-one years the population had more than doubled, and the natives found themselves outnumbered by the newcomers.

But worse was yet to come. A Five-Year-Plan of immigration was begun in 1936. It brought the Japanese population up to 62,305 in 1937 and 73,028 in 1939. This is the last year for which figures are obtainable. If the rate of increase of these years has been maintained, and there is every reason to believe it has been since the war has undoubtedly brought many civilians as well as garrisons to the Micronesian bases, the Japanese population of the mandated islands stands in 1944 at approximately 100,000.

In the meantime the native population, which had so long held its own at 50,000, sagged, perhaps under the terrific pressure of the Japanese flood, and by 1939 had dropped to 40,406.

Thus in a single generation the natives, who by immemorial tenure might have been supposed to have a right to all the elbow-room their small islands afforded, were overrun by an alien population more than twice as large as their own.

Immigration did not do all this. Indeed if immigration were stopped tomorrow, the situation would continue to grow progressively more acute. A rapid increase of Japanese would take place even without immigration.

The Japanese birth rate is one of the highest in the world. The native Micronesian birth rate is one of the lowest. In 1934 Japanese births in the islands were 1,714 and deaths 475, the natural increase being 1,239. Native births were 1,562 and deaths 1,637, causing a natural decrease of 75. As noted above, that decrease has since been greatly accelerated.

Japan's rapid settlement of Pacific islands has been a matter of concern to all nations surrounding that ocean. Spain's tenure worried no one—except the natives, and, perhaps, Spain. By the time Spain reached her arm all the way around Asia there was very little strength left in the fingers. Spain could not rule the islands, much less develop them. She was continually involved in bloody wars with the natives. Nor were the Powers much concerned when Germany bought the islands, for they were too far from Germany to be dangerously used. Germany did better than Spain. She produced order. She did some trading in copra and phosphate; but she found it not profitable to transport them halfway around the earth to Germany. But when Japan took the islands there was a flutter of international excitement. Not, as some Japanese have thought, because of any discriminatory feeling toward Japan—but because Japan was in a position to make significant use of the islands. There was no German immigration to the islands. An old resident on Palau remembers that there were fifteen Germans there (three officials, five priests, five sisters, and two traders). Today there are an estimated 15,000 Japanese. Then, in all these islands, there were not more than 100 Germans; now, 100,000 Japanese.

That is the difference. Japan took the islands seriously. Spain and Germany never did.

United Nations victory will not settle the problem. The question will remain: shall the Japanese occupants of the islands be allowed to stay? Many of them are innocent farmers, fishermen and businessmen. It is too bad to have to rout them out of their homes. But they must be prepared to pay the penalty for their nation's rape of Asia.

Japanese infiltration would not stop with Micronesia. Even before the war Japanese were multiplying in the islands of Australasia and Polynesia. There were 25,000 Japanese in the Philippines. Davao in the Philippine island of Mindanao was a tropical Yokohama. Japanese were pouring into the Dutch islands, despite restrictions. We were surprised to learn that steamship fare from Japanese Palau to Dutch Celebes was half rate.

"Why?" we asked the ticket agent in Palau.

"Our government has decided that Celebes is a good place for Japanese."

The government subsidizes the steamship line. Therefore when the government orders that the fare to Celebes shall be cut in half to encourage Japanese colonists to go there, the line obeys.

We later went to Celebes. As we approached the island, Captain Amano waxed lyrical about it.

"A paradise. The Japanese don't know much about Celebes. They think it's a small island. And they suppose it's too hot—because it's on the equator." He hunched his shoulders against the chill wind that cut across the deck. "As a matter of fact, the climate is cooler than in Palau or Yap. And anything will grow. Just right for sugar and cotton. The Japanese go to Brazil, because they know about it. But if I had my choice between South America and Celebes, I'd go to Celebes."

Ashore, we took an automobile ride, the captain with us. The road mounted terraces to the high plateaus of the interior.

"So many different elevations," commented the captain, "that anything can be cultivated. By the sea, the finest coconuts in the Pacific and all manner of tropical fruits. Higher, potatoes. Above that, tea. And on the cool uplands, rice."

We returned to town and looked into the stores. Voile and lace— they formerly came from Switzerland. Now from Japan. And here is the famous Java chintz. It is supposedly from Java. But it came from Osaka. Of course you can buy it in Java, but it will still be from Osaka!

Souvenirs of Menado (made in Japan!). Japan makes the world's souvenirs. In Colombo you may acquire a wooden elephant as a souvenir of Ceylon. It was made in Osaka—but, by agreement with the manufacturers, it is sold only in Colombo.

"Once when I was in New York," says Captain Amano, "I went to the top of the Woolworth tower. I saw a souvenir, a metal tray, with a picture of the Woolworth Building embossed upon it. I bought twenty of them, brought them back to Japan, and distributed them among my relations. One of them turned up his tray and found on the bottom, in very small letters, 'Made in Japan.'"

The war of course immeasurably quickened Japan's economic infiltration into the former Dutch and Australian islands. Japanese workers by the thousands have poured in to man the oil wells and war industries, open shops and accelerate trade. Japanese bosses run the plantations. The Japanese are working their way into the warp and woof of daily economic life.

It is very well to say that they will all be expelled at the war's end. It will be easier to expel them than to insure that they will not come back. They have had a taste of the riches of these lands. They have learned how to develop their resources. They will leave no stone unturned in their effort after the war to dominate Asia economically. And we, for our part, have no wish to prevent legitimate economic development. How to be fair to Japanese trade, and at the same time keep the Pacific from becoming a yellow man's ocean to the complete extinction of the brown and the exclusion of the white, may well rack the brains of postwar administrators of liberated lands.

The Japs talk of a hundred-years war. By that they mean that the decision in the present war, even if against them, will not stop their program of expansion.

They even have schools of expansion in their great cities—where prospective emigrants are prepared for life in the South Seas.

I met a graduate in Palau.

"When do you intend to go back to Japan?" I asked him.

"Oh, I won't go back. You see, I've been trained for Palau."

"But you'll have to go back some day to find a wife—unless you take a brown girl."

"No brown girl, please," he laughed. "No, I get my wife from the brides' school. She is coming now—arrive next week."

"Have you ever seen her?"

"Oh no, certainly, no."

"Then how do you know she will suit you?"

"Oh, that is very safe. You see, I send all my thoughts [he meant characteristics]. The president of the school, he picks a girl with the same thoughts. So everything very happy."

The brides' school in Tokyo trains girls to become the wives of colonists. Men who have gone to the islands write back for mates.

A Japanese newspaper defending the system says, "Untrained women are not qualified to be sent as wives, and the sending of unqualified women is deplorable. There is need for knowledge of the history, geography, climate, customs and other aspects of the countries in which they will live. Even the British, who are famous for their colonizing ability, advocate special training for women who will live abroad."

But I doubt that the British have ever got to the point of shipping out women professionally molded and modeled to fit mates they have never seen. Yet such apparently blind matings, in which trait for trait is dispassionately matched by go-betweens, are the rule in Japan.

Where the Jap goes he expects to stay. He does not interbreed with the natives, whether they be Polynesians or Californians. He establishes a little Japan. This generalization is too sweeping since there are many sons or grandsons of Japanese immigrants in the United States who are loyal Americans. But in general the Japanese are more cohesive and exclusive than any other people. Let them become numerically dominant in any island or country and they will expect ultimately to become politically dominant as well. Therefore we cannot countenance

the two-mile main street of Palau the rare thatch hut looks out
place among Japanese stores, telegraph poles and radio towers;
mono and foreign dress have banished the lava-lava.

Looking from the lush gardens of Koror across the lagoon to t**
mountains of Babeldaob. The latter island is flanked by one **
the best naval bases in the Pacific. (See Chapter XXI).

their becoming the most numerous element in the islands of the Pacific unless we are prepared to see these islands become and remain a part of Japan.

XX:

I Become a Spy

ON PALAU we did not have the liberty we had enjoyed on Yap. There we had gone anywhere we pleased without the slightest surveillance. Which led me to the conclusion that Yap was not intended for use as a major base in time of war. Of course when war actually began, some coastal batteries were probably mounted on Yap.

But Palau was a different story. Plainly something was brewing here. That was very evident in the dark suspicion that looked at us out of every Japanese eye.

I had not thought of becoming a spy until the Palau police put it into my head. They had a training course which turned innocent foreigners into spies.

Chief instructor was a smiling young police officer, by name Toyama-san. In black-and-white *yukata* he strolled in one evening to lay a map on the missionary's table.

First lesson: "You cannot go there," he said, indicating a spot with his pencil. And to quiet a natural suspicion, he added, "But there are no fortifications—nothing." Another point. "Cannot go . . . but there is nothing." Four other spots. "Cannot go," jabbing the points vigorously with the pencil. Then, each time, a disarming wave of the hand. "But there is nothing—nothing—nothing."

Anything better calculated to fire the student's curiosity and zeal for learning could hardly be imagined.

I took down the names of the six forbidden spots and determined to visit all of them.

The next morning I called upon Mr. Kodama, Vice Governor-General of the entire South Seas government.

After I had recounted the restrictions of the police, Mr. Kodama said, "I don't know why they should do that. We have no secrets here. You may go anywhere. But have you seen Captain Konishi? You had better see Captain Konishi."

Captain Konishi was naval attaché. He delivered sailing instructions to the merchant ships and prepared the way for the Japanese warships which occasionally visited Palau. The extent of his power was not quite clear. Some said that he was on a par with the civil authorities, if not superior to them . . . just as the army and navy in Japan accept no dictation from Parliament or Premier but are answerable to the Throne alone.

However that may be, he was the soul of modesty.

"I am only a naval officer," he said when I asked for permission to move freely through the Palau group. "That is a matter for the Governor to decide."

Mr. Toyama was eager to know the result of the interview.

"What did Captain Konishi say? May you go?"

"He said he would accept the Governor's decision. And the Governor says I may go anywhere. Therefore I may go anywhere."

But I had been a little too logical in my deductions. It was not so simple as that. When I sought to go to the nearest of the forbidden points, the island of Arakabesan, there were polite difficulties.

The best way to see Arakabesan was from a plane, and it seemed to me that this might be arranged since there were two seaplanes lying in the harbor.

So we made a social call upon Captain Konishi at his house.

This time he received us in shirt and suspenders (a sign of increasing confidence, I thought, for the first time he had barricaded himself behind gold braid).

With Western directness I immediately stated my mission. There were rumors abroad that Japan had fortified the islands. I wished to be able to write positively, "There are no fortifications on Palau." To say that, I must see. I was too lazy to climb every hill on Arakabesan.

122

Could a plane be placed at my disposal for half an hour so that I might fly low over this area?

Captain Konishi gave no sign that he considered the request extraordinary. He bowed slightly, made a little sound of agreement deep in his throat and asked whether the bean candy was to our taste.

It was. Munching *yokan,* we discussed the versatility of the bean— used to make everything from cake to buttons, from milk, cheese, butter, soup, salad oil and ice cream to varnish, enamels, oilcloth, linoleum, glue, soap and electrical switches.

When the bean's possibilities had been exhausted I re-ventured my request.

The Captain bowed, considered, and inquired whether we liked *sashimi* (raw fish). That started Mary who is a *sashimi* gourmand . . . yes, the red more than the white. *Sashimi* made from bonito was splendid. Ah, but, put in the Captain vivaciously, had she tried bass *sashimi?* When he had been stationed in San Francisco he had had *sashimi* made from bass . . . delicious. There is good bass fishing on the Pacific Coast.

Yes, I said, and speaking of fishing, it was interesting how airplanes were used to locate schools of fish. And speaking of airplanes, would it be possible to arrange for an airplane over Arakebesan?

He nodded gravely. Now take dried fish. We really should see the making of *katsubushi* on the shores of Malakal. And turtles. He showed us a fine specimen in the *tokonoma.*

There were many other distracting things about the room. Wooden tattooed dolls made by the Mortlock people, carved faces from Mortlock, an ivory nut from Ponape, a necklace of white and black disks made from sea shell and coconut shell respectively, the great Tritonium shell which the natives use as a trumpet.

Finally there was nothing left in the room to discuss except the visitors. He successfully got them talking about themselves. Still I did not forget to inject my question, each time a little more weakly. It always reminded him of something really interesting.

When two hours had gone by in this delightful fashion and it was positively necessary to leave to make the dinner hour at Frau Siemer's,

I rose and placed both hands upon the table as if about to deliver an address. Mustering all the powers I had of direct and succinct statement, I put my request.

Captain Konishi expressed mild surprise, as if he had only now understood me. The airplanes . . . unfortunately they were not naval planes, but government mail planes. He had no power. It would be necessary to apply to the Governor. But why go so soon . . . please come again. Take along these little souvenirs.

We came away in a very happy frame of mind. We had enjoyed our visit immensely (the Captain, the Calpis, the hibiscus reflected in the pool in his garden) and agreed that Captain Konishi was a splendid fellow and would some day be an Admiral.

Over the *obstkuchen* I told Herr Siemer of our visit.

"He did not like to disappoint you," said the missionary. "He is a very kindly man."

I believe it.

Although my naïveté was now so blunted that I no longer expected to get a plane, we went that evening to call upon Vice Governor Kodama in his beautiful home on the shore of the lagoon. He received us jovially. He had cheeks like apples and was the most genial host imaginable. Unfamiliar with English and not wishing to force us to converse in Japanese, he sent a car to the other end of town for Mrs. Shisatomi who had learned English in Hawaii. She came with her baby, too young to be left at home. Two other officials were called in. We sat about a conference table, the baby nursing quietly during most of the interview. Occasionally the mother must rise and jiggle the fretful child, translating meanwhile . . . or attend to him on a chair under the horizon of the table top, never quitting her interpreting.

Now, the Orient has two ways of countering unwelcome questions. One is to talk of something else. The other is to answer the questions directly but expect the visitor to be sufficiently polite not to apply the foot-rule of reason to the answers. In either case the underlying motive is courtesy—the desire to decline without hurting the feelings of the visitor.

Mr. Kodama answered my questions in a very forthright manner.

Airplane? Very dangerous. The pilots were men of little experience. The planes had been here only four months and the men were not yet accustomed to the peculiar air currents above Palau. So they refused to take up passengers. He himself, Mr. Kodama, had wished to go, but could not. Too dangerous. With his hands he demonstrated how violently the planes wobble—and laughingly used the word *jishin*, earthquake.

I agreed that the air currents must be dangerous indeed if they could not be learned in four months. But I offered to sign a paper assuming all responsibility in case of accident.

No, even so, the responsibility, he said, would be theirs. If I did not care for myself, they did. Also it would be necessary to board the plane from a boat and disembark into a boat . . . very difficult.

I thought I could manage.

He feared not.

Very well, I said, doubtless he was right. Then might I pass around Arakabesan by boat and land where I pleased?

He was very sorry. As I doubtless knew, at the southern end of the island an airport was being built for the forthcoming air mail service to Tokyo. Much blasting. Very dangerous. During the operations no visitors, not even Japanese, were allowed.

But if I went under proper supervision? And landed at a safe distance from the blasting?

It was a very small island.

A mile long, was it not?

Yes . . . but all roads led to the same place.

I saw that it was time to agree that it must be very dangerous, and did so, shivering a little.

Moreover, went on Mr. Kodama, there was a leper island nearby. That was another danger that made it inadvisable to visit Arakabesan.

What, I said, the small island I had noticed half a mile north of Arakabesan? Was it a leper island?

Yes.

Then that settled it. I wouldn't take the risk. Lepers! I thanked him for warning me in time.

125

I turned the conversation to the magnificent bird of paradise from New Guinea which stood in the corner. Mr. Kodama showed us other treasures. His magnetic, cordial manner, his zest and zeal (and, above all, his tact) made apparent why he is universally popular among officials and civilians in the islands.

As we were about to go, he said earnestly, "Have you had any unpleasantness in Palau?"

"On the contrary, our visit has been very pleasant."

"I hope that any unhappy incidents will not unduly disturb you."

He was so genuine about it. I replied that we had lived in Japan a long time, and that when anything unpleasant occurred we thought of all the pleasant things that had happened.

"*Arigato!*" He bowed and smiled.

We walked home through the deserted main street under the tropic moon.

Mary mused. "What a blow to our leper friends in Korea who entertained us in their homes, if they knew that now we can't stand a leper half a mile away!"

"Yes," I agreed. "But it would have done no good to argue him out of his genial mood into an ugly one."

A shadow came slipping along behind us. Upon challenge, it turned out to be a policeman, following us, he claimed, for our protection.

The stranger was not permitted to feel neglected. The New Yorker who complains of the difficulty of finding a policeman should delight in Palau. There the procedure is simple. Step out of your door, go ten paces in any direction, and lo! a policeman behind you.

The gentleman will be courteous in the extreme, cordially interested in knowing where the foreigner may wish to go, and eager to extend "every facility." His sole mission is to be helpful. I have never in my life been subjected to so much sheer helpfulness.

"They look sharp on white people," remarked a Palau chief.

The white visitor was rare and he generally stopped over only for the hours his ship was in port. An official entertainment committee offered to show him the sights of Palau. He was whirled off to a geisha house, there was much drinking and dancing and the gentle charms of the island Circes detained him until someone looked at his watch.

"Oh! Time to get back to the boat!"

The rare and extraordinary visitor who actually wished to stop over from one boat to the next was permitted to do so, but he was the object of unremitting curiosity as to why he should maroon himself here when he didn't have to. Something funny about it. Better keep him provided with every facility.

Two German professors on vacation chose to paddle about in a rubber boat. A government pinnace containing police and sandwiches followed them everywhere lest they should get lost or go hungry. One day they paddled off through a mangrove canal too shallow for the pinnace. They came back at night to find a row of anxious officials seated on their doorstep, and their lack of consideration in causing so much uneasiness to their guardians was brought home to them in no uncertain terms.

An American artist's motor failed and his small boat drifted from Hawaii to Palau. That was indiscreet of it, for he had no landing permit and nothing to show that he had not drifted there by intention. His arrival was the sensation of the island. The motor was repaired but he had no money to pay for the repairs. His request that he be allowed to remain until he could get the money was politely refused. He was given a farewell dinner with speeches. Every facility for his departure was accorded to him and the finest government launch towed him in his motorless boat well outside the reef. He then proceeded to drift, with better judgment this time, to American soil, landing some weeks later in the Philippines. He was later reported to be feverishly painting pictures along the Mindanao coast to earn enough money to retrieve his motor. He held no grudge against the Japanese, in fact considered it all worth while for the thrill of sudden importance he enjoyed on Palau.

The complaint of a German that he had been shadowed reached the Mandates Commission at its meeting in October, 1935. Mr. Ito, the Japanese representative, explained that the traveler in question was tubercular, therefore the Japanese wanted "to take good care of him."

It was quite probable, Mr. Ito suggested, that this "care" had caused the German "to mistake Japanese hospitality for surveillance."

As for the famous case of Colonel Earl Ellis of the United States Marines who died mysteriously while investigating conditions on Palau, the Japanese protested indignantly that there was no truth in the rumors that he was "liquidated." Ex-champion Gene Tunney, visiting in Japan, asked about this after my return to Tokyo.

"Nobody knows," I said. "But they say Ellis drank himself to death."

"Pretty hard, don't you think?" said Tunney. "Look at the efforts I've been making all these years!"

Tunney's efforts have not been too serious, but it was reported that Ellis broke under the tropic strain and took heavily to the bottle when his boat did not come on time to carry him away. Excess led to fever, it was said, and fever to death. But a less official version is that he was neatly poisoned by the Japanese. Whatever the truth or falsity of conflicting reports, it is at least certain that an American Marine investigating a Japanese island was bound to find himself an unwelcome guest.

A British army officer wearing many medals stopped for a day on his way to New Guinea. He came to the missionary's house . . . and five officials with him. When he stepped into another room, or to the outhouse, he was accompanied. Three officials sat in a row by the edge of the tub as he took a bath. Doubtless they feared he might escape through the drain.

XXI:

The Palau Naval Base

WE HAD been on Palau for some weeks before the restrictions began to let up. Perhaps the authorities were gradually becoming convinced of our harmlessness. Certainly we showed a great interest in fauna and flora—and that interest was genuine. Also, remembering our promise to scientific societies desiring ethnological data, we studied native customs.

Possibly my notebook helped to break down suspicion. The missionary warned me that it would be read daily during our absence from the house. His two houseboys, though natives, were, he had reason to believe, acting as spies for the police. Sometimes I left the notebook on the bedroom table, sometimes at the bottom of the deepest traveling bag or dresser drawer. Always I found it where I had left it; but not exactly. The slight change of position was just enough to show that it had been removed and replaced.

I was amused one day when the Secretary for Foreign Affairs used a phrase from my notebook, evidently not realizing where he had picked it up. I complimented him on its aptness, and he was pleased.

No information of a geographic or strategic nature went into the notebook. It was preserved in other ways. The pages overflowed with birds, flowers and folkways. Now and then there would be a pleasant word about one or another of the officials who were honoring us with so much attention.

So the absent-minded professor with his hand-microscope and records of cephalic index, and his pretty and popular wife, were allowed a little more rein.

We saw Arakabesan, though not minutely. A boatride along every foot of its shores, but no landing, gave a fair idea of its future. Statements by natives who had been employed on the island, and the missionary who had visited it, filled out the picture.

Arakabesan (on some charts called Ngarekobasan) was being conditioned as an air base. The island is something short of two miles long. It has no great elevations and could be leveled, but had not been at the time of our visit. At the southern end a just-completed hangar big enough to house a Zeppelin stood about 150 feet back from the shore. The ground sloped gently from the hangar down to the beach. A long pier was being built with a ramp at the end extending deeply enough so that even at ebb tide seaplanes might come up from the water. Not far from the hangar large storage facilities were being constructed for gasoline. A village which had stood on this spot had been demolished and the natives packed off to shift for themselves as best they could elsewhere. All other settlements on the island had been evacuated.

A sign of the importance attached to Arakabesan was the bridge, a mile long, which was being constructed from islet to islet across the lagoon to connect Arakabesan with the headquarters island, Koror.

"If you should visit the *Nanyo* next year," said the governor, knowing very well that that would never happen, "you may come by plane, land on Arakabesan, and ride in a motor car across the bridge to Madelai pier."

But the pretense that the entire work was merely a civilian project was belied by the position of Arakabesan. The place for a commercial airport would have been on Koror itself. There was plenty of space on the flat uplands. Then no bridge a mile long and costing some millions of yen would have been necessary.

The peculiar virtue of Arakabesan was that it guarded one end of the naval base. It stands at the southern end of one of the two most magnificent fleet basins in all Micronesia.

A companion island at the same end of the basin is Malakal. There too a major operation was being performed. Hills were being blasted to bits and roaring bulldozers were levelling the elevations, dumping the surplus material into the sea, thus substantially extending the area of the island. Reduced to a plain, it would make another good airdrome.

Later I saw signs on the great island of Babeldaob that further air facilities were in preparation. Babeldaob flanks the fleet basin.

It was not until 1939 that regular commercial air service was established by the Japan Airways Company. Seaplanes of the company then flew twice a month to Palau, stopping at Saipan.

But one plane twice a month would hardly require the extensive airdromes being built at great expense along two sides of the Palau base.

On one of the Japanese ships, I had seen in the wheel house a Japanese navigation chart of the Palau waters and noticed with curiosity that while depths were given in all other places none were recorded in the large basin. I asked the captain about it.

"We don't need to know the soundings there," he said. "Merchant ships don't go there."

"You mean, it's for warships?"

The question was indiscreet and the captain flushed. "Certainly not. The League mandate forbids military use of the islands. We would not think of disobeying the League."

"Of course not," I agreed piously. "Then why are no soundings given?"

"Because," replied the annoyed captain, "the lagoon is so shallow that it is closed to navigation."

But on an old German chart that I came upon in the missionary's house, the depths in the great lagoon were plainly marked. Nowhere was the water too shallow for large ships.

Palau is a volcanic chain of islands ninety miles long and about twenty wide. It comprises 26 principal islands and well over a hundred lesser ones. Adjacent to the shore is a fringing reef. Several miles out from shore is a barrier reef. It is a natural torpedo-proof breakwater protecting anything that is behind it. Behind it lies a sixty-mile-long lagoon. What portions of this have been dredged we shall find out when we get there; but the part already sufficiently deep for any naval use was the great basin ten miles long and up to three miles wide lying between the reef and Babeldaob, blocked at the north end by hills and at the south by fortified Arakabesan and Malakal.

Naturally I wished to traverse this basin. Herr Siemer contrived a good excuse. Another German missionary, Herr Fey, lived at the north end of Babeldaob. We would all go to visit him.

Seeking permission, we were told that we could go—but by the open sea, up the east coast of the island. Frau Siemer protested vigorously at the idea of an ocean trip in a small motorboat. She was very plump and could not help rolling with the boat; and the shifting of her cargo made her most uncomfortable. She knew from experience that she would become desperately seasick.

We won consent to go up the west coast through the basin.

"But you will take no camera, please," police officer Toyama warned. "And no pencil and paper. And no field glasses. And I will go with you."

So he did. Also Secretary for Foreign Affairs, Hayashi.

At dawn we came down to a pier near the Siemer home on Koror. The pier is a quarter mile long in order to span the fringing reef and has a lighthouse at the end, "for fishermen," said Hayashi. But the pier did not end until it had reached water seventeen meters deep. A vessel of that draught would be a most amazing fishing boat.

Thence we passed westward through a channel called the Toagel Mid varying in depth from 11 to 22 meters, according to the German chart—which of course we did not take with us but consulted again upon return. This channel opened directly into the great fleet basin. There we turned north, following the shore of Babeldaob. (Variant spelling Babelthuap and Baberudaobu. I suppose there is no island in Micronesia that is not confusingly spelled in at least two and sometimes half a dozen different styles.)

There was no glimpse of a colorful coral floor here. The water beneath us was a deep sullen green. The consecutive soundings from south to north as noted on the chart were 18, 44, 20, 44, 35, 48 and 20 meters.

The barrier reef on our left protecting the basin against attack from the open sea was no slight wall. In some places it was ten miles wide.

Behind us lay busy Arakabesan and Malakal, the boom of blasting coming to our ears over the sound of the motor.

On our right was Babeldaob, the largest single island in all Micronesia with the exception of Ponape. It is 27 miles long and eight miles in greatest width. It is picturesque and hilly but has no elevations much more than 600 feet. Parts of it are heavily wooded with fine timber; but there are also open uplands suitable for pineapple, tapioca, and airfields. The island was very sparsely inhabited. And yet I saw wide, straight, level roads starting from piers at the shore and running back into the interior through country where there was not a sign of life. What were they for?

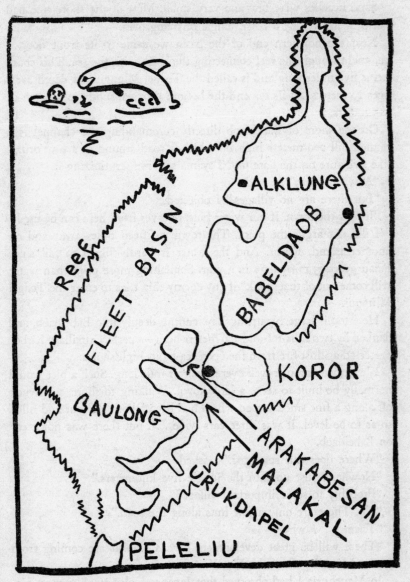

PALAU

133

Sand beaches were few and very small. Most of the shore line had been taken over by a black tangle of mangroves.

Near the northern end of the basin we came to its front door, a channel through the reef connecting the basin with the sea. This channel is five miles long and is called the Toagel Mlungui. Its depth averages 20 meters. At its sea end the bottom drops abruptly to a depth of 415 meters.

On the shore of Babeldaob directly commanding the channel is a domed hill 200 meters high up which a road wound to a low drum-like structure on the bare top. Toyama saw me scrutinizing it.

"A water tank," he said.

"But there are no villages," I objected.

"It's for the town. If our water fails, reserves from here can be used."

I did not argue the point. The town is fifteen miles away and on another island, Koror. And the water is hardly likely to fail since Palau gets 265 rainy days in a year. Something more grim than water will come out of that "tank" if any enemy ship tries to enter the Toagel Mlungui.

Here too is large Ngatpang Bay, cutting deeply into Babeldaob, and flanked by two hills 196 and 170 meters high—a perfect auxiliary harbor protected against fire from the open sea by its high shores.

We landed at a pier well over a quarter mile long. Such a pier would normally be built to serve a large town. Walking to shore, we struck off along a fine smooth road which had been laboriously cut and filled so as to be level. It was three cars wide . . . but there was not a car on Babeldaob.

"Where does this road go?" I asked.

"Nowhere. Just up into the jungle five kilometers."

"Probably to some important village?"

"No. There are only a few huts along the road."

"Then . . . why?"

"There will be great development here. Colonists are coming from Japan. It is all part of the Five-Year Plan."

In Manchuria I had observed that Japanese colonists, like most pioneers, have to make their own roads—and they are usually pretty crude affairs. The construction of a perfectly graded three-car highway for colonists who had not yet arrived was to say the least a remarkable example of Nipponese foresight. Would the guileless Japanese later discover that the roads were useful feeders from inland ammunition dumps and stores to warships in the fleet basin?

We walked up the highway for some distance, then turned off on a jungle trail to the village of Alklung. Missionary Fey's house was a two-story affair of native wood, constructed by Christian natives, the mangrove posts roughly squared off by the none-too-sharp Palau adze made of the shell of the giant clam. Downstairs was the church, upstairs the living quarters. We ascended to sit down with wiry Fey and his buxom young frau to a strictly German meal. For if the Englishman wears a boiled shirt in the jungle, the German clings to his *sauerkraut* and *obstkuchen,* ignoring the fresh taro, breadfruit, coconut, mangoes, pineapples and papayas all about him.

They were good people, the Feys. They too were cut off without support, the Nazis having forbidden the society in Germany to send any more funds to its missionaries overseas.

But Fey worried, not about himself, but about his country.

"The campaign against the church in Germany is a bad sign," he said. "It means a tendency to throw away idealism for brute force. Brute force is a weak thing. It always gets licked in the end."

"Don't you think," said the *Nanyo's* dapper little Secretary for Foreign Affairs, "that brute force can sometimes be used to accomplish a good purpose? For example, Japan's purpose to liberate Greater East Asia from oppression. Remember your own Christian crusades."

"The crusades got nowhere," said Fey. "Aggression always defeats itself."

Hayashi shook his disbelieving head.

I wonder if he is beginning to believe today.

. .

On another day we voyaged up the opposite side of Babeldaob. Here the picture was quite different. While the west coast was protected by the deep and wide fleet basin, the east coast was also protected, but by a narrow lagoon too treacherous to be waded and too shallow for landing boats except at high tide. And, judging from the miscalculations of our boatmen, it is hard to figure the exact arrival of high tide in these intricate, mangrove-choked waterways.

Leaving Koror, we wound for two hours through tight passages between attractive islets fringing the Babeldaob shore, then for fifteen minutes through a dense mangrove swamp by way of an artificial canal. Now the lagoon became more open and rather rough. Mrs. Siemer began to roll and asked to sit next to the gunwale. She needed it when, the tide ebbing rapidly, we were forced to go outside the reef for ten minutes.

This was off the village of Melekiok. Here the appearance of the shore line changes. The mangroves give way to lovely palm-covered sand beaches. The lagoon was jade green where sand-bottomed, purple where rock-bottomed, blue where deep, all these colors accented by the gleaming white reef.

The island was less hilly on this side. There were great open uplands covered with grass and few trees.

After four hours we arrived at the village of Ngiwal (the Japanese call it Oniwaru) and climbed a trail through palm groves to the high lonesome house built by the man who had started German mission work in Palau. But Herr Länger had gone home to Germany disheartened when his daughter and wife both died. Memorial crosses for them stood in the yard overlooking palms and ocean. The wind whistled through the empty windowless house.

Hungry, we were depressed to learn that Mrs. Siemer had brought along nothing better than a can of salmon. But she sent a brown boy up a tree for coconuts, opened them, grated the meat, strained out the juice into the fish, and transformed the lowly salmon into a dish for the gods.

Herr Siemer had sent word through the village that he would preach in the church at seven. Seven came and went. At eight the missionary still chatted.

"Aren't we due at church?" I asked.

"Oh, I'm all ready to go. But I don't hear the bell."

"Bell! Does the congregation have to call the preacher to church?" Somehow this appeared to go backward.

The missionary laughed. "It must be confusing," he said. "But it's a system we have here. It's a contest. We see which can outwait the other, the missionary or the congregation. I announce service for seven. But I don't go to the church at seven. What's the use? I would find it empty. So I have a man there who will signal me by ringing the bell when the people begin to come. Of course, even then, I don't go. I wait until he rings the bell the second time, which is supposed to mean that all the people are assembled. But still I don't go, for my man is in league with the elders and rings the second bell when there are still only a few gathered. After the third or fourth bell, I may think about going."

The first bell rang at eight-fifteen. The second at nine. The third at nine-thirty. We went down to the church. It was empty.

The congregation had won, palms down. What folly for a German even to think of trying to compete with a Kanaka in delay!

After uncounted bells the people began to drift in. Through the velvet darkness they came, each carrying a torch made of strips of the "fruit leaf" which lies close to the nuts on the coconut tree. The strips are bound together to form a long slender bundle, and fired at one end. It is not held erect, but horizontally, the arm hanging at the side. The swing of the arm as one walks helps to keep it going.

It is a rule that he who goes abroad at night must carry a torch. It serves as a sign of honest intentions. Without torches, people move too quietly on their bare feet and are too dark in color to be visible. You feel as if surrounded by ghosts. You can see nothing, yet hear faint rustlings and breathings.

Upon arriving at the church, each beat out the fire of his torch on the ground.

The benches filled. At ten the service got under way. There was a savage edge not only in the features of some of the parishioners but in the way they cut stridently into the songs. Once started they had no desire to quit. Ngiwal being a village where evening entertainments are unknown, this was cinema, vaudeville, concert and wake all in one.

Even the babies were present, and in full cry. The missionary's words got rapt attention despite competition. When he was hoarse, the service ended formally, but continued informally with bursts of wild song from various groups—Christian words set to native tunes, some of which had known a bloody or obscene past.

Then torches were reluctantly lit for home-going. The king invited us to come to his house the next day. The king was in a shirt but no trousers because the night was warm. He was a bloodthirsty-looking wretch but we were given to understand that he had long ago repented of his record of two hundred and eighty heads and was now a staunch pillar of the church.

XXII:

Headhunters and Englishmen

"*Ungil dutau!* [Nightingale]" the king said when we arrived at his house the next morning. The Palau nightingale has the sense to sleep at night but sings cheerily in the morning, hence the morning greeting means, "May you be as happy as the nightingale."

On the shelf were a few heads. He apologized for not having more, but the Japanese are zealous collectors of these trophies. He took one down and demonstrated with professional authority how a head should be severed. Drawing his two-foot-long cutlass-like knife from its carved wooden scabbard, he caressed the imaginary neck with the keen blade.

"The blow should come from behind, not in front," he said, illustrating with knife and head. "If you strike in front, your man may protect his neck by lowering his chin; and even if you do reach his neck, the muscles may slow up the blade so that it will not have force enough left to cut the backbone. So you strike from behind, sever the backbone first. The rest doesn't matter. You will have plenty of time to cut the muscles and skin after the man is dead. And notice that the blow should be slanting, not straight."

On the same principle, apparently, as the diagonal stroke of a razor.

"Some white people say we are cowardly because we always attack from behind," went on the king. "It is not so. It is just that we know the right way to do."

Palau head-hunting was never conducted for the purpose of displaying courage. The man sent out by his tribe to get a head of the enemy tribe was expected to go about it like a sneak-thief. Far from openly challenging anyone to battle, he would lie in wait among the bushes beside the trail and spring out behind a fisherman plodding under a load of nets, or a woman carrying home taro, or a child chasing a butterfly. Upon his return he received the same praise whether the head was that of man, woman or child.

"What difference did it make?" said the king. "A child eats as much as a man. There were too many people and too little food on these islands. We made war so that we might eat. If we could stop a young mouth from a lifetime of eating, it was even better than stopping an old one."

But the desperation of hunger paused short of cannibalism. There is no record that human flesh was ever eaten on Palau.

The king took us to the nearby All Men House. Before it was a circular stone platform called *ailiuth*. At its center was an *olgal,* a stone with a hollow in its upper surface forming a stone cup.

When a "warrior" returned from a successful foray, the head he brought was placed in this cup. Then the tribesmen gathered on the *ailiuth* and danced about the head, clapping their hands. Toddy made the occasion merrier.

A delegation was organized and sent on a tour of neighboring friendly villages. At each the proud trophy, perhaps the tousled head of some youngster, was placed in the local *olgal* and became the center of festivities lasting two or three days. The village fed the delegation well, paid it some money for its service in reducing Palau's food problem, and sent it on its way to the next village.

"But I suppose you were especially proud when you got the head of a chief," I said.

"No, no!" The king was shocked. "That was forbidden. We would kill a chief, but not cut off his head. That would be a disgrace."

Like depriving a general of his sword. So apparently there was some honor even among cutthroats.

He took us through an overgrown path (asking us not to speak of it to the Japanese policeman who would fine them for not keeping it cleaned out) to the grave of the giant of Ngiwal. The story of the giant of Ngireumelas is well known among the natives of the Palau Islands and probably has some basis in truth. It seems that about one hundred years ago enemy villages which resented the adeptness of Ngiwal experts in picking off heads united to punish this mischievous village. They killed all the males and decreed that there should never be any more. Thenceforth every man-child born was to be killed.

But one woman who bore a strong son tattooed him as a girl and dressed him as a girl. He grew to great size and single-handed subdued the enemies of Ngiwal. Now he sleeps in a grave so long that when the five-foot king lay down upon it, touching his toes to the footstone, there was a gap of four feet between his head and the headstone.

. .

Next to the giant, the tallest dead of Palau are the English. Many are buried here. Their tombstones are gray with age, for the English preceded the Japanese, the Germans and even the Spanish. Their blood runs in the veins of many a dusky islander and their speech lingers in his mouth.

Back on the island of Koror near Herr Siemer's home lived William Gibbon. Eighty years old, he was a living history of Palau. He had been here during English, Spanish, German and Japanese times. And his father before him.

His father lay in a grave in the front yard of William's thatch home. William could usually be found sitting on the flat gravestone translating English into the Palau tongue so that the few natives who could read their own language might learn something of the outside world.

Perhaps his work was a reflection of his own longing to know something of the outside world, the world from which his father had come. For William himself had never been beyond these islands.

"My father was an Englishman," he said proudly. Then, becoming more explicit, "He was the son of an Englishman and a colored lady. He was born in Saint Kitts, but he was brought up in England. He became a sailor on a man-of-war. Later he shipped on a whaler."

"How did he come to live on Palau?"

"Well, you see, my father didn't get along with the captain. So when this whaling ship came to Palau, the captain said to the king, 'You'd better keep this man on shore.' The ship went off without him. Every day for many years my father went to the mountaintop and scanned the sea for vessels. None came. So he made his home here, married a Palau princess, had children, ten of them. Then he couldn't leave."

Of the ten children of the marooned mulatto, William is the only survivor. He has added to the mixture of nationalities and races by marrying the half-caste daughter of a Palau woman and an American buccaneer-trader, Captain Clark. Captain Clark, in Spanish days, had his own schooner and his business was salvaging wrecks. He one day walked about on the bottom of Hongkong harbor inspecting a vessel; a davit, swinging in the current, struck and broke the window of his diving helmet, and his Palau daughter never saw him again.

William has six children. He has tried hard to teach them his beloved English, but they are content with the Palau language and a smattering of Japanese. He still insists that they are English children. And he sits upon the grave as if clinging to the past—the far past, even before his English grandfather married a colored lady of Saint Kitts.

A death chant rises from a group of men seated on the stones before a house nearby. A chief has died. They will bury him in the front yard. It is the custom.

"The Japanese want us to take our dead away," says William. "We want them near. We cannot understand it that the Japanese are willing to burn their dead, to lose them. You have seen the death fires?"

Yes, I had seen the solitary spot on a hill overlooking the sea where the Japanese cremate their dead. It is a weird sight an hour before dawn when the burnings take place. Under an iron roof is a great furnace. Fuel goes into its lower door, the boxed body on an iron tray goes into the upper door and rests upon an iron grate. About the furnace are tables where relatives and friends may drink . . . in typical Japanese fashion glossing over their misery with merriment. When the burning is over, the tray is removed. It contains ashes and bones. For some reason the ashes alone are respected—the bones join a promiscuous heap on the hillside. The ashes are presented before a simple stone shrine and prayers are offered.

At a safe distance is an open-air grill upon which the bodies of "blood-sick" natives, victims of plague, are burned; the motive in this case being sanitation rather than veneration.

Now and then the local king would come and sit on the gravestone with William. He was a roly-poly old monarch not unlike the legendary King Cole. His royal robes were a bit scant. But he never appeared among his subjects without his shirt. Trousers he scorned as being unsuited to a tropical climate; and without a doubt he was right. He liked to sit on the gravestone because it was cool against his skin.

"This is good stone," he said, patting the great slab of calcite. "The Yap people even use it as money!" He laughed heartily over the absurd customs of the Yaps. "Have you seen real money?" he asked, suddenly serious.

I suppose it is every man's ambition to see, before he dies, some real money.

"No," I said, "I have never seen real money."

"I'll show you some."

He waddled away to his thatch palace, calling lustily to the queen.

"The queen keeps the money," explained William. "It belongs to the whole village, this great money. Of course every family has some small money of its own."

He went into the house and brought out a box. It contained small objects carefully wrapped in absorbent cotton.

"This is a *kluk*," he said, disclosing a white and green stone about the size and shape of a large bead. It was pierced by a hole so that it could be worn on a string around the neck. "It is worth one hundred yen in Japanese money. The *kluk* is the unit of exchange of this currency, like the English pound or the American dollar. This small piece is a *klesuk*, or half a *kluk*. These glass pieces are still less valuable—they are worn by the little girls."

The king arrived with a strongbox. He brushed away William's slight possessions with a gesture and spread out on the gravestone a magnificent display of large, vari-colored stones.

Most of the pieces seemed to be a sort of porcelain, worn as if by sand and wave.

"What is this material?" I asked.

"We do not ask that," said the king. "It was given to us by the god of Palau." (And the king is a deacon in Herr Siemer's church!)

"That guess is as good as any," agreed William. "Professor Kramer from Germany and Professor Hasebe from Tohoku Imperial University have been unable to identify this material. It doesn't seem to have originated in this part of the world. Some think it may be meteoric."

The king picked up a beautiful green specimen. "This is worth seven *kluk*. Its name is Chalbuchop."

"Every piece in Palau has a given name," said William, "like a man."

"This yellow one is Nglalemesall. It is worth fourteen *kluk*. And this one is Nglalemiaur. It is five hundred years old." He displayed a beautiful round red piece the size of a golf ball.

"This is the price of a canoe. This, the price of a house. This, the price of a village. And these," turning reverently to the greatest pieces, "are beyond price."

"We buy and sell with the small pieces," William said. "But the great pieces are not used for trading. They change hands only when captured in wars between villages. Even if we were faced with starvation we would not spend them. We would rather die. You are now looking at the finest money of this kind in the world. It is used only in Palau, and this village of Koror is conqueror of all other villages and the richest in Palau."

Every piece has a hole so that it may be strung and worn on state occasions by the queen and other noble ladies—never by the men. But while it is displayed by the women it belongs to the men.

But there is another currency, exclusively for women. It consists of small trays of tortoise-shell. They become immediately worthless in the hands of a man, but a woman may use them in trade with other women, or dowry her daughter with them when she marries.

"Now, these pieces are worthless," the king said of two large yellow stones. To a novice, they looked as good as the rest. "We keep them only as curiosities, to show the difference between real money and false. An Englishman named Emery thought he would get rich, so he brought in a lot of pieces like Palau pieces. He said they were from Arabia. He tried to sell them for copra and bêche de mer. But the people wouldn't take them. They could see that they were nothing like the money from god."

He replaced the gems and carried the strongbox back to the custody of the queen.

"The women appear to be very important in Palau," I commented to William.

"A man without a wife is nothing in Palau," said William. "He is helpless. Taro is our chief food, and that is in the hands of women. It is against custom for a man to work in the taro patch—he would rather go hungry. A man who is not married is nobody. He is like a beggar. He must eat any scraps given to him by his relatives."

It was almost as if he were describing the unhappy lot of the widow in India instead of that supposedly free and favored individual, the bachelor.

"I am a poor man," said William, "because I have many sons and few daughters. Daughters mean riches in Palau. The women of Palau are stronger than the men—yes, in body as well as in mind. They have always worked, while the men have spent their time at the *abai* [club-house] with the slave women. It has become the custom in Palau for the women to support the men. A man with brothers and sons has nothing but expense. A man with many daughters and sisters and a wife or two is a rich man. So every man gets married as soon as he can —and then prays for daughters. He is disappointed if a boy comes.

There have been cases of infanticide here, but it was boy-babies, not girl-babies, who were put out of the way."

The man's life is not entirely parasitic, for he must do the building and the fishing. And the latter is not without peril. One day an automobile came up the street, its running boards and fenders loaded with excited men talking animatedly with the passengers within. News was shouted ahead and people flocked to see, bringing the car to a halt. Inside were four famished Palau men who had just been rescued after twenty days adrift in an open boat. Three of them were insane.

The motor of the fishing boat had failed and the trade wind had carried the craft to sea. There was no food or water in the boat. The two Christians prayed in their way and the two non-Christians addressed the spirits of their fathers. Whose prayers did it was a difference of opinion, but something brought a bunch of coconuts alongside, and on another day two sharks followed the boat. They were speared and the raw flesh served as food for three days. Three of the men drank sea water and became "sick in the head." A small sail improvised from gee-strings accomplished little. Ships sailed by. The speck of a boat, although it contained a whole world of torture, was too small to be seen. After twenty eternal days, a *Nanyo Kohatsu* steamer picked them up.

"The history of Palau has been one long fight with the sea," William said. "Not only the Palau men but the Englishmen know that to their grief. You know that too, don't you, Elizabeth?" He spoke to a woman who, except for her dark color, would have passed as a New England schoolteacher. She lives in William's house. "Elizabeth Lewis," said William, "is English too. Her father, Captain Lewis, was taken by the sea. Elizabeth has married twice—two Englishmen—the sea took them both. Her father left her fine houses and possessions. The sea rose in a typhoon and swept everything away. Now she has nothing. But," he added, as if this made up for having nothing, "she is clever. She can speak English, German, Japanese, Chamorro, Yap, Lamotrek, Uleai, Mokomok, Truk and Palau. You can't beat an Englishwoman!"

We were to find more traces of the English in Peliliu, southernmost island within the Palau reef. The trip to it gave us an opportunity to

145

complete our observation of the strategic waters of this remarkable archipelago.

If we had thought the fleet basin large, what were we to think of the inland sea thirty miles long and up to ten miles wide stretching from Koror to Peliliu? The only reason this may not be used will be because it may not be needed, the fleet basin affording ample space and facilities for the Japanese navy.

Standing between this southern sea and the northern fleet basin is strategic Malakal, one of the forbidden points at which Toyama had originally jabbed his pencil. We did not land on Malakal but passed close to it from one end to the other. The process of leveling and extending the island was being vigorously carried out. There was a fishermen's village in process of demolition. Farms on the upper slopes were being cut into. There were two wooded hills less than two hundred feet high. They were destined to disappear. The depth of water around the island was recorded on the German map as averaging about thirty meters. No battleship could ask for more. If the island has been converted into an "unsinkable carrier" its planes will furnish convenient air cover to ships in either basin.

The next island passed was Urukdapel, long, irregular, a veritable stone pile, quite uncultivable and uninhabited. Its shore was an abrupt, undercut cliff. It seemed of no use either to farmers or to soldiers, except perhaps for a few batteries which could readily be concealed beneath its enormous boulders.

Along the coast of Urukdapel are hundreds of small islands, abrupt, steep, each one a miniature fortress. Densely wooded, each looks like the bushy head of a giant savage protruding from the sea. The effect is heightened by the fact that the waves have sharply undercut the island, forming a neck. Under the chin your boat may be sheltered if a sudden rainstorm sweeps the lagoon. Here and there are caves and tunnels eroded by corkscrewing breakers. Although the sea is protected by reefs, a thirty-mile stretch of water can become pretty rough.

Occasionally the launch chugged through a high arch, skeleton of an island otherwise worn away.

This inland sea is quite as beautiful as Japan's own Inland Sea and as picturesque as Matsushima.

We passed the fantastic all-elbows islands of Ailmalk and Aulong, then skimmed over jade-green shallows of inexpressible beauty, past dredges hard at work, to the Peliliu pier. Near by was a great phosphate drying house, for Peliliu is a phosphate island. Good roads cut through the jungle. There was even a narrow-gauge railroad. As if in protest against such desecration of the forest, gorgeous red-and-bronze-green roosters similar to some in our chicken yards but much more powerful of wing, flew from one lofty treetop to another, screaming as they went. Their voices were drowned out by the horns of trucks and the whistles of the small locomotives that pull the phosphate trains. The Japs had arrived in once peaceful Peliliu.

The natives have caught the contagion of progress. Later we were to see on Koror a sports meet in which young men from Peliliu took part. These annual games include javelin-throwing, broad jump, hop, step and jump, running high jump, pole vault, shot-put, relay races.

As you watch, the team from Peliliu carries off the honors.

"Fu-re! Fu-re! Odesangal!" they shout.

"What is that 'Fu-re'?" you ask.

Your Japanese companion looks at you in surprise.

"Why, it's your own word," he says. "You use it in America!"

Light breaks. "Fu-re!" is the closest approach the Japanese syllabary can make to the sound of "Hooray!"

"And why are they shouting for Odesangal? I thought they came from Peliliu."

"Yes. But the real name of the island is Odesangal. It was always defeated in battle by the other islands. They reduced it to serfdom. They contemptuously called it 'Peliliu' which means 'Under House.' When these sports were begun the 'Under House' saw its chance to show its real merit. Its boys went into hard training. When they come here they fight with all their might. The result is that every year they take off first honors. They have changed the attitude of the other tribes toward their island. Now they have discarded the name of 'Under House' and shout for Odesangal."

Mingled with the sounds of progress on Peliliu as represented by locomotives and trucks, there came the wail of a funeral ceremony. We plunged through the thicket to a small village. The old king, noseless because frambesia had left only a great hole where his nose had been, came out to meet us. He was surprised to hear English. He could not speak it, but told us through an interpreter that the just-dead old lady over whose corpse the neighbors were chanting "should have stayed alive to talk English to you. Her husband was an Englishman. He wrote books in German. He became a native chief, put away clothes, wore a lava-lava, carried a basket, and a chisel on his shoulder, chewed betel nut, spoke our language well."

"Was his name Kubary?" I asked, thinking I recognized the great erratic ethnologist in this description. Johann Stanislaus Kubary was a Pole, but because of his background and training he passed readily as an Englishman.

"That's it. Kubary. A great man. We liked him. We gave him good women for his wives—this one here, one in Koror and two in Ponape. But one of the Ponape women went with another man. When Mr. Kubary found it out, he killed himself. Too bad—to lose such a fine man for a woman."

The missionary said, "In the most unexpected corners of these islands I find traces of the foreigners of long ago. Many old women have said to me, 'My husband was an Englishman.'"

On the trip back to the main island the line behind the boat snapped taut and we hauled in a four-foot-long barracuda. To land it and get a rope through the gills was a struggle. One of the crew was nearly knocked overboard by a sledge-hammer blow of the great tail.

After the fish had been subdued, Dr. Sekine of the Palau hospital, who was with us, pried open the great jaws to reveal a remarkable set of great, razor-edge teeth.

"Those teeth cause us a lot of trouble at the hospital," he said. "Many natives are bitten by barracuda. We have had several victims die. Loss of blood. Anemia."

This fish possesses another formidable weapon in the shape of jaws that taper down to a sharp point. The fish hurls itself through the water like an animated spear, stabbing its enemy. Since the great barracuda often attains a length of eight feet and moves with the speed of a torpedo, its piercing force is terrific. The hulls of fishing boats are sometimes punctured. Not content with this feat, one barracuda, during our stay in Palau, thrust his beak not only through the hull but into the gasoline tank, spilling all the fuel and setting the boat adrift.

On our port bow rose again the hilly little island of Aulong. To anyone who has reveled in the tales of the early explorers of the Pacific, this is one of the most romantic spots in the South Seas. And another reminder of the English. For it was here that Captain Wilson's East India Company ship, the *Antelope,* was wrecked in 1783.

XXIII:

First Taste of "Civilization"

CIVILIZATION, chiefly in the form of rifles and smallpox, came to Palau in a storm on the night of August 9, 1783.

The *Antelope,* schooner of three hundred tons, ran aground on the coral reef. Captain Wilson ordered compass, food, water, arms, and ammunition put into a small boat and took off at dawn for a small island three miles distant. It was found to be uninhabited. The ship's goods were gradually transferred from the wreck to the island, and the crew set about the building of a new schooner.

But they were not to remain undisturbed. On the twelfth, eight natives appeared and a Malay who understood English. They brought a request from the king that the strangers should visit him upon Koror island. Matthias, the captain's brother, courageously offered to be a hostage to fortune and went with the natives.

He was received cordially by the king, Abba Thulle. After being regaled on honey tea, coconut meat and taro cakes, he was given a sleeping mat and a block of wood intended to serve as a pillow. What with the hardness of the pillow and the wonder of the admiring throng which stood about him all night (for he was the first white man they had ever seen) he got little sleep. Moreover a fire was kindled just outside his room . . . he feared he was to be burned alive, and prayed to God. He did not know that a fire is always made in honor of a guest. He returned to camp none the worse and had favorable reports to make concerning King Abba Thulle.

These auspicious beginnings were promptly spoiled when six natives under cover of night visited the wreck and stole a supply of medicines. But retribution followed them swiftly. Thinking the medicines were food, they drank them down, and all died. Native respect for the visitors grew. They were credited with mysterious power.

So the king thought it wise to visit Captain Wilson. He came naked, but was distinguished by the iron axe he carried on his shoulder. The common people used axes made of shell.

Captain Wilson ordered his crew to fire a welcoming salute. The king and his followers, terrified by the explosion, began to run to their canoes, but finding themselves unharmed, returned full of curiosity about the thunder-sticks. The captain showed them how these strange tubes could be used to break a twig on a distant tree, or kill a bird, although no arrow was seen to pass from the tube to the bird.

A bright idea came to the king. Could not this tube be used to kill men also? The captain complimented him upon the idea, adding that it was not entirely original—others had thought of the same thing.

The king returned the next morning and asked if he could borrow five guns for five days. He was expecting some enemies and wished to surprise them. Wilson lent him the guns and ammunition.

The king's enemies came upon him, one thousand strong in one hundred and fifty canoes. The wild shots of the king's inexperienced marksmen did little damage to the enemy but did happen to pick off one of the king's own men. This so astounded the enemy that they fled. The king's men buried the accidental victim and celebrated a great victory.

Next, the war was carried into the enemy's territory. Some of the

Englishmen were persuaded to go along to operate the rifles and the results this time were more positive.

Wars continued, with English help, until the tribes in all directions were under the sway of King Abba Thulle. It does not seem to have disturbed the king that Captain Wilson raised the British flag and fired three times, thus claiming ultimate sovereignty for Great Britain. The king was more powerful than he had ever been before. And on all surrounding islands were the evidences of his prowess—taro fields burned, coconut trees cut down. Civilization was wonderful. The king resolved that his own son should go to England to reap more of the benefits of enlightenment.

The ship was finished. Its hull was painted with red and yellow clay presented by the king. The king asked Wilson to take his second son, Leeboo, to England with him, and Wilson consented.

While the savage prince dreamed of life in England, one of the Englishmen, Blanchard, dreamed with equal ardor of the joys of life on a savage isle. The captain finally consented to leave him behind. Before sailing away, November 12, 1783, Captain Wilson presented the king with five rifles, five shotguns and a barrel of powder. Blanchard, who was an expert rifleman, would teach the king's men the use of these armaments.

The king was overjoyed. He made Blanchard a chief and gave him two women and a forest. Blanchard removed his clothing, tattooed his body and made every effort to revert to type. Leeboo put on clothes, whitened his skin and learned English.

After four months in England, Prince Leeboo caught smallpox and died. After seven years in Palau, Rifleman Blanchard was killed in battle—by a spear.

In 1790 two English ships, the *Panther* and the *Endeavour,* were sent from Bombay to Palau. Two of the men who had been with the *Antelope* were on board and were recognized by the natives. The king was saddened to hear of the death of his son, but was pleased with the gifts showered upon him—four cows, two oxen, two Bengal sheep, eight goats, five Bombay pigs, three ducks, two geese, one Sumatran wild duck, two hens, one rooster, eight pigeons, two parrots, ammunition, silverware, grindstones, spoons and saws. In return for these gifts, the king thought it not too much to permit the British formally and officially to raise their flag, declare Palau British territory, and build a fortification of stones on Arakabesan. It was called Fort Abercrombie after the governor of Bombay.

Again, one man was enamored of simple savage life. It was Captain McClure of the *Panther*. He turned over the *Panther* to the next in command and stayed on Palau. It is thought that he had ambitions to become the king of Palau. He kept with him twenty rifles, twelve revolvers, twelve axes and a large amount of explosives. His dream of paradise was short-lived for he came away from the island ill and died an obscure death.

And so, out of this adventure with the English, Palau had gained rifles, livestock and an assortment of the best civilized diseases. The rifles rusted, the livestock died, but the diseases lived on. The English had gained an empty sovereignty, for there was no way to make use of it. The fort fell to ruins. The British Admiralty forgot Palau. Spain later nonchalantly picked it up and found no trace of the English except a few buff-skinned descendants of Blanchard and McClure and considerable smallpox, tuberculosis and syphilis.

"No good," was the comment of the present king of Koror, a direct descendant of Abba Thulle. "We like to have foreigners come. It is exciting. They show us new things. But sometimes I think it would be better if no foreigners had come—no English, Spanish, Germans, Japanese, anybody. This is an island. People on an island are supposed to live their own life. It must be so or the gods would not have made it an island. Don't you think so?"

I couldn't answer. It seemed so, indeed. And yet, in a world so crowded and so swiftly traversed, are there any islands any more? Perhaps we are condemned to world brotherhood whether it is good for us or not.

A head-hunting king regales Herr Siemer and the author with stories of the good old days. When an enemy's head was taken it was placed in this cupped stone and the entire tribe executed a war-dance around it . . . then took it on a triumphant tour of the villages.

A costume that would be approved by sun-bathing enthusiasts; but the doctors contend that the tropical native could do with less ultraviolet and more protection against bronchial troubles and skin affections.

XXIV:
Palau Is the Sword's Point

THE samurai sword which slashed so deeply into the southern Pacific had its handle in Japan, its blade in the Marianas and Carolines—and Palau was its fire-hardened point.

Palau was the nearest Japanese outpost to the Philippines. The nearest to Singapore. The nearest to Australia. The nearest to the Netherlands Indies.

There is a Japanese saying, "A drawn sword must taste blood." After a samurai had once taken his sword from its sheath he was considered an arrant coward if he replaced it unbloodied.

Japan could not resist the temptation to use the sword placed in her hands by the Versailles Conference—the sword tipped with deadly Palau.

Whether or not English civilization was good for the natives, it is probable that if Britain had held Palau Japan would not today be running hog-wild in the Pacific.

Occupation of Palau centered Japanese attention upon the Philippines, next door. The nearest Philippine coast is only five hundred miles away, two hours by plane. It is significant that the first Japanese air service in the South Seas was to Palau, with a spur to Davao, Japanese colony on the Philippine island of Mindanao. Also the steamship fare to Davao as well as to Celebes was cut to a nominal figure in order to encourage economic infiltration of Mindanao by Japanese civilians.

The Nippon Yusen Kaisha steamers which served the mandate were ordered by the government to sidetrip a few hundred miles to Celebes and to Mindanao—thence back into the mandate.

The ships lost money on every trip to these ports, but the government said they must go and covered their loss with a subsidy. The road must be kept open so that trade and immigrants might flow into these rich islands. The government sent not only the Nippon Yusen Kaisha to Celebes but also the Osaka Shosen Kaisha, the Nanyo Yusen Kaisha, the Ishihara line, the Sanyo Kabushiki Kaisha, and tramp steamers.

Japan's trade with the Netherlands Indies was greater than that of Mother Holland herself. It doubled between 1931 and 1936.

Japanese immigrants were not moving as briskly as Japanese cotton print dresses. It was not the fault of the Japanese government. By cutting the already very low steamer fare in half, Japan demonstrated that while she was anxious to have her people go to the mandate, she was twice as anxious to have them settle in Dutch and Philippine territory.

Mindanao is the richest and second largest of the 7,083 islands of the Philippines. It was the farthest Philippine island from the American seat of government in Manila; but the nearest to the Japanese seat of government in Palau. Boat service from Manila was incredibly poor. By the ordinary schedule it took a week to get to Davao. But the fastest Japanese liners from Palau required only two days. Small wonder that American influence in Mindanao was negligible. In the hills five miles back of Davao I met many Bagobos who had never before seen an American. But they knew all about the Japanese. The great industries of Mindanao, particularly hemp and lumber, were in Japanese hands. The harbor of Davao swarmed with Japanese ships. An American ship was a great novelty.

Davao is situated at the head of the deep, mountain-flanked Gulf of Davao, which must have appealed to the Japanese as a potential naval base. The busy city is seen against a magnificent back-drop composed of the volcanic Mount Apo, 9,600 feet high, loftiest crest in the Philippines, covered with stage snow. But this white material, although it suggests wintry cold, is really a reminiscence of infernal heat. For it is sulphur, cast out by the boiling volcano.

It did not take the visitor long to discover the other active volcano of the Philippines . . . Japan. Those who live on the flanks of a volcano are usually nervous, and there was almost hysteric nervousness in Davao. The wildest tales were current. That the Japanese were fortifying Mount Apo! That they were smuggling in arms and ammunition.

That there was a tunnel five kilometers long under the hemp planta-tions leading to a secret arsenal where ammunition was being manufac-tured. That planes were being massed in Palau for an air attack upon the Philippines.

"Have you heard any news about the war?" a young Filipino, a uni-versity graduate, asked me.

"What war?"

"The war between Japan and America."

It was as close as that!

The Americans, he said, had made an airfield a kilometer from his house and every day twenty American bombing planes were using it. They were getting ready for a counter-attack upon the nearby Japanese stronghold, Palau.

Most of the rumors were just smoke. Yet, where there was smoke there was fire.

The fire was that Japan, with characteristic lack of subtlety, was plainly preparing for Japanese occupation of Mindanao. It was evident to any visitor to Davao, but seemed absurd when mentioned in the cool government offices of Manila and received no attention in Washington. Twenty-five thousand Japanese thronged Davao streets. The Japanese consul was the unofficial governor of the city. The mayor elected under American supervision was a puppet of the Japanese.

According to Philippine law, the Japanese could not buy land. They neatly circumvented the law by buying through Philippine dummies.

The very few American plantation owners were forced out. The Japanese bribed the wild Bila-an tribesmen to descend from the hills and loot the American plantations so severely and frequently that the Americans, unable to get protection from the Philippine constabulary, which also was under Japanese influence, sold out and went home. All this caused not a ripple in the American press.

And the feeder through which more and more Nipponese power was siphoned into the Philippines was Palau.

When the day came for armed attack upon already thoroughly infil-trated Mindanao, it came from Palau.

Much the same drama was enacted in the case of Borneo, Celebes, the Moluccas and New Guinea. All these fabulous islands were within easy reach of the Palau naval base. The farthest of these, Borneo, was but 1,200 miles away, bomber-plane range. New Guinea was only six hundred miles distant. The very stiff and long resistance which has been put up by Japanese forces in New Guinea may be largely credited to Palau.

"Palau is the spigot of our oil barrel," remarked a scout for the *Nanyo Kohatsu.*

He did not mean that there was oil in Palau but that Palau was so placed that it could be used to tap the oil riches of the Indies. The Nipponese navy has long been acutely conscious of the importance of Japan's path to the oil lands. Wrote Commander H. Sato in Brassey's Naval and Shipping Annual for 1927:

"One half of the oil import of Japan is drawn from the Dutch Indies; the freedom of that sea route will be absolutely necessary for her power of resistance."

Directly south of Palau 1,400 miles is Australia itself. Japan had good reason to hope that the Palau swordpoint would pierce the "empty continent" where only seven million people hold a land nearly as large as continental United States.

When I asked the governor why the government for all the Japanese *Nanyo* had been established on Palau, he mused a moment and then replied,

"Palau is near everything that matters."

I do not know how well we qualified as spies. We had seen most of the six forbidden spots, and many others perhaps quite as important. We had amassed quite a bit of information to be turned over finally to those who had a right to it. The fact that we had been accompanied everywhere by Japanese officials strongly suggested that there were still other places worth seeing and things worth knowing. But the authorities evidently feared that we were becoming more interested in geopolitics than in entomology and ethnology.

When we had been in Palau for a month the governor said,

"You are the only visitors who have thought it worth while to stay

156

with us so long. We have been greatly honored. I am sorry to learn that you are leaving us tomorrow."

We too were sorry to learn that we were leaving, but promptly fell in with the suggestion. Remembering the fate of the U.S. Marine who had overstayed his welcome, we sailed on the *Yamashiro Maru* the next morning.

XXV:

Buried Treasure

Long ago some wanderers in the Pacific cached a fortune on the island of Angaur. The Japanese have been digging it up and carrying it off to Japan at the rate of a million dollars a year.

This might seem very romantic if the treasure were bullion or pieces of eight; the fact that it is in the form of bird droppings may detract somewhat from the romance, but not at all from the value of the guano.

This material, rich in phosphate, was laid down on the flat coral island of Angaur some ages ago. Possibly two million years were required to do the job, since the deposits are forty feet deep. It is being mined at the rate of 70,000 tons a year. There is said to be enough to last twenty-five years more.

It goes to Japan for use as fertilizer to perform the favorite Japanese trick of magic, making one acre do the work of twenty.

We landed and walked back along narrow railroad tracks to the interior of the island. There, for square miles, the surface of the island has been taken off to a depth of forty feet. The mined area is girdled by a white cliff of phosphate which the picks and shovels are gradually driving back.

Where the phosphate has been entirely removed, the coral reef upon which it was laid is exposed—pockmarked by great holes where the diggers for phosphate have painstakingly picked the reef's teeth.

Swarms of monkeys in the surrounding jungle protest against the daily encroachment upon their domain. Every time a ton of phosphate comes out a tree must fall. Ultimately Angaur will be nothing but a bare, jagged reef.

The phosphate is broken up with a pick, then loaded into dump cars. Little locomotives left from German times and bearing Berlin name plates haul the cars to the drying house. The phosphate goes onto an endless belt, which drops it little by little into a great revolving cylinder twelve feet in diameter and sixty feet long where hot air from a coal furnace thoroughly dries the material. Then it is carried away on another belt to be dumped into a storage shed. When a ship arrives the phosphate takes another belt journey up a fantastic bridge projecting over the sea high enough to clear a ship's superstructure and drops through a mammoth tube into the ship's hatches.

The workmen come on a contract for about six months. Alone—no wives or children allowed—the island is too small. The Japanese claim that labor is not forced to come, but only "persuaded." The word has a slightly sinister sound.

We are used to thinking of Japanese incomes as low. They are lofty compared with Kanaka incomes. A steep sliding scale of wages is in operation on Angaur. The average daily wage of the Kanaka is 0.77 yen; of the Chamorro, 1.41 yen; of the Chinese, 2.13 yen; of the Japanese 3.19 yen.

The laborers live on shelves in a long wooden shed like a loggers' bunkhouse but not so comfortable—yet much more airy, light and sanitary than the average Kanaka hut. They may enjoy pool, ping-pong and table games in a dingy clubhouse. But their lives are dreary, womanless and homeless.

Angaur has always had an unhappy reputation among the Micronesians. It has been known as "The Village of the Dead." Its rather unearthly guano waste is thought to be the promenade of ghosts. Angaur is a sort of purgatory. All the dead come here to be tested for an indefinite period, after which those who qualify are taken to heaven, called *babluades* or "the village over us." Angaur is thought to be a place of terrible agony of spirit in the uncertainty as to whether heaven or hell is to be the final destination. When a person is mentally distressed it is said that he is suffering Angaur. These native beliefs do not make employment on the island any more agreeable.

Angaur is valuable as a treasure house but of no military importance. The *Nanyo* has been so little known that while some of its strategic features have been underestimated others have been greatly exaggerated. The author of a book on "War between Japan and the United States in 1925" had much to say of "the great naval base of Angaur." There is not even a bay in the coast of Angaur, much less a fleet base. There is not even anchorage. A ship loading phosphate must be ready to sail at a moment's notice in case of sudden storm.

XXVI:
How About the Brown Man?

"MY PEOPLE all die," a chief lamented. "Long time ago, only old men died. Now young men die."

That has been the common experience of the Pacific islanders during the last fifty years. The young men have been dying.

The population of the Marquesas has shrunk to one-tenth of its former size. That of the Solomons to one-quarter. The hundred thousand inhabitants of the Marianas before the foreigner came had dwindled to 3,000 in German times. The native population of the Marshalls, 15,000 before the Germans took the islands in 1885, has dropped by a third. There is but one native in Sonsorol for every two twenty years ago. Two thousand natives of Kusaie before American whalers came roistering ashore dropped to 200 before the end of the Spanish regime. The population of the Yap group has faded from about 13,000 in early Spanish times to 4,000 in 1939. Death and desolation on Tahiti caused a native poet to lament:

"The leaves are falling on the sand,
The sea shall swallow coral strand,
Our folk shall vanish from the land."

Some say that the native population would have dwindled even if the white man had never entered the South Seas. Certainly they are wrong. But it is equally a mistake to claim that it is all the white man's fault. The truth lies between.

The white man is not to blame because the Yap Kanakas wash the body of a dead chief in water and then drink the water. Thinking thereby to quaff the great man's strength, they actually take over and spread his infections.

The white man did not teach the natives to plunge a fever patient into the sea, or to lay one suffering with chills against an open fire.

Native medicines are sometimes effective; more often they are nullified by superstition. The prescription does not depend so much upon what ails the patient as upon how it came to ail him. If your rib is broken, the *machamach* must first know how it happened. If a coconut fell upon you as you lay under the tree, you get one medicine. If you were struck by something falling from a roof, quite a different medicine. If you fell and hurt yourself upon the stones, still something different.

In other words, the medicine is not planned especially to mend a broken rib but to appease an angry spirit. And since the spirits of tree, roof and stone are different, different medicines must be employed.

Promiscuity at an early age and abnormal sex practices then and thereafter make men impotent and women sterile. Four women out of ten in Yap never bear a child and the others have only one or two in a lifetime.

Habits are irregular. Bedtime is anytime. If the argument is good and the toddy lasts, there may be no sleep for anyone in a Yap home until morning. Meals are catch-as-catch-can and the farmer is not supposed to eat until he returns from his plantation in the evening lest the gods of the crops be annoyed by his gluttony. Then weariness and gorging give him indigestion. Also, his food is wanting in variety. Particularly, it lacks protein. If his water is rain water which has streamed down the trunk of a tree and been diverted into a jar, well and good. But it is easy to neglect to take advantage of a rain in this way. In that case the water comes from an infected pond or taro patch.

Then the moot question of clothing. Ultraviolet has taken the civilized world by storm. Sun baths are the rage. Nudist colonies flourish. Bathing suits are cut low and lower.

I reminded Dr. Nagasaki, head of the Yap hospital, of these facts.

"Why then," I asked, "do you advocate clothing for the natives?"

"The ultraviolet rays are valuable," he said. "But in this latitude, and living an outdoor life, everybody is likely to get plenty of ultra violet, even through light clothing. On the other hand, the bare skin is exposed to skin diseases. And on chill, rainy days one is more likely to catch cold if unclothed. Weak children, especially, need protection. Bronchial troubles are partly due to the lack of clothing. You have seen the men sitting directly on the damp ground."

Yes, I had. But I recalled the scene in the Spanish mission when a hundred Kanaka maidens switched their grass skirts under them and sat down on the cement floor. The voluminous grass bustles make excellent portable cushions.

"But perhaps you noticed that those skirts were green," said the doctor. "They are made fresh for the Sunday service. Being green, they are damp. One skirt may actually contain a quart of water. We have frequently put these skirts on the scales. They weigh fifteen or sixteen kilograms. They are too heavy on the abdomen and their dampness is dangerous. Nothing at all would be better. And thin cotton dresses would mean more for the health of Yap women than all our medicines."

It's a pity. The picturesque costumes of the world seem destined to disappear and their place to be taken by cotton dresses and coats-and-pants.

The foreigner is not responsible for the damp, black hole of a house in which the people of many of the Micronesian islands choose to live. The small door-windows with overhanging shutters resemble low-lidded eyes. Little light can get in through that narrow squint. In bad weather the house is closed as tight as a drum. The air, if it may be called air, becomes a thick purée of smoke, moisture and human exhalations. The enormous thatch roof is a reservoir of dampness. The floor consists of poles laid on the ground. The family lies on the floor as on a grill, the earth-vapors rising through the cracks.

No wonder that the traveler in the jungle who wishes to know whether a house is near, stops and listens for a cough.

So much for native negligence.

But that negligence runs back some thousands of years. If it had been sufficient to wipe out the race, then the race would never have developed in the first place. The Polynesian peoples would not have multiplied and spread, as they did, from southeastern Asia over all the great island world of the Pacific. They were such a vigorous race that it took more than their own follies to kill them off.

Other follies were necessary, and the white man supplied them.

Dark, damp houses did no great harm until the Spanish brought in tuberculosis. That disease found the living conditions of the Kanakas exactly suited to its purposes. Today more than fifty per cent of the deaths on Yap are due to tuberculosis.

It is agreeable to blame everything upon the Spaniard, the German, and the Jap. Candor compels us to admit that the English and Americans were far from blameless.

One of the best accounts of the early nineteenth century in the Pacific is contained in a rare volume called *The Islands of the Pacific,* written by the Reverend James M. Alexander in 1895:

"It became proverbial that in coming to the far away Pacific many men, even from the best circles of society, hung up their consciences off Cape Horn and seemed to conclude that God did not rule west of America.

"In 1843 three English vessels visited the island Vate of the New Hebrides and there took by force a big quantity of fruits and vegetables and two hundred hogs. The natives made resistance and a fight ensued in which twenty-six natives were killed and the remaining ones were driven to take refuge in a cave. The crews of the ships then piled wood at the mouth of the cave, set it on fire and suffocated all within. The next year the crew of the Cape packet were massacred at this island.

"At Mare, of the New Hebrides, three natives once swam off to a vessel that called for sandalwood and while bargaining got into an altercation with the Captain. He fired on them killing two; the third swam ashore. A few months afterwards the crew of the *Lady Ann* were massacred at this island.

"The early missionaries at Hawaii remarked of some of these traders that they made their vessels like floating exhibitions of Sodom and Gomorrah and that their influence was only to make of the Hawaiians a nation of drunkards.

"During the year 1860 three Captains came to Port Resolution of Tannia in the New Hebrides and gleefully informed Mr. Paton [the missionary] that to humble the Tannese and to diminish their number, they had put on shore at different ports many men ill with measles. As Mr. Paton remonstrated, they exclaimed, 'Our watchword is, Sweep these creatures away and let the white men occupy the island.' They then invited a chief by the name of Kapuku on board and confined him for twenty-four hours, without food, in the hold among natives ill with measles and finally sent him ashore without a present to spread the disease. The measles thus introduced spread fearfully and decimated the population of the island. In some villages, men, women and children were stricken down together and none could give food or water to the sick or bury the dead.

"The Captain of a small vessel would sometimes get clearance papers from Sydney for trading in copra and trepang, and then cruise to kidnap the natives who would come off in canoes with supplies. Sometimes he would assume the guise of a missionary. Painting his vessel white that it might resemble the mission packets, he would approach the island with a white flag flying and arriving in port, go ashore dressed like a respectable gentleman, wearing spectacles and carrying an umbrella over his head and a Bible under his arm. As the natives joyfully flocked to meet him he would invite them on board his ship and into his cabin and then suddenly seize and manacle them and put his vessel to sea amid the cries of their relatives and friends in the surrounding canoes.

"In 1890 the ship *Alma* took four hundred natives of Micronesia to

Guatemala and two years afterwards only 180 of them were living, the rest having died of fevers contracted in the malarious swamps of the plantations."

The damage begun by the white man has been continued by the yellow man.

"The Japanese who came to Palau spread tuberculosis," said Dr. Sekine of Palau. "The disease is old in Japan. Therefore the Japanese have some immunity from childhood. But the natives are virgin soil for it and can't resist."

Tuberculosis, gift of the white man and the yellow, is the chief cause of the high native death rate.

The low birth rate is also chargeable mainly to the outsider. The inability of Yap women to bear children is said to be chiefly due to venereal disease. And venereal disease was the longest memory left to the Kanaka maiden who stood on the shore and waved good-by to the American whaler. The Spanish also spread this plague. Today it is being perpetuated by Japanese *oiran,* prostitutes and geisha who have become infected in Japan and come to the islands to rot and die.

A German radio operator brought leprosy to Yap forty years ago. Dysentery was introduced in Palau before Spanish times by English traders.

"I became sick with it," says a Palau old-timer who was a lad in those days. "I nearly died. Every house was shut up. It was a terrible disease . . . terrible. Our village buried five or six men every day. Funeral processions were always passing. More than half the people of the island died. Oh, it was terrible. When I talk of it, the hair stands up on my skin."

This epidemic, which cut the population of Palau in half, was followed by others almost as serious.

The yellow man came on the scene to see all the damage wreaked by the white man and to wreak a little more himself. With all the Exhibits A, B, C, etc. of the past century's sorry experience laid before him, what has he done about it?

Whether prompted by altruism or self-protection, he has done a good

164

deal. The islands were not a safe haven for Japanese so long as they remained a pesthole.

There are eight government hospitals in the Japanese mandated islands, with a staff of twenty-five physicians, seven pharmacists, twenty-three midwives and nurses, and seven assistants. In addition there are several hundred medical depots; which means simply that first aid materials and mild medicines are placed in charge of a village chief or king and dispensed free by him (generally for the wrong ailments) to the suffering neighbors.

The hospitals are not merely hospitals. They are made responsible for the public health. They train as well as treat. Each year every hospital selects the ten brightest girls from the graduating class of the local school, puts them in white caps and smocks, drills them for one year in the wards, then sends them back to their native villages. There they become the special pain-in-the-side of the *machamach* who resent the growing confidence of the people in these amateurs who do not even know the words to say with a sting-ray wand. These girls are not constituted district nurses. They are unpaid; they marry and settle down. But the ailing make a path to their door.

No one has ever charged the Japanese with being remiss in public surveillance of private affairs. Through such watchfulness, distressing as it may be to the individual, epidemics are reported and checked almost before they begin.

"I can't sneeze without the *junke* [native policeman] making a notch in his stick," complained one native.

Sanitary conditions are being forcibly mended. Natives are mobilized to build concrete water tanks, and iron roofs from which rain water may run into the tanks. Traveling physicians motorboat from island to island to diffuse sanitary knowledge among the natives by means of popular lectures and magic lantern and cinematograph shows.

Lepers, usually hidden by relatives, are ferreted out and consigned to a small "leper island" where they are scientifically treated. Hostels have been established for tubercular patients. School children are being taught prevention. Microscopes are making the rounds of the villages so that natives may acquire a first-hand horror of the tubercle bacillus.

"Model houses" are being built. The government pays one-half the cost of construction, then dictates what shall be done. The roof must not be of thatch, but of corrugated iron. (Farewell to romance!) There must be real windows and doors. The floor must be raised a meter from the ground so that air may pass freely beneath it, but not through it. It must be a solid floor, not a sieve. And there must be beds for sleeping.

"Why?" I asked the Japanese, "when you yourselves sleep on the floor?"

"But the native floor is not clean."

The new houses are a serious artistic loss. They are iron-lidded wooden boxes on stilts. It is small consolation to the poet, the artist, and the photographer that these houses are the greatest single contribution to the health of the natives. "Man shall not live by health alone," grumbled a painter from Kyoto, dismayed by iron roofs.

There is less progress in clothing the natives. Those of the western Carolines seem determined to resist this indignity to the bitter end. On a cold day the man who owns a pair of trousers may use it as a shawl, the legs tied under the chin. School children are given clothes and required to wear them in the classroom; which they obediently do, then leave them in their desks.

The hospital's scouts coach expectant mothers on child care. The new-born babe should not be washed in the sea and then left, naked, to dry in the trade wind. Nor is a banana leaf sufficient protection for an infant. The hospital now issues a large bath towel to envelop each new-born.

An increasing number of women come to the hospital at the time of confinement. There the child gets a fair start in life. Although this service is free, many women cannot be persuaded to accept it, so strong is tradition and dislike of the Japanese.

Infant mortality during the first year after birth was sometimes reported during the Spanish regime to be as high as eighty per cent. It has been reduced by half.

The remarkable success of salvarsan in the treatment of frambesia (yaws) has helped the hospital to win its race with the *machamach*.

Patients who have been relieved regard salvarsan almost as a fetish capable of curing anything from baldness to a broken leg.

Some remain stubborn in their fear of the hospital, particularly the old men. The only way to bring them is to make them fear more the consequences of not coming. So they are told that if they refuse to come while alive they will be brought when dead . . . and laid on the dissecting table, for the advancement of science. They dislike the idea. For it would mean, according to their lights, that they would not go to the aerial village, the native heaven. Their ghosts, harassed and earth-bound, would annoy the neighbors. So, by one device or another, resistance to medical science is broken down.

Respect for the hospital has increased since the former free policy has been abandoned and nominal charges have been made for most treatments. But still the fees can hardly be called exorbitant.

We visited the Yap hospital to get a sea thorn extracted from Mrs. Price's foot. Dr. Yoshida performed the operation and charged the princely sum of twenty sen. (Six cents, for what would have cost three to five dollars in New York.) At that, we were overcharged. While Japanese and foreigners are expected to be able to pay twenty sen for a treatment, the natives pay only four. If they cannot afford that, they are treated free. The total expense of the Yap hospital is 35,000 yen a year. The income from all patients, Japanese, Chamorros and Kanakas (not forgetting the twenty sen from the only American patient the hospital has ever had) is less than 3,000 yen.

Whether the Kanaka wants to be benefited or not, he is being taught to go to the hospital when sick, to keep his house and village clean, to eat better foods, to work, and to study.

True, the work is for the Japanese, and the study is to make him an obedient subject of the Emperor.

Before the Japanese regime, mission schools were relied upon to teach the native. Only two government schools were built, one in Saipan and one in Truk, but the latter had not been opened when the Japanese navy arrived in 1914.

The navy built six schools and navy officers turned teacher. In 1915 teachers from Japan took their place. By 1922 the number of schools had become seventeen. Today there are twenty-five schools for natives.

Native school attendance in 1936 had reached ninety-eight per cent in islands such as Yap where communication is easy, but stood at a little more than fifty per cent in Truk. It is not practicable to build a school on every one of the 245 small islands of Truk, and going to school by canoe over miles of stormy lagoon has its difficulties.

The schools supply books, pencils, clothing, and sometimes food also, without charge. The cost of native education to the government is more than four times the total of the poll tax received from natives.

Knowledge of Japanese institutions and Emperor-worship are taught in every school. Every expedient is used to discredit the white man and his civilization. It is proclaimed the duty of all Asiatics to expel the "foreigner" and unite in a Greater East Asia Co-Prosperity Sphere under the leadership of Japan.

The Japanese language is taught in these schools. No instruction is given in the native language. The result is not wholly satisfactory. After five years of school (in some islands it is only three years) the graduate cannot easily read a Japanese newspaper and finds a magazine or book quite impossible. Nor can he read in his native tongue. He is a man without a written language. He can speak Japanese imperfectly but soon forgets what he knows of it when he returns to the jungle.

The native gets no higher education. He is trained for manual labor. He is not allowed too wide a horizon. He studies an arithmetic of coconuts and pigs, a geography that concerns chiefly his own islands although it never slights Japan, the natural science of his jungle and lagoon, ethics stressing the "virtues" of obedience and hard work. Nor is it all book-learning. The girls learn how to cook, sew, care for babies and nurse the sick; and the boys learn agriculture in the school farm and at the experimental station.

The graduate farmer is supplied with land without cost for three years, seeds, implements and everything else, sometimes even including zeal. He is encouraged, if not compelled, to raise something besides taro-potato. His path is hard, but paved with bonuses. If he prefers leisure to the earning of bonuses, he is liable to spend some leisure in

168

In the fabulous lagoon of Truk, forty miles wide, great fleet base.
This island was Dublon but the Japanese preferred to call it
Natsushima, Summer Island. (See Chapter XXVII).

In an island without streams, the only safe drinking water is the rain that trickles down the trunks of trees and is diverted into a jar.

jail. If he should have a new, light, airy house built high above the ground instead of his low, dark, tuberculosis-breeding cavern of thatch, the government offers to pay half the cost—and is reluctant to take no for an answer. Roads, piers, clubhouses, community plantations and other public works require the labor of each man. He may take his choice between payment and punishment. Thus by a curious system of reward and compulsion, the government overcomes to some degree the lassitude of the tropics.

No man likes to be protected against himself. So the Kanaka does not appreciate the restrictions upon his alcoholism; particularly when he sees the Japanese enjoy full liberty in this regard. Liquor is forbidden to the ruled but not to the rulers.

Petty officials impose upon natives. "That's a nice bunch of bananas. Bring it around to my house." No pay.

I am glad to give credit to the occasional honest and humane executive. Governor Tanaka, upon first taking office in Ponape, called a mass meeting of three thousand natives.

"Don't give any official anything," he told them, "unless he pays you. And if he mistreats you, report at once to me."

The average executive is not of high caliber. He resents having been exiled to the islands. He is likely to drink more than is good for him and to loosen up his inhibitions, the restraint of homeland customs being removed. Under pressure from Japanese adventurers who have invaded the islands in search of easy money, he milks the natives dry for benefit of his friends. There is no place in the new economy for the brown man, except as a wage slave. And Japan even sends in wage slaves of her own to replace him. All industries are in the hands of Japanese. A native so unwisely enterprising as to start a shop or factory would soon find difficulty in getting supplies or machinery. His shipments would be unaccountably damaged in transit. When affairs had reached a fairly desperate stage, a Jap business man would appear with an offer to buy his outfit for perhaps a tenth of what it was worth. If he was prudent, he would accept with alacrity. If he stood on his "rights," his place might be destroyed some night by thugs or a fire.

If he protested to the authorities he might be branded as disloyal and subjected to "questioning"—the Japanese euphemism for torture.

"It doesn't pay to make trouble," say the natives.

It must be said that such treatment is not reserved for the natives. Unlucky Japanese are as summarily treated by the *Kempeitai*, Japanese Gestapo. The forcing of "confessions" from innocent persons is an art as highly developed in Japan as the tea ceremony. But the Japanese can hope for justice in the courts. The Micronesian cannot.

"The Japanese don't pay," said a native baker on Palau. "I used to be a sailor. I learned to bake on an English ship. After I came home and the Japanese came I thought here was a good chance to bake bread— some of the Japanese like it. So I got a little store and some ovens. The Japanese liked my bread but would not pay me for it. So I went out of business.

"Then I tried being a contractor. There was a great demand for labor. So I would get men to work for the Japanese. I would have to pay the men—but the Japanese wouldn't pay me. So again I had to quit. I won't try again. It's no use."

Wage scales differ sharply for the chosen people and the subject race. The Japanese carpenter or shipwright receives four yen a day; the native one or two.

The net result of a policy of banishing disease and teaching industry but at the same time depriving the people of the fruits of either health or industry is an accelerated decline of the native population. Some 400,000 Micronesians were progressively reduced by the Spaniards to a few tens of thousands but recovered somewhat during German rule. When the Japanese took the islands the population was growing. However, it soon reached a standstill at 50,000, where it remained until 1939. Then, according to the *Japan Year Book*, it dropped from 50,868 in 1938 to 40,406 in 1939. No explanation is given of this sudden decrease. We can venture none, and must wait until the islands are again accessible before we can learn whether there was active deportation of "undesirables," or whether the 1939 figure was the result of a census whereas the former figures were estimates, allowed to remain at approximately the same level during years when the population was actually dying out with increasing speed.

Just as some plants cannot live in the same soil with certain others, so the Micronesians could hardly exist in the face of the Japanese torrent that increased the Japanese population of the islands from about 300 in 1914 to 73,028 in 1939!

The total expenditure of the mandate government is about five million yen a year. Of this, the government estimates that about one and a quarter million yen is spent on matters of direct benefit to the natives.

"What do you mean by 'benefit'?" I asked the *Nanyo* treasurer, but he only stared, uncomprehending.

Of course there is always the question as to whether the Kanaka might not be benefited most by being let alone. That is too deep a question for the Japanese—but not too deep for an old chief who had a wide reputation as a cynic and a sage.

"Benefits!" he said. "Too many benefits! Before the foreigners came we lived at peace. The forest fed us—simply but sufficiently. We did not work. Is work a virtue when there is nothing to be gained by it? Neighbors were friendly, children were obedient. Life was a trade wind without gusts or squalls. But now comes struggle—the struggle to make money. Money for what? We do not need clothing—the sunshine clothes us. We do not need an iron roof to carry rain water into a cement tank. The water that streams down the trunk of a tree can be turned into a jar. We do not need farming tools of iron and steel. We can make our own from the shell of the giant clam. We do not need alarm clocks and phonographs and electric lights. They spoil the sounds of the forest and the light of the moon. We do not need the telephone —we can talk to those on faraway plantations through the shell-trumpet. We do not need schools. The father can teach his children all that is necessary for our simple manner of life. We do not need hospitals. This is a small island—if some did not die there would soon be too many people, too little food. But our young men are upset by the idea that they must do something, even if it is something useless. On the athletic field near the school a track has been made where boys may run around in a circle. That is what civilization is—running around in a circle."

XXVII:
Japan's Pearl Harbor—Truk

NAVAL men estimate that Truk may be the strongest base in the Pacific with the exception of Pearl Harbor.

The sea approaches are dangerous because of reefs and currents.

Coming from the Palau group through a maze of islands, we sighted on the afternoon of the third day the low island of Enderby to starboard and Pulap to port. Between them the chart indicated extensive shoals. The captain enumerated several *Nanyo Boeki Kaisha* boats which had been wrecked here, and the *Kasuga Maru* of the *Nippon Yusen Kaisha* had run aground. She had, however, been patched up, got off under her own power and put in at Ponape for repairs.

Matters are further complicated by an erratic forty-mile-a-day current, the direction of which can never be foretold. It may flow against or with the ship or strike either beam from any angle. During our passage it was throwing us to port. The pencilled course on the captain's chart showed odd sidesteps, each representing a correction that had been made after an observation had shown the ship to be fifteen miles or so off her course, due to the current. In weather when observations are impossible, the chartroom wizards may be able to "prove" by everything that is reasonable that the ship is in deep water at the instant when she is about to end her career on a reef.

Entranced passengers lined the rail as we sailed throughout Northeast Pass into the wonderful atoll of Truk. For Truk far excels Tahiti in exotic beauty.

I had always thought of Truk as an island. Instead, it is a cluster of 245 islands in a vast iridescent lagoon surrounded by a coral reef. The

Note: These chapters were written just before the American attack on Truk, February 17, 1944. The forecasts made seem to have been fairly well borne out.

surrounding reef is 140 miles long. The lovely island-studded lake it encompasses is some forty miles across.

All these islands were once one great volcano high above sea level, according to the geologists. Streams cut the mass into many separate mountains. Then the land subsided, leaving only the tops of the mountains above water—and these mountaintops are the 245 islands of Truk.

The great volcano had been bordered by the usual fringing reef. As the land sank, water separated the reef from the land, forming the present lagoon. Of course the reef sank too, but the polyps were still busily at work and built new coral on top of the old, thus keeping the height of the reef constant. The result is a rim of coral with an outer slope of about thirty degrees dropping to a depth of three miles. This natural breakwater is a few hundred feet wide but at places broadens to form small islands covered with coconut palms.

These flat coral islands are in sharp contrast to the high volcanic islands inside the lagoon, some of them five to ten miles long, many very small. They are towers and minarets, clothed from sea to summit with breadfruit and banana trees, coconut palms, scarlet bougainvillea and crimson hibiscus, brilliant against the deep blue South Sea sky. Some islands slope up gently from sand beaches. Others rise abruptly in steep cliffs.

We entered the Eten Anchorage, a triangular harbor formed by the three islands, Dublon, Fefan and Uman (called by the Japanese Natsu, Aki and Fuyu). We anchored about a mile offshore. Native boats swarmed around the ship.

The question had constantly harassed us—how to get ashore on Truk. It would probably be more difficult here than elsewhere. We would not ask for permission. There would be no refusal, only an interminable series of excuses, obstacles and delays. And to ask for permission would be to acknowledge the right of the authorities to stop us. We could not recognize such a right, since the privilege of free access had already been granted by Tokyo and was required by the terms of Japan's mandate.

We worked out a dozen schemes. We might have saved our brains; the problem solved itself.

A handsome Polynesian climbed aboard. He stopped short when he saw a white man, then came to me, all smiles.

"You are American?" he asked eagerly. "For twenty years I have not seen an American. My name is Fal. I used to be a chief—now no more. There was an American missionary here. His name was Logan. That was long ago, before the yellows came. He was a father to me. He taught me English. He was good to my people. I swore I would do anything for an American. You will come to my home?"

"If you can get us off quietly," I said. "The captain wouldn't want us to land."

He looked around. "Everybody is up forward. Go aft. I'll have my boat there. It has a little cabin. Slip into the cabin and no one will know you are aboard."

In ten minutes we were flying toward shore in Fal's big outrigger sailing canoe.

"Take us straight to the governor," I said to Fal. The best way to flout authority is to pretend to respect it. It wouldn't do to wait for police to pick us up and take us before the governor of the island. We had best go to him under our own power and present our credentials.

We avoided the docks and landed on a quiet beach on Dublon. Above us towered a hill crowned by a building in German style. It had been the residence of the German governor and was now occupied by his Jap successor.

We climbed up, called a polite *"Ohaiyo,"* the Japanese equivalent of a knock on the door, were admitted by a bewildered attendant and met the much astonished Governor Yamaguchi. After the first *"Sa!"* he covered his surprise well. He expressed great pleasure that we should consider his poor islands worth visiting.

"I am afraid you will be disappointed," he said. "There is nothing of interest here."

Tea was brought in, and we talked. Suddenly there came a blast from the harbor.

"Your ship!" exclaimed the governor. "It is sailing!"

"It is just going to Kusaie," I said, "and will be back in a week."

"A week!" he gasped.

But there was nothing for it. We were Truk's unwelcome guests for a week.

I came near staying there forever at the bottom of the Truk lagoon.

We were assigned to Fal's care and lived in his log-and-thatch home. Fal stood in well with the Japs. They had made him a *soncho* or administrator over several dozen villages. The Japs trusted Fal—as much as they trust anyone. They did not dream what was in his heart.

"The Americans will come back some day," he said. "Until then we can only obey."

Fal took us on endless trips among the myriad islands. He refrained from drawing too close to military features because a small police motorboat always followed us at a distance of half a mile or so. Even at that the police finally decided that we were learning too much.

But those days on the Truk lagoon! If I should be reliably informed that heaven was closed to me but were allowed to choose any other spot in which to spend eternity, I should think twice about Truk. Assuming, of course, that the place were de-Japped.

Its name is not musical, but its sea, land and sky are a symphony. Its forty-mile-wide lagoon sheltered by a white girdle of coral is paradise for a yachtsman. There are no disturbing swells and billows, yet always a breeze.

You sail over broad lakes, shoot through narrow passages between islands, skim past sleepy thatched villages on palm-shadowed beaches, drink sunshine, relish the spray, and haul in barracuda over the lee rail.

And below, what a pageant! The lagoon floor is a garden of coral and algae, of sea fan and oarweed, of bright blue sea moss and red sea cucumbers, of ultramarine starfish and of swimming fish in all the colors of the rainbow. There are corals like sponges and sponges like corals. There are green sponges, geranium-scarlet sponges, marigold-yellow sponges.

You get color-dizzy and look back at the plain blue sky for relief.

And again the grim note is struck, for in some parts of the mighty lagoon the bottom drops away and there is a reef-protected basin which seems to be big enough for every battleship, cruiser, destroyer, transport and submarine of the Japanese Fleet.

There are occasional gaps in the encircling reef. The polyps were not thinking of the convenience of the fleet when they left these openings. They were expressing their disgust for fresh-water streams coming from the islands. In these currents the polyps die, for they cannot

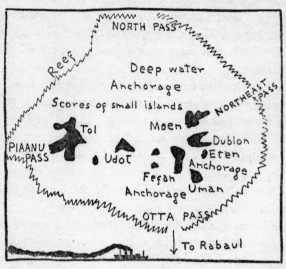

TRUK

find their proper food. They thrive only in the salt sea, when it is of proper temperature and depths.

Where the gaps are not wide enough or deep enough, they have been enlarged by man.

The Japanese town is on the eastern end of Dublon. The houses cling to a hillside, facing Eten Anchorage. Climbing through the town and descending into the valley behind it, one passes a school (for Japanese pupils only) with gateposts inscribed with the names of those Japanese citizens who contributed to build it and the exact amount given by each, a rather tacky *shikenjo* or experimental garden, a fine hospital in a charming garden, an airfield and radio station, a con-

176

spicuous hill on which the *shicho* or governor's headquarters are an inviting target (if this building had been erected by the Japanese instead of by the Germans it would have been artfully concealed in a valley), and come at last to a fine church on the far edge of the three-mile-wide island.

This was a Christian church built by Americans of whom no trace now remains except the grave of Robert W. Logan, missionary of the American Board of Commissioners for Foreign Missions, who translated the New Testament into the Truk language—and won for America the undying friendship of men like Fal. Our native friend was silent as we visited this grave near the house of the vanished Americans on a lovely hill overlooking the sea. But garrulous enough was the host who served us with refreshments on the mission veranda. He was the new missionary, the Reverend Kawashima, serving under the *Nanyo Dendo-dan* or South Sea Mission with headquarters in Japan. This mission, though Christian, or shall we say because it is Christian, is substantially subsidized by the Japanese government. Japan believes in Christianity—for Micronesians; it helps to make them meek and pliable.

"But doesn't the government support Shinto priests in the islands?" I asked the missionary.

"Very few. Shinto is a warlike faith. Shinto may do for the Japanese, but not for these people. It would lead them astray. Not that I have anything against Shinto. I am a Shintoist."

"You are both a Christian and a Shintoist?"

"Of course. Why not?"

"You don't find any conflict between the conception of a Christian God and the conception of a God-Emperor?"

"Not at all. The Christian God in the form of Christ was a great prophet and we deeply honor him. He was an Oriental, crucified by the West but accepted by us of the East. There is a tradition, you know, that he came to Japan and honored the *Tenshi* [Emperor] as his father and father of all mankind. It is said that he died in Japan and is buried there. But God still lives."

"By 'God' you mean the Emperor?"

177

Mr. Kawashima smiled at my crudeness. "I can hardly explain to one not brought up in the same religious atmosphere. No, we do not think of the reigning Emperor as God. What we revere is the Godhead which began with the Creator, Izanagi, continued in Amaterasu, the Sun Goddess and her grandson, the first Emperor, Jimmu, and flowed through all his imperial successors to the present day."

It was an odd kind of Christianity. Japanese Christians who have been under the direct instruction of American or European missionaries do not share this bastard theory—or, when they do, keep it to themselves. But since the exodus of the white missionaries, the government has worked zealously to make Christianity serve national policy. And the most outspoken exponents of the new creed are the missionaries sent to condition all Asiatics for Japanese hegemony. In Micronesia, in the Netherlands Indies, in Malaya, Thailand, Burma, Indo-China and China they are at work. Whether they are Christian pastors, Shinto priests or Buddhist monks their message is substantially the same. Japan has but one faith—faith in Japan.

XXVIII:

The Truk Lagoon

DUBLON is a hive of Japanese activity. Certain other islands show little change except in their names. Of course they were already named in quaint South Sea style, but the names did not fit snugly into the Japanese syllabary. So the empire-builders undertook the task, and, judging by the results, they could have done with a little help from the pullman-christeners. At least the latter have imagination. The islands have not been named One, Two, Three, but only narrowly escaped that fate. The four principal ones are named after the four seasons, Spring Island, Summer Island, etc. (in a clime where there are no seasons!). Seven others have the days of the week pinned to them, although just what similarity there is between this island and Monday, or between that one and Thursday, it is impossible for a mere novice in these arts to tell. Then come the flowers. There is Cherry Island (although the island has never seen a cherry, except in a can), Chrysanthemum Island, Iris Island and so on. Flowers, not of the South Seas but of Japan.

I said there were no seasons. That needs a word of qualification. Such terms as spring, summer, autumn, winter, are meaningless absurdities where there is only summer. Nor is time marked off into periods of life and death. Every season is a growing season. The only outstanding change is in the direction of the wind. For six months the steady trade comes from the east and northeast, and then, for six months, from the west and southwest. So the natives, logically enough, think of two alternating years, each six moons long, the East Wind Year and the West Wind Year.

We land on Monday Island (Getsuyo-to, formerly Udot) and walk across it. It is a bower of loveliness. Smiling natives step out of the path into the long grass, bow profoundly, and announce their own age by their greeting.

"Buenos dias!" says the oldster who learned his foreign talk when the Spaniards were here.

"Guten morgen!" says the middle-aged.

"Ohaiyo!" says the youngster with Japanese schoolbooks under his arm.

They are a gentle folk with sometimes beautiful faces and always broad smiles, revealing white teeth—shockingly white, they seem, after one has become accustomed to the jetblack canines of Yap and Palau. There is no betel-chewing on Truk.

Music drifts down the glade from a forest-hidden hilltop where there is a German mission school for girls (soon thereafter to be taken over by Japanese). The tunes are German hymn tunes, but reduced to soothing tropical cadences by the use of mandolins and guitars, softly fingered. The natives have an excellent ear for music. They melt the strident strains that come from lands where trains roar, into melodies appropriate to a land where the loudest sounds are the rustle of palms in the trade and the purl of the lagoon upon the beach.

We have a sunset repast of native foods, then take to the boat again. Some natives on the beach sing us a parting song as we draw away from Monday Island. It will still be two days before we can sleep . . . we must pass Tuesday and land upon Wednesday.

We really do not care how long it takes. It is an impossibly beautiful night. The moon is full, and a full moon in the South Seas is the richest gift of the sky to man. You could read small type with ease, but who wants to read small type on a night like this? The deck is bathed in milk. The jib and mainsail float above like smoke. Orion blazes overhead, trailing brilliant Sirius. They show off to as great advantage as gems laid out on a pad of blue velvet on a jeweler's showcase. At one end of the sky is the North Star and at the other end will soon rise the Southern Cross. The horizon is cushioned with white puff-balls of clouds, their crests snowy in the moonlight. The bow-waves sparkle like fountains. The coral colors of the lagoon-floor melt liquidly one into another. We flow along with amazing speed, for the wind, though gentle, is abaft the beam. Our half-clothed native friends, perched, singing, on the weather rail, look like statues of marble and bronze combined.

Past black Tuesday. And, too soon, to mountainous Wednesday (Tol). We land on a grass-grown pier. Then, through the forest, along silver trails against which the gaunt fingers of breadfruit leaves are sharply silhouetted. Past sleeping thatches. To a house smothered in bougainvillea on the edge of the lagoon. There to wash, eat, sleep.

This is thirty miles away from the ship harbor but still within the lagoon. The Japanese hand is lightly felt here. But the people are not untouched by the outside world. Our hosts back up their wash-bowl with a wall-cloth on which a German missionary lady has embroidered in blood-red silk the words, *"Gewaschen im Blute des Lammes!"* One instinctively looks critically into the wash-bowl . . . but the water is clear and fresh and does not deserve the gory imputation.

Before the Germans, the Americans were here. The Truk language is sprinkled with English words. They are particularly interesting because they give us an index to objects not native to the islands but brought in by American missionaries and traders. The words include money, clock, bicycle, towel, white-shirt, jacket, stockings, shoes; pig, cow, calf, cat; lamp, stove, table, soap, flour; school, lesson, book, ink, pen; cigarette, devil, Satan and hell.

Some of the words are modified, of course. Matches has become masis. Bible, Paipel. Sunday school, Sonte skul. Trousers, rouses. Button, butch.

The word pillow has been taken over along with the soft object it designates. But the word bed has not been accepted, because the bed itself is not yet used.

Life remains simple. Food, shelter and a shirt—that is life. One shirt lasts a year. Shelter comes from the pandanus. Food is all about, and is always served cold. That may be because that congenitally lazy human being, man, does the cooking.

For a unique reversal of social custom may be seen here on Truk. The men have changed places with the women. They have not yet taken to bearing the children, but they care for them and look after the house while the women go fishing. The men cultivate the fields (women's work in the islands behind us). On Friday the men gather a week's supply of food. On Saturday they cook it all in great pots, slaving over the fires while the women make the day a holiday, strolling and playing. Ordinarily no food is cooked on any other day. That prepared on Saturday is eaten cold throughout the week. The men give various reasons for this. It is too much work to make daily fires. The climate is so warm that hot food is unpalatable. No forks are used, and hot food would burn the fingers. Even on Saturday, cooking day, food is allowed to cool before it is eaten.

But it does not take many meals of cold fish and cold potato to make one glad to sail to the main island and have a hot *sukiyaki* dinner with Governor Yamaguchi.

He stages a native dance for us and takes us to the school to see the handiwork of Truk children. I admire a childish drawing in colored crayons, and it is now on the wall beside me. It represents a palm-fringed shore and lagoon and some men approaching in a boat upon which two immense Japanese flags are flying. Native children on the shore are ecstatically waving their arms in welcome. "The pleasure of the natives when the Japanese came to Truk," explained the teacher. Evidently the portrayal of this pleasure was a class assignment since the teacher allowed us to look through a stack of some forty such drawings. They were all on the same theme and differed only in such matters as the degree of ecstasy and the size of the flags.

It is to be hoped that when the Yanks land it will not be necessary to make a school assignment of "the pleasure of the natives when the Americans came to Truk." Nowhere, I believe, will the newcomers receive a more cordial welcome. Fortunately the education of Truk was not left to the American whaler. Thanks to American and European missionaries, practically all the 16,000 natives of Truk are Christian and friendly to people of other Christian lands. They will not take up arms, having none. They have been disarmed both materially and spiritually. But they will give refuge and comfort and silence where needed to the friendly invaders. That sort of aid, as the Japanese found to their advantage in Malaya, may be more valuable than armed support.

XXIX:

How Strong Is Truk?

INVADERS of Truk may be surprised not by the defenses but by the lack of them. That is, defenses of the stone and steel variety.

They need not look for a fortification of the type of Singapore, Gibraltar, or the Maginot Line. The Japanese doubt the value of fixed fortifications and prefer mobile defense in the form of planes and ships. Certainly there will be shore batteries and anti-aircraft. But the chief defense of Truk has been supplied by Nature.

This is more or less true throughout the mandated islands. Japan did not build great fortifications, not because the mandate forbade such installations, but because they were not needed. There is no necessity for stone bastions where there are already rock cliffs several hundred feet high; no need for a sea-wall where there is a reef.

Wilhelm's *Military Dictionary* includes in its definition of the various types of fortification the "natural fortification" which "consists of those obstacles which nature affords to retard the progress of an enemy; such as woods, deep ravines, rocks, marshes, etc." In that sense, the islands are heavily fortified. Not only are some of them perfect natural bases for destroyers and submarines, but, in the words of Admiral Suetsugu, "These islands are naturally built aircraft carriers."

Truk was born to be a naval base. The naval engineers were the coral insects which built a wall around Truk 140 miles long and many hundred feet thick. This coral reef has a rampart some fifteen feet high along its outer edge, because there the waves break and the coral polyps love to work in the oxygenized surf. Behind this rampart, batteries are protected against the fire of an enemy fleet.

Landing boats would be confronted by a cliff of knifelike coral under pounding swells. Palms hang out over the cliff and snipers concealed in the tops would have no difficulty in picking off many of the occupants of the boats.

After perhaps heavy loss, a landing would be made on the reef. Perhaps nothing would please the defenders more, for the landed forces would then be the target of batteries on the island peaks. The invaders would be faced by a lagoon with the nearest important island about four miles away. How would the lagoon be crossed?

But suppose an effort is made to bypass the reef and enter the lagoon through one or more of the channels. There are only four of these and they would certainly be well mined and covered by fire from the reef as well as from the hill batteries. The hills of five of the islands are over a thousand feet high, thus providing good locations for both anti-aircraft and guns trained on the low-lying reef and invading surface ships.

A high island guards each channel. Dublon looks down upon Northeast Pass, Uman upon Otta Pass, Tol upon Piaanu Pass and Moen upon North Pass.

Once in the lagoon, Allied ships would be at the mercy of the "coral mine fields" which are quite unpredictable and uncharted by foreigners except long ago by Spaniards and Germans. Their charts are useless now because coral does not stay put. The polyps have been building rapidly in some places, slowly in others, not at all in still others. Man has added to the confusion; the Japanese have dredged coral from certain areas and deposited it elsewhere. Without charts, not only warships but even small PT boats could not navigate the lagoon safely.

Airpower will perhaps solve the puzzle. But not easily, for, as at Munda, planes will have difficulty locating targets because of the dense vegetation. Japanese warships will not be concentrated in one basin as in the ordinary small naval roadstead but well dispersed among the 245 islands from the peaks of which anti-aircraft will intercept attacking planes.

The Japanese make good use of their "natural fortifications." Fuel storage tanks are camouflaged and submerged in the lagoon. The lagoon surface is a smooth field for seaplanes. Bomb-proof hangars will probably be found tunneled into cliffs. I witnessed the reduction by noisy bulldozers of an island three hundred feet high to a level field for landplanes. The island was Eten, and doubtless other islands have since been treated in the same way.

But despite all obstacles, air power will spell the doom of Truk. With Rabaul in Allied hands, land-based planes can easily span the 800 miles to Truk. A radius of a thousand miles, or even 1,200, 2,400 round trip, is not beyond the reach of present planes, and new ones will be capable of much greater range. At the same time other planes will presumably be coming from the east, possibly Jaluit, 1,200 miles, Enewetok, 750, Kusaie, the same easy distance, or Ponape, 430 miles away. The lesser of these distances are practicable even for fighter planes. Air cover for the bombers will also be supplied from the decks of the six carriers which the Japanese announce they have "sunk or absolutely sunk," whatever that means, in the battles of Bougainville.

XXX:

One Comic Adventure, One Not So Comic

"WILL you go shark-hunting?" someone called at dawn outside the hut that had been placed at our disposal.

It was Fal. He held a *kap,* the remarkable Ponapean yam, four feet long, under one arm and a harpoon in his other hand. He gave me the potato.

"This," he said, "will keep your woman busy while we go fishing."

My wife was not particularly pleased with this arrangement, but Fal considered the trip too dangerous for her.

Incidentally, she had the last laugh when I arrived home looking as if I had been dragged across the bottom of the lagoon at the end of a troll.

Leaving her with the potato and some dusky neighbor women who were eager to show her what to do with it, we went down to the lagoon.

Fal's boat was a canoe carved from a single log, fitted with a starboard outrigger of bamboo and a sail made of plaited pandanus leaves.

We set out, both paddling, until the morning breeze should come up. The surface was smooth. Objects on the floor of the lagoon were as clear as articles in a show window.

A pancakelike sting ray lay on the bottom, languidly waving the flexible tail of which the Spaniards used to make riding whips to quicken the movements of the natives. Its deadly spines stood erect, waiting for an incautious bather.

Cobalt and orange *mamo-tik* swam in and out of the miniature forests of coral.

The poisonous bladderfish blew itself up like a balloon as the paddles disturbed it.

The garfish, which has been known to leap into small boats and stab fishermen to death with its lance, swam idly by.

Fal laughed at the *paikop,* a fish with a homely flat face.

"When we want to make fun of a person," he said, "we call him a *paikop*-face." Evidently the expression was equivalent to our "pie-face."

Young octopi, delicacy of the Japanese, hungrily searched about with their tentacles. The big dangerous ones would be in deep water.

Where rocks projected above the surface, climbing fish hopped and crawled.

I reached into the shallows after a brilliant blue starfish.

"Please, no," warned Fal. "It is called 'a little bit of the sky.' We say that if you take it out there will be a heavy rain. Perhaps it is only a superstition." He shrugged.

Fal had shipped all over the western Pacific. He had picked up English and, along with it, the suspicion that some of the beliefs of his own little island were absurd. But he was taking no chances.

Chugging motorboats passed us, making for the open sea. They were after bonito. The Japanese have made a big industry of it, for every Nipponese family must have a scraping of bonito in the soup.

We saw a mother-of-pearl diver fix his goggles over his eyes and dive from his small boat while his companion remained in it, spear ready, to defend his partner against sharks.

We were passing over a slightly submerged part of the reef that separates the lagoon from the ocean.

"Want a drink?" asked Fal.

He dipped his coconut shell into the water where it appeared to be boiling up through the sea from a hole in the reef a few feet below the surface.

The water was perfectly fresh!

"A spring," he said. "Very popular with fishing parties."

Suddenly we were no longer over the reef. The steep submarine cliff on the ocean side dropped to unseen depths. Fal prepared to hunt shark.

He used no bait—only a rattle! He dangled a string of coconut shells over the side and clattered it against the gunwale. Fishermen for bonito do something similar. They rap on the sides of the boat, or keep the motor running, to attract the fish.

For nearly an hour Fal patiently rattled. Occasionally a dim shape would rise from the depths, only to sink again. But at last one rose until it took the form of a tiger shark some fifteen feet long. The irregular bands or splotches on its body give it its name. But the name fits its disposition also. There is no more dangerous shark in the South Sea.

He came up until his dorsal fin cut the surface. He swam back and forth a few times, taking in the situation. I manipulated the rattle now; Fal stood with the harpoon poised. He might have been in bronze. He did not move or speak.

The shark swam off. I thought we had lost him and wasn't sorry; then he suddenly came gliding back within three feet of the rattle. The harpoon zinged and sank into his back.

One surge of his tail like the push of a big propeller, and he was off. The coil of line fastened to the harpoon spun out of the tub.

We grabbed our paddles and turned the boat in the direction taken by the big fish. Fal clamped a piece of wood upon the line where it smoked out over the bow. The boat began to gain headway.

At last the five hundred feet of line had all snapped out. The end of the line was tied to a thwart. As it came taut, our craft leaped ahead and we went wildly careering through the waves. Surf tumbled into the boat. I began to bail with a coconut shell.

Suddenly the line went limp. The boat slackened, I breathed again. But Fal was alert.

"Hang on!" he cried.

Snap, jerk, whirl, and we were off in a new direction.

The shark repeated this maneuver frequently. But he was growing less vigorous. Fal had begun to take in line. Gradually the thrashing fish came into full view.

Suddenly he dashed straight under the boat to the other side. The line tightened around the hull and turned the canoe upside down before Fal could more than half say, "Look out!"

We came up to find ourselves in a turmoil of bloody water whipped up by a frenzied shark. There were other gray shapes shooting through the water now; the blood had attracted more sharks. Our lives could not have been pawned for two cents at that moment.

Fal saved the situation. He drew his knife from his belt and cut the line. The wounded shark fled, the others following his bloody trail. At least we saw no more of them.

But there was a slightly harrowing experience still ahead of us—swimming to the reef through waters known to be a favorite haunt of the big gray torpedoes of the deep. Legs tingled with expectation that steel jaws would close over them at any moment.

And one could not help thinking of the giant octopi that lurk in deep holes in the outside wall of the reef.

The octopus is not so turgid as he sometimes appears in the aquarium. He can shoot like a comet through the water, trailing his tentacles behind him, and once he takes hold of his prey he does not let go.

We righted the canoe and pushed it ahead of us. It was impossible to empty it, for the bailer had been lost. Two hours of this, and we felt the solid reef under our feet. Then we could hoist the canoe and empty it. The soaked sail was unfurled and sluggishly carried us across the lagoon.

Chill and dripping, we climbed the hill, to find the women still grappling with the giant potato and inclined to be very merry over our tale of the perils of the deep.

Our sojourn on Truk just escaped an unhappy ending. I was wary of treachery, always slightly haunted by the mysterious death of Colonel Ellis and of two British officers who had been too observant.

"Look sharp!" was Fal's way of warning me.

"Is my wife in any danger?" I asked him.

"No, only you."

The reason for that distinction was not that the Japanese have any spirit of chivalry toward women. Quite the reverse. They hold women in contempt as unintelligent creatures quite incapable of harming them.

But for inordinate conceit, they would have learned from their own wives and mothers how badly mistaken they are in their estimate of women. Japanese women are distinctly of a higher cut, both mentally and morally, than the men.

But, whatever the reason, it was a satisfaction to know that only one of us need "look sharp." I sniffed at every cup and glass put into my hand. But the party planned for me was quite different.

We had seen a great deal in the Truk atoll. Everywhere we had been followed at a distance by the police. I do not doubt that a complete dossier of my movements lay before the governor. When I saw him his cordiality was more extravagant and less sincere than ever. I told him enthusiastically of our shark-hunting trip.

"I am so glad you are enjoying our islands," he said.

A day later Fal took me aside where we could not be overheard. "They kill me if they know I tell you this," he said. "They want me to take you sharking again."

"I have no objection to that!"

"But they tell me not to bring you back."

The canoe was to upset, he told me, and I was to be most unfortunately drowned. It was all very simple, from the Japanese viewpoint.

Fal could not refuse. That would immediately convict him of complicity with a foreign spy. He must make at least a good show of trying to lose me.

We laid a plan by which I should escape drowning by a sufficiently narrow margin to convince the authorities that Fal had done his best. But if the plan slipped a little and the drowning happened to be too thorough . . . ? It was with a tingling spinal sensation that I set out with Fal on this strange errand.

We harpooned a shark at last. Standing in the canoe, the better to manipulate the line, we were wrenched in a wild, tipsy zig-zag across the lagoon.

Half a mile away was the usual police boat. Binoculars were trained upon us. We waited until we came within swimming distance of Dublon Island.

"Now!" said Fal, as the boat twisted.

I fell overboard. It was plain to the eyes behind the binoculars that

Fal could have cut the line and returned to save me. He did not. I called after him and stretched out an appealing arm, but in vain.

Thrashing violently to keep off sharks, I started toward shore. It was slow work for I am not a good swimmer. More than once I wondered if we had not made our little act a bit too realistic. Gray shapes scudded by. At last I stood on the beach.

I went to the governor that evening and complained of Fal's negligence. The governor seemed much distressed. "I shall see that the Kanaka is properly punished," he said and promptly wrote out an order, presumably for the police.

The police did come to see Fal; when they left he told me they had complimented him on his effort and instructed him to try again.

But our ship came the next day.

It is now safe to tell of Fal's trick upon his Jap masters, for he is secure in the Polynesian heaven. He escaped from the Micronesian islands to the Solomons where American boys reported him and other brown chiefs fighting at their side. He fell fighting.

XXXI:

Ponape, Pacific Crossroad

I DO NOT know how we would have fared in our attempts to land on other islands if we had not acquired a princely patron.

A young man in amber glasses and golf pants asked us to join him in a game of deck golf. He spoke English surprisingly well. When I remarked on it he said that he had spent some time in England. It was only later that we learned he had been educated at Oxford. He had a frank friendly manner, quite different from the clamlike inscrutability of many Japanese. He did not play deck golf with consummate skill and Mary soon put him in the "pool." She was called "nasty" for her pains.

When he had gone to his cabin, the steward came to tell us rather breathlessly that he was Prince Saionji, grandson of the last of the Genro, the elder statesmen who guided the policy of the nation until the militarists seized power. At this time his grandfather was the most influential and most respected man in Japan, hardly excepting the Emperor.

The young prince, not yet thirty, occupied himself in the treaties department of the Japanese *Gaimusho,* Foreign Office. He was distinctly pro-American and pro-British and loved to talk with anyone acquainted with Europe or America. He had various fine plans, one of them to establish a university like Oxford in Japan.

We soon found that we had gained a powerful ally. We were of course the only American passengers on this ship, as we had been on all the others, and the closely enveloping Japanese atmosphere had sometimes been very oppressive. Now the lowering brows lifted, the Japanese politeness one reads about began to take the place of the more usual Japanese rudeness, and suddenly nothing was too good for us.

Land on Ponape? Why of course. A radiogram was sent to the governor and he radioed back that a house had been placed at our disposal.

Ponape is the largest of the 1,400 islands of the Japanese mandate, and covers about 146 square miles. A vast lagoon surrounds it, rimmed by a reef. Some fifty islets dot the lagoon.

In addition to the ship basin afforded by the lagoon, there are no fewer than six excellent harbors cut deeply into the island itself, and the chief harbor is guarded by majestic Chokach, a fortified island 900 feet high.

The Spaniards made Ponape their headquarters, not only because of its central position in Micronesia, but because of its relation to other lands. It has been so much a crossroad of the western Pacific that its people are a blend of Polynesian, Melanesian, Papuan, Malay and Japanese.

Some of the group's lore may be founded on fact. It is so close to New Guinea, says one tale, that crocodiles washed out to sea by the rivers of that great island have drifted over to it. It is close enough to Hawaii, says another, so that ancient Ponapeans venturing long distances in sea-going canoes saw "the midnight sky red with a great blaze of fire as if of a million torches," and, terrified by erupting Kilauea, made haste to return to their own land. It is near enough to Tahiti, Samoa and the Marquesas so that there are many similarities of language.

And its present masters make full use of its proximity to Rabaul and the Marshalls.

Ponape is impressive as one approaches it by way of the twisting channel through the reef to spacious Ponape Harbor. The island is mountainous and wildly picturesque. It plays its role well as an island of mystery. Its appearance is more ominous because of the inky clouds that habitually roll across its ranges. Lightning crackles and thunder roars around the mighty Rock of Chokach overlooking the harbor.

This huge natural fortress, two-thirds the height of Gibraltar, drops away in basaltic cliffs so steep that they can be scaled only in one place where the Japanese have constructed a dangerous trail. Without doubt heavy batteries are mounted on the flat crown.

More than once in the past this rock has been used as a stronghold. In German times a governor noted for his harsh methods came to Ponape to put down a native rebellion. When he had the king arrested and flogged, the islanders retaliated by assassinating him, his secretary, and all of his higher officials. Then they fled to Chokach and pulled themselves up by lianas to its summit. But German soldiers trained in wall-scaling tactics climbed the precipice and captured the natives. Some were executed, others deported to Palau.

Lofty Ponape attracts the storms. Rain descends in torrents as we draw near looming Chokach. A severe rainstorm is almost a daily event in Ponape. It has the dubious distinction of being one of the best-watered islands in the entire Pacific. Anything will grow here, including mold and madness. Telephone poles sprout branches.

Under thumping rain, a launch takes us on a half-hour trip through shallow passages between islands to the docks of the town. Busy streets, teeming with Japanese, climb the hillside to a high point crowned by a *shicho,* government building. It is a frame structure in German style. Genial Governor Fushida (transferred from Saipan where we had first met him) shows us about the humming offices where heavy-spectacled eager young Japanese brush columns of ideographs into ledgers and chatter in high-keyed self-importance; then walks with us down a street of bustling stores a mile long ("There was nothing but jungle here a year ago," he says) to our home-to-be. It is a two-room German house with a veranda commanding an astounding view of the island-studded harbor, towering Chokach, and the gleaming white reef. Fruits of every description droop from the trees around the cottage. Rain is still coming down relentlessly. We are almost used to it by this time. A man is slashing out some jungle undergrowth that is encroaching upon the garden. "It comes in at the rate of a foot or two a day," says Governor Fushida. "And perhaps you haven't believed the stories you've heard about Ponape telephone poles sprouting branches. Well, look at that one." Sure enough, the pole before our house was rapidly reverting to type.

"But I'll tell you something stranger than that," he went on. "The director of our experimental farm stuck his walking-stick into the ground. It was made of green wood. That was two years ago. Now it's a tree."

We looked apprehensively at each other for branches. The long rubber boots which had been supplied to us for wading through Ponape mud were buried up to the ankles and might even now be throwing out roots.

The Spaniards called Ponape "the garden island" and made it their headquarters for all Micronesia. An early visitor described the island as "of a prodigious and inexhaustible fertility. Sago-palms, bananas, mangoes, orange and lime trees, grow in greatest magnificence. Great beds of wild ginger carpet the ground, sending up a pungent aromatic reek from their trodden leaves. . . . There is no lack of food in the land, for yams and taro are zealously cultivated."

That was in Spanish times before the Germans and Japanese began the agricultural development of the island. Now extensive plantations of tapioca and rice as well as scientifically cultivated coconut groves and oil palms have been added to the natural products of Ponape.

Man's life is largely fashioned by the plants around him. Many of his habits and superstitions are determined by the trees and shrubs; and this is curiously illustrated in some of the folkways of the Ponape natives.

The jungle is their medicine chest and source of magic. A decoction of the leaves of the *inot* is prized as an aphrodisiac. The *yol*, a giant convolvulus, is said to enable a woman to accomplish abortion. The

PONAPE

chenchul facilitates childbirth. The astringent *ioio* is a specific for sore throat. Take *ingking* for colic. The seaweed *kom* is a narcotic. The pounded bark of *tupuk* will heal a wound. The bush-weed *or* will reduce fever. *Par* is a tonic. *Ngi* will cure dysentery. It is claimed that *maikon* purifies the blood. *Kava* brings drunken oblivion; and the highly poisonous, quick-acting *kiti* makes suicide almost a pleasure.

Black paint comes from the candlenut tree or *chakan,* varnish from the *ais,* thatch from the coconut or pandanus, shutters from a lovely reed-grass called *alek,* house-posts from the giant fern, *katar,* perfume from the polypody fern, *kitau,* boats from the *pulok,* flutes from the reed *ro*—and clothing has been until recently so commonly made from tree bark that one word for clothes is *kun-ne-kai* meaning skin-of-trees.

Dean of the plant world of Ponape is the giant banyan. It starts life on a shoestring, as a slender vine twining among the branches of a tree and feeding upon it. This parasitic vine drops aerial roots which clasp the trunk of its host and finally strangle it. The original tree dies inside the new one which now has its own roots firmly in the ground. The vine has become a tree. From its rapidly spreading branches it continually drops new aerial roots to sway in the breeze until they finally reach the ground and worm their way into it, each forming a new trunk to support the constantly expanding canopy. The insignificant little sprig that came to dinner and stayed may at last cover an acre, blotting out all other growth.

Where vegetation is rank and dank, animal life is apt to be vigorous and wicked. It is so in Ponape. There are no dangerous four-footed animals—they have never been able to get there from the mainland. But it would perhaps be easier for an airman dropping into the interior of Ponape to defend himself against an occasional tiger than against the myriad of small barbed stinging things.

The ubiquitous flea is bitterly called "woman of corruption." There is a small, sand-colored scorpion with a venomous sting. Centipedes are common in the thatch and under the reed-grass flooring of the huts and they can inflict a very painful bite. The natives have a different name for the centipede by day and by night. This is because of some forgotten religious taboo. Just as the Japanese must not call their Emperor by his name, Hirohito, so the Ponapean must never use the actual name of certain sacred animals. The centipede is supposed to be inhabited by a spirit which will be deeply offended and retaliate with a severe nip if you fail to use the proper ceremonial names for the insect. By day it must be called *Man-en-ran,* The Creature of the Day, and at night, *Man-en-pong,* The Creature of the Night.

You need not fear the large black, red-spotted skink unless you are dead. This uncanny alligator-like beast haunts burying grounds and feeds upon corpses.

There is a vicious green eel, the *macho,* which is amphibious. It may be encountered by anyone wading through the salt-water marshes which belt the island of Ponape. When it does not find what it wants under the surface, it climbs a mangrove tree and waits to pounce upon any prey passing below. While we were in Ponape a man bitten by a *macho* was brought to the hospital. He died after two days.

A cruel chief murdered his wife and children. His neighbors chased him into a swamp where he escaped by changing into an eel. This, according to the native legend, was the origin of the deadly *macho.*

There is another savage eel to be found in fresh water. It sometimes attacks persons fording or bathing in the mountain streams. Here again, the real name, *it,* is taboo and the animal is addressed by the more respectful name, *Kamichik,* The Terrible One. On the Kiu uplands, 3,000 feet above the sea, there is a lake filled with this writhing death. Christian natives of Mortlock identify this eel as the serpent of the Garden of Eden.

Another creature too much feared to be addressed familiarly is the skate. Its real name, *pae,* must not be spoken and it is reverentially called Queen of the Sea-bottom.

The queen, as becomes royalty, does not exert herself unduly. She lies passively on the bottom and waits for her dinner to be served. She is protected, like the sting-ray, by a bared bayonet projecting upward from her back—and if a wading marine steps on this poisonous saw-toothed blade, nothing short of a surgical operation will get it out of his foot.

The large octopus is rare inside the lagoon. He prefers the depths outside the reef. But the coral shelves in the lagoon are the home of The Favorite Wife of the Flame Tree, as the sea-slug is respectfully called. The variety found here is able to sting the flesh with its feelers and eject a poison that will cause blindness. This is a form of bêche-de-mer, a dainty much prized by the Chinese.

Naturally not all is danger on Ponape and there are hundreds of interesting harmless animals—but the visitor does well to learn first the ones that may do him harm. The others may wait until the days of peace when the student takes the place of the soldier, sailor and marine.

XXXII:

The Defenses of Ponape

LIKE a castle surrounded by a moat, Ponape is circled by a lagoon walled by a coral reef. The lagoon is from one to four miles wide. Much of it is a shallow and almost impassable mangrove swamp. The mangrove has a peculiar habit of sprouting what look like branches but turn out to be roots, descending through the air until they reach the mud.

Naturalist David Fairchild's description of the mangroves of other islands in his *Garden Islands of the Great East* applies also to those of Ponape:

"The stilt roots which shoot out in all directions from the trunk, often as much as ten feet above the mud, and curve downward into it, anchoring the tree securely, are most difficult to climb over. They cannot be cut easily, and your muddy feet slip off them continually. You cannot walk erect through a mangrove swamp; you must use both hands and feet. Indeed, mangroves form a barrier as difficult to get through as a barbed-wire entanglement."

Where the shallow lagoon is not choked with mangroves it is studded with reefs of live coral growing so rapidly in some places that charts, even if available, would be useless unless new. Violent cross currents caused by the tides add to the difficulties of navigation.

Not all of Ponape's moat is shallow. In six places harbors pierce the reef and swamp and provide access to the shore or shelter for defending ships. These harbors are Ponape, Chokach (or Jokaj), Ronkiti, Mutok, Lot and Metalanim.

The first two of these harbors are in effect one harbor, since they join to form a magnificent fleet basin fully ten miles long and from one to two miles wide. In the heart of this stands Chokach Island with its

900-foot, cliff-faced rock. Also the harbor is commanded from heights on the main island. Ranged like carefully placed sentry boxes along the shore of the fleet basin are four summits, the lowest at the western end, eight hundred feet high, the highest a mountain of two thousand feet overlooking the best part of the fleet basin on the east.

Moreover, all harbors around the island and the seas beyond them are commanded by the central peak of Ponape, Totolom, with an elevation of 2,579 feet. From this peak the distance to all parts of the reef averages less than eight miles, well within the range of big guns.

The several dozen rocky islands in the lagoon afford good protection for ships from sea attack. Ships of the greatest draught can be accommodated. The depth of the basin averages twenty fathoms; and in some places exceeds forty.

It is possible that interior Ponape may be the scene of the stiffest land fighting in the Micronesian archipelago. No other island is so rugged, has such deep valleys, high peaks, abrupt precipices or dense jungle. The natives have a superstitious dread of the interior, but the Japanese have penetrated it to start plantations and, doubtless, install armaments. Because of the difficult terrain there are only forty miles of roads as contrasted with 171 on much smaller Saipan. Streams of any kind are almost unknown in Micronesia, but there are rivers on Ponape, tumbling down to the sea from upland lakes. American whalers used to come to Ponape for fresh water. Picturesque waterfalls are numerous. One we saw at Metalanim drops sheer three hundred feet.

The thousands of cliffs are penetrated by caves. When the natives rebelled in 1901 they found safety in these caves against the shells of German cruisers. They will doubtless be used again by the Japanese. With a facing of concrete such a cave makes a strong pillbox or machine-gun nest or cache for ammunition.

Forts of the formal sort are rarely built by the Japanese, but there is on Ponape a fort left over from the Spanish regime. It is still in good repair and will probably be used. It stands on a hill overlooking Ponape harbor. Several acres are enclosed within a high stone wall six feet thick, on top of which defenders may crouch protected by a three-foot escarpment. There are two heavy iron gates. Inside the compound is an old Spanish roundhouse, solidly built, with gun-ports framed on the inside by the brass ports of some Spanish ship. In another corner is a small prison made of great blocks of stone and as dark and putrid inside as the worst dungeon of the Inquisition. One end of the compound is occupied by a large Catholic church in Spanish style.

Also within the fort is a native school facing a large playground. From the veranda of the school we viewed a native war dance. Stout Ponape youths removed their straw hats, Osaka-made shirts and pants, smeared themselves with oil and dabs of paint and adorned themselves with wreaths of the lovely fragrant white flower with yellow center called on Ponape the *Pomaria* or "Smell of Mary." Their well-oiled naked brown bodies flashed in the sun as they fought with staves to the rhythm of a shouting chorus. The chants or songs were stirring. The performance without a change would be a sensation on the New York stage.

The dance was in honor of Prince Saionji. His face wore a strained, almost horrified expression as he watched the blood-chilling ferocity of the savage dance and the very evident relish these head-hunters would have for real battle.

"Good men, if they are with us," he remarked. "I'd hate to have them against us!"

XXXIII:

The Uses of Massacre

B Y ALL odds the most warlike natives of Micronesia are the Ponapeans.

They made plenty of trouble for the Spaniards and Germans. They have made trouble for the Japanese—and will make more.

The fort of Ponape was built for the express purpose of protecting the Spaniards from the natives. It was the only island of the Carolines on which the Spaniards found a fort necessary.

In the old cemetery near the fort a gigantic mango tree broods over the graves of dons and huns killed in native uprisings. The wooden Spanish crosses have mouldered and become undecipherable. Granite stones commemorate the German governor Gustav Böder and three of his aides killed by natives October 18, 1910. The Japanese dead are buried elsewhere.

It is interesting that the first white men to take up residence on Ponape were Americans. They were missionaries of the American Board and they came in 1852.

The next visitors were also Americans, but not bound on so holy an errand. They were New England whalers, coming ashore to raise hell with native women. But they met their match in the warriors of Ponape and soon chose easier conquests on other islands. Therefore the Ponapeans do not remember Americans with bitterness, but rather with a certain degree of affection since the missionaries did them no harm and some good. However they were never deeply dented by Christian doctrine and are practically as savage today as before the first white skin was seen on the island.

The third visitation was also American. During the Civil War certain Union ships fled to the refuge of Ponape Harbor. The Confederate cruiser *Shenandoah* caught them there and burned them to the water's edge.

So the Spaniards were comparative late-comers. It was not until 1886 that the Spanish flag was raised at what was called Ascension Bay, now Ponape Harbor.

The Spanish Capuchin priests did not get on well with the Americans from Boston. In 1887 Mr. Doane, head of the American Board Mission, was deported to Manila.

Two weeks later the resentful natives rose in a massacre of Spanish soldiers and their Filipino mercenaries, captured the fort and killed Senor Posadillo, the governor.

In 1890 there was another massacre. The Spaniards took revenge by burning native villages and slaughtering the inhabitants. Believing

Ponape's great rock of Chokach, 900 feet high, typical of the "natural fortifications" consisting of mountains, harbors, lagoons and reefs, which make the Micronesian labyrinth of great strategic importance.

A fortification that would be of little use to-day but was essential during the bloody struggles of the Spanish overlords with the natives of Ponape.

that the American missionaries had encouraged the natives to resist Spanish oppression, they ordered the Americans out. The American corvette *Alliance* exacted seventeen thousand gold dollars as compensation for the expulsion of the Americans, then took them to the island of Kusaie.

That did not end the trouble. Eight years later when the Spanish-American War broke out, a Ponape chief friendly to the Americans and head of the mission schools inherited from the missionaries, led a revolt. He was promptly imprisoned, but his followers carried out a terrible massacre of Spaniards.

Perhaps the Spaniards, having suffered so many bitter humiliations in Ponape at the hands of savages, were not too sorry to lose the island to the United States at the close of the Spanish-American War. But when the United States refused to accept the fruits of victory, Spain sold Ponape along with the rest of the islands to Germany.

Rebellion continued under the Germans, the most savage being that of 1910 already mentioned. It occurred on Chokach Island in the shadow of the great rock. A young German overseer in charge of a road-gang struck one of the men with a whip. In ten minutes he was dead. When the news got to headquarters, the governor and a squad of soldiers boarded a sloop and came across the bay to Chokach. It was assumed that the natives had no firearms. But guns captured in Spanish days had been concealed and the governor had no sooner set foot on shore than he fell with a bullet through his head. A general massacre followed. Not one German was left on the island.

A few weeks later a German warship happened to call at Ponape. The only foreigner the crew could find was a London gipsy called "Joe of the Hills" who lived with the natives. He was forced to tell the story of the massacre. German vengeance followed. The inhabitants of Chokach were rounded up, the ringleaders shot, and two hundred deported to the bleak island of Angaur to work in the phosphate mine.

The same fates, death and deportation, have been meted out by the Japanese, but rebellions continue. The native population is in 1944 estimated at about ten thousand as against six thousand Japanese. In the town of Ponape the Japanese are in the majority and are safe enough. Strolling along the main street of Ponape, one might think himself on Tokyo's Ginza. In a modern department store we sat in armchairs and listened to phonograph records from Tokyo and saw a naked savage, whose children had been taught in school to brush their teeth, buy for himself an Osaka toothbrush complete with tongue scraper for twenty-five sen.

The town natives, and natives who come to town, are meek enough. But let a Japanese step two miles out of town and he will be courting trouble, if not death.

The native is friendly when fairly treated, but revengeful when imposed upon. And he *is* imposed upon. He is stern stuff compared with the gentle folk of Tahiti. Young men slash their arms and burn holes in their breasts to show their contempt for pain. When reaching marriageable age they endure the mutilation called *lekelek,* the excision of the right testicle. They cut their flesh in elaborate patterns with knives and keep the wounds open until ridged cicatrices result. Some of these designs are quite artistic and all of them are evidences of considerable physical courage.

In warfare, a sling plaited out of strips of hibiscus bark is used with deadly effect. The sling-shots are stones more or less egg-shaped but coming to a sharp point, and they strike point first. A war-club of solid stone is also used; and a war-ax made out of the stout shell of the giant clam. The native bow is taller than a man and the arrow is tipped with the poisonous spine of the sting ray. The same spine tips the murderous twelve-foot lance which the Ponapean uses as deftly as any Knight of the Round Table.

The native warrior is denied firearms, but filches them whenever he can and makes trouble for his Japanese masters. He uses a shell trumpet to signal from village to village, and a message will pass from one end of the island to the other with the speed of a telephone call.

The Ponapean loves war dances where mock battles are fought to the music of drums five feet high covered with the skin of the sting ray. For these dances he oils himself from head to foot. The method of preparing this oil is odd, to say the least.

I saw four old women sitting like witches around a big pot. One was stirring. The other three were chewing! Beside them lay piles of dried fish heads. Periodically they would cram several fish heads into their mouths, ruminate like cows for a few minutes, then expel the mash into the pot.

Braving the smell, I approached near enough to see that the pot also contained shredded coconut. With this the masticated heads are stirred, pressed, and kneaded. The mass is then taken out and spread in the sun for a few days. During that period wayfarers will do well to observe a three-mile limit.

Finally the oil is squeezed into small calabashes and applied to the skins of tawny warriors. There it serves the double purpose of reflecting the sun in dazzling fashion and causing the grip of any opponent to skid hopelessly.

The hardy Ponapean sleeps on a wooden floor and uses a wooden pillow. It is literally a block of wood cut from the trunk of the pandanus tree. The wooden pillow of Japanese women has been offered, but was rejected because the thin pad on top of it made it unacceptably soft.

The native women have as hard a life as that of the men, sometimes harder. They must do all the work while the men make war, or, when not allowed to make it, sit and talk about it.

Anything that goes wrong is the fault of women. All bad habits are pinned on them.

"A woman's fault" is the expression for a lie. "A woman's peering" means curiosity. Conspiracy is "a woman's whispering." Favoritism is "a woman's choice." Fury is "a woman's angry voice."

And yet, women remain in demand. The braves marry young. Marriage is a quick and easy process. The prospective mother-in-law briskly rubs coconut oil into the bride's bare back. This is "the anointing." Then a wreath of flowers is placed on the bride's head and the ceremony is finished.

The groom has had nothing to do with it. The girl seems to have been married to her mother-in-law. And, in fact, that is about the way of it, for she is the virtual slave of her husband's mother.

If that worthy dowager does not get on with her, there is an early divorce, or exchange of wives may be practised. This consists of trading wives in the hope of finding one more congenial to the husband—or to the mother-in-law.

The ancestor worship of the Japanese is nothing new to the Ponapean. His own religion consists in being terrified, day and night, by the unseen spirits of his ancestors who haunt the woods, the mountains, the swamps and reefs, and are under the floor and in the thatch roof, conspiring to punish the living for not doing sufficient honor to the dead.

Heaven, to the native of Ponape, is a submarine cavern far beneath the gorgeous coral floor of the lagoon. It is full of lovely sights and the blessed odor of fish oil.

Hell is another cavern, but under the cold earth, a place where one shivers forever in mud and gloom. It is guarded by two devils, women, of course, one holding a gleaming sword and the other a torch.

Besides the spirits of ancestors, celestial gods crowd the air of Ponape. There are "The Little Angel from Heaven" who dropped a piece of *kava* root from a feast of the gods in the clouds, thus conferring the heavenly joys of drunkenness upon mortals; the moon-goddess; the god of dances; "The Lady of the Sword"; the god of carpentry; the god of the jungle; the rain-god (perhaps the hardest working of all the gods of Ponape); the god of the breadfruit tree; the god of the coconut; the sea-goddess; "The Lady Who Loves the Holy Places." Any of these good gods may do harm when so disposed, but the particular agents of evil are "The God Who Makes Dizzy," "The Lord of the Morasses," the god of the sting ray, the god of famine, the goblin of the woods, "The Fairy with Long Iron Teeth," and, worst of all, *Loki,* Satan himself.

Very apt and picturesque are the names the Ponapean has given to his diseases. Tuberculosis is "The Lady who Shrivels Men Up." Itching is "Quick-Skin" and smallpox is "Peeling Skin." Squint is "Eye on One Side." Leprosy is called "The Foreign Skin" because of the white patches.

Ponape language skilfully imitates the sounds of things. Who cannot hear the cackle of fowls in *ketiketikak,* the cooing of doves in *kingking,* the sound of liquid shaken in a cask in *monomonoi,* the patter of rain-drops in *patapatar,* the splash of paddles in *tautau,* the banging of a door in *teteng?*

In studying the Ponape language one is struck by its similarity in some respects to Japanese. For example the Japanese language is full of honorifics. Each person must be addressed according to his degree. In Ponape also, you dare not call the hand of a chief and the hand of a commoner by the same name. The former is *lima,* the latter *pa. Kumikum* is a chief's beard, *alich* a subject's beard. A chief's eye, tooth, mustache, all have names so distinct that one might suppose Nature had devised for him something completely different from the eye, tooth and mustache of the commoner.

This is not a peculiarity of Ponape alone. Stevenson has given a diverting description of the manner of speech jealously reserved for the elect in Samoa:

"For the real noble a whole private dialect is set apart. The common names for an axe, for blood, for bamboo, a bamboo knife, a pig, food, entrails, and an oven are taboo in his presence, as the common names for a bug and for many offices and members of the body are taboo in the drawing-rooms of English ladies. Special words are set aside for his leg, his hair, his face, his belly, his eyelids, his son, his daughter, his wife, his wife's pregnancy, his wife's adultery, his dwelling, his spear, his comb, his sleep, his anger, his dreams, his pleasure in eating, his cough, his sickness, his recovery, his death, his being carried on a bier, the exhumation of his bones and his skull after death. To address these demigods is quite a branch of knowledge, and he who goes to visit a high chief does well to make sure of the competence of his interpreter."

The Ponapeans cling to their language and their ways more zeal-ously than any other Micronesians with the exception of those of Yap. They have resented and resisted the Spaniards, Germans and Japanese. They gave their hand in friendship to the Americans because Ameri-cans never exploited them. The missionaries accomplished little on Ponape so far as the extension of their faith was concerned; but we can thank them if the day of opportunity finds the Ponape warriors ready to fight for their own freedom in confidence that that freedom will be preserved under whatever administration is later provided for the Pacific islands.

XXXIV:

City of Ghosts

Iᴛ ɪs a stormy morning a few thousand years ago. Magnificent canoes, shaped somewhat like gigantic, sea-going gondolas, bravely decorated, move in procession through the water-streets of Nanmatal. Some are double canoes with a platform between. On these decks maidens dance. Time is kept by the lion-roar of great drums, five feet high, shaped like monstrous dice boxes, and covered with the skin of the sting ray. In one canoe is King Chau-te-leur and his priests. He has proclaimed this festival in honor of the completion of his city. Flowers rain down from the hands of women who line the crests of the battlements high among the tops of the palm trees.

The procession halts at Nan Tauach, The Place of Lofty Walls. It is a fortress designed as a safe resting place for the royal dead. The small islet is girdled by a great rampart. Within it is another, almost as strong. Within it, at the center, is a deep vault covered by gigantic slabs of rock. The king and his priests, to the thunder of the drums, carry certain chests up the long flight of steps from the water's edge, through the towering gates, and down into the vault. The bones of past Chau-te-leur kings, brought here from far over the seas, are laid to rest.

. .

"I want to dig in the ruins of Nanmatal," said Prince Saionji. And it came about that we were invited to accompany him on his expedition.

206

At dawn of the appointed morning, the rain was as usual thundering down.

Dripping officials bowed before the Prince.

"Would you prefer to wait for better weather?" they asked.

"When do you expect better weather?"

"*Sa!*" apologetically. "We don't expect it."

"Then we'll go now."

Nanmatal is on the east coast, half a day by launch from Ponape town. After three hours in the tossing launch we change to open canoes and enter the seldom-visited city of the dead. Shallow draft is necessary because huge blocks have fallen from some of the structures into the water streets. Nanmatal was an island Venice. Canals were, and still are, the thoroughfares.

Abruptly from the water's edge rise beetling castle walls made up of vast natural prisms of basalt larger than the stones used in the Pyramids. The mighty building blocks which compose these barbaric structures make the English castles or those of the Rhine seem delicate and ladylike in comparison. The ferocious appearance is heightened by the fact that there has been no effort to join the stones. I have tried unsuccessfully to insert a knife-blade between the perfectly matched stones of Inca structures in Peru. Here one might insert a hand or a head with ease. The difference is that the Inca stones were tooled to fit. But no tool has touched these stones. The material would have defied Inca implements. And the old-time ax of the South Seas made of Tridacna shell was too brittle to chisel this igneous rock.

Then how was the material hewn into these great blocks? It was not hewn. It was used just as nature made it. In many parts of Ponape may still be found basalt fashioned by the fires of long ago into the form of massive columnar prisms, generally six-sided, sometimes five-sided, sometimes eight-sided, often twenty-five feet or more in length and from three feet to twelve feet in diameter.

Thus the building blocks were ready made and only needed to be transported. But what a mighty task to transport them! Most of them were brought fifteen miles or more from the neighborhood of the great cliff of Chokach. Craft very different from the present canoes must have been necessary. To raise the stones to their positions must have been a herculean task even with the aid of an inclined plane and unlimited manpower.

And this was no isolated fort, nor even a walled village. It was a city, made up of about fifty fortified islets extending over eleven square miles. Most of it is now hidden by the advancing jungle.

How the past speaks here! So evident is the hand of man that one expects to see men appear around any corner. The natives have an unholy dread of coming near the place. Even our Japanese companions were awed and silent.

We landed at Nan Tauach and entered a court through a gateway flanked by two cliffs built of monster stones that looked as if they had come from the Giant's Causeway.

The Prince saw a hole and, against the protests of his associates who were under the eerie spell of the place, dropped into it.

"What did you find?" we asked when he returned to the surface.

"Ghosts!" he replied.

We came to the central vault, the tomb of the Chau-te-leur kings. It is still covered by cyclopean slabs weighing many tons. Thousands of years hence they will doubtless still be there. No souvenir hunters will care to remove them. Descending a moldy stone stairway beneath one of the stones we entered a half-dark crypt, frightening the bats. Large bones, skulls and jewels have been taken by former excavators, notably Kubary and Christian. But our efforts were rewarded by the discovery of fragments of shell axes, necklaces, bracelets, shell needles and fragments of bone. The objects found and measurements and observations taken by the Saionji group, together with past studies by Kubary, Christian and others, make certain facts increasingly evident.

It seems clear that this city was built up out of the lagoon as a Venice, and is not a land city that has sunk. Was it built by the race now here? It is hard to believe that people content with palm thatch for all buildings, private or public, could even have conceived, much less have erected, these structures. Stone barricades and walls are not unknown among the Polynesians but usually they are made of the sort of stones a farmer takes from his field and piles in a fence. It would be easier to build a whole fort thus than to move just one of these blocks from its place in the mountains to its place in the castle. There is no record of the brown people ever having made use of the mammoth basaltic prisms in any of their buildings.

The city appears to have been constructed by a black race. This conclusion was reached by Kubary on the basis of measurements of calvaria, or skull-tops, found beneath the ruins. The measurements were found to be entirely different from those of the modern inhabitants of Ponape and showed negroid characteristics. It is evident that these were people of a superior civilization. The structures are reminiscent of another black marvel, the palace of St. Christophe in Haiti.

There is no history of the ruins. They are remotely prehistoric so far as the people of Ponape are concerned—people whose collective memory runs back only a little way since, being illiterate, they have no written records. But while there is nothing that can be called history there are legends that have been passed down from generation to generation and may contain some truth.

According to these traditions the usual fate of success befell the city. The walls were strong, fighting was unnecessary, the people lived luxuriously and became soft.

A savage invader, Idzikolkol, came one day to the island but was so awed by the formidable ramparts that he made haste to be on his way. As his warriors were launching their canoes, a native woman came to speak with him. She had been cast out of the king's household and jealousy prompted her to reveal the military weakness of the city and to instruct Idzikolkol as to how he and his men might enter the palace and take the king unaware.

The brown warriors overran the city, slaughtering the inhabitants. Some of the women they took as wives. That is said to be the reason for a noticeable black strain in Ponape blood today. The old civilization was stamped out. The island metropolis was abandoned. The brown race established itself in the jungles of Ponape, there to remain practically unchanged to this day.

Soaked to the skin and smeared with the mold of ages we took to the canoes once more. A special vessel had been brought from the nearest *Nanyo Kohatsu* station for the prince. Upon the platform, poised atop the gunwales of a native canoe, had been perched a wicker armchair. The prince, who would have much preferred to sit in the bottom of the canoe, was forced to accept this lofty and unsteady throne. An official stood on the platform behind the chair, his feet braced in order to preserve his balance, and held an umbrella over the noble guest. Did the Chau-te-leur kings when they traveled through these water-streets go in any greater state?

At the *Kohatsu* station wet clothes were peeled off, there were dry kimonos to slip into, a bonfire of coconut shells, hot *saké* and a lunch of huge balls of rice wrapped in seaweed and concealing in the core an inconceivably sour plum.

It is all very Japanese. Here at Metalanim, not far from the ancient battlements of Nanmatal, is a modern tapioca plantation and factory. A Japanese town is going up. Five hundred Japanese immigrants are at work. Thousands more are said to be on the way, for Ponape is the largest of all the mandated islands and the most fertile.

The black race scorned the island and built themselves a stone city in the lagoon. The brown race lived on the soil but they were not of the soil. The yellow race dig and plant and grow with their crops. They have been taking root in the South Sea islands as no other race has ever done in the past. What a pity that Japan's industrious farmers could not have been let alone by their militarists. The world would have had no objection to a Pacific peacefully developed by Japan. Legitimate enterprise by anyone, anywhere, is for the good of all.

XXXV:

Sunday Morning in Kusaie

HERE at last is the tropic paradise of one's dreams.

We cast anchor at dawn in the snug harbor of Kusaie. Only half a mile wide is this harbor, and as beautiful as an Italian lake. Its still surface reflects romantic mountains that stretch up out of a dark dawn and terminate in sharp stabs of rock blazing in a scarlet sunrise. The fire gradually creeps down the slope, igniting the tops of magnificent palms like matches, one after another.

These mountains stand hand-in-hand in a semicircle around the little port. They are on the main island of Kusaie. The other semicircle is made up of the small island of Lele, for without its co-operation there would be no harbor. Lele is but an hour's walk around, low, luxuriant, with many sand beaches. In its still morning beauty it looks like a model in wax for exhibition purposes rather than a real island. Hospitable-looking thatch homes nestle in its groves. Canoes line its shore. Yonder on a little point stands a white church, as primly as if cut out of cardboard.

The captain is cursing, of course forsaking the Japanese language to do it. One must go to English for choice epithets. This is no dream world to him. He wants stevedores.

"Sunday morning," he growls. "Everybody will be going to church!" as if that were the greatest crime in the calendar. "We have to sit here and twiddle our thumbs until they get done with their psalm singing." He glared at me as if it were my fault. And it was—or that of my compatriots.

Americans have had a good deal to do with Kusaie. Americans damned it, Americans redeemed it.

Whalers from Boston and New Bedford circled South America to get into the Pacific, "hanging up their consciences off Cape Horn." They picked up more men along the Pacific Coast. Life aboard a whaler was too hard to attract men. Therefore they were shanghaied. Knocked on the head, they woke to find themselves in the forecastle of a ship, seabound. Many of the men recruited in this fashion were a rough lot; and if they were not, the life made them rough. The ships were provisioned for three years and put in at no ports lest the men might escape. Summers, the whale-hunters operated in northern waters. Winters, they sailed to the South Seas to rest and riot. When they stepped ashore after months of confinement on a small whaling vessel, they were wild men. Anyone who has spent six months on board ship can perhaps hardly blame them.

Kusaie was discovered by Americans in 1806 and named Strong Island after the governor of Massachusetts. Thus whaling captains of New England learned of the island and thereafter made its beautiful harbor a rendezvous.

"I can remember seeing twenty-two whaling ships in this harbor at one time," King John of Kusaie later told me.

The whalers indulged in wild orgies on shore, abducted Kusaie women, and left a legacy of foreign diseases. The population dwindled from about two thousand when first discovered to two hundred in late Spanish times.

Here, according to an account written in 1899 by the ethnographer, F. W. Christian, "the famous 'Bully' Hayes, the modern buccaneer, played fine pranks after losing his beautiful vessel on the reefs, half frightening the lives out of the peaceful Kusaians by landing a number of fierce and warlike Ocean and Gilbert Islanders, who brewed huge quantities of coconut-toddy, and set the whole place in a ferment with their carousals and mad orgies. Night after night they kept it up, alternately drinking and fighting. Murdered men's bodies were picked up on the beach every morning, and the poor natives of Lele fled in terror of their lives."

When the American buccaneers of the whaling fleet had done their worst and only a pitiful remnant was left of the Kusaie people, there came other Americans, also buccaneers in a fashion, and also from Boston, to repair the damage done by their countrymen.

It was a romantic and pioneering venture. American Sunday-school children contributed their dimes to make possible a great square-rigged sailing ship, named *Morning Star,* which should carry their missionaries to the South Seas to convert the heathen. Of course there were

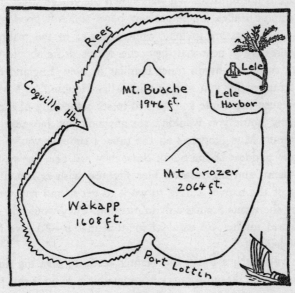

KUSAIE

plenty of heathen in Boston. But they did not wear grass skirts and lop off heads. Surely it was the buccaneer spirit in so far as it means the fascination of far seas, the courage to sail them, and the boldness to make captives, that prompted both the children and the missionaries. The project gripped the imagination. The Micronesian mission thereafter never lacked for funds. As soon as one *Morning Star* was wrecked, another was fitted out. There were five in all. Finally commercial sailings in the South Seas made special ships unnecessary.

For eighty-four years missionaries of the American Board of Boston have been at work in Kusaie. Let us go ashore and see the results.

We are taken off by Arthur Herrman, lone American planter, the first American we have met in all the Japanese islands. Evidently Kusaie agrees with him—he is portly and jovial. On the copra-scented pier we meet Mrs. Herrman, a native of Kusaie, more jovial and more portly. One look at her beaming and enlightened countenance and we conclude that the missionaries have done a good job.

Her face is not unusual. We walk down the village street through a sea of seraphic smiles. There are low bows and soft good mornings. All the inhabitants are in long white robes as in the realms of the blest. Houses are so neat that they ache. Music drifts about—whistled, hummed, twanged—hymn tunes familiar in New England churches.

"I've arranged for you to stay with Miss Hoppin," says Mr. Herrman, "because you wrote you wanted to see something of the natives. Around my house you wouldn't see anybody but Japanese. But the natives are at Miss Hoppin's all the time. I suppose you've heard of her—white goddess of the South Seas, they call her. She's just about God to them, and no mistake. Her slightest wish is law. If I want anything of the natives I have to work to get it and pay well for it. Anything she wants she has only to mention. They would do anything in the world for her. So would I for that matter—I'd give my right hand for her."

When you catch a tough old planter ready to give his right hand for a missionary, that missionary has something. Who is this paragon? If we are expecting to meet a looming, booming personality we are mistaken. A cunning little old lady, as neat and bright as a new pin, her gray hair encompassed in a coronet of snow-white shells, awaits us on a bit of an islet just big enough for her and her house in an enchanting grove of palms, mangoes, papayas, banana trees, breadfruit, scarlet hibiscus and lavender bougainvillea. This world of loveliness is not two hundred feet from shore to shore. It is connected with the island of Lele by a grass-grown causeway. Over that causeway stream the natives day and night; coming to bring coconuts, or coming to get medicine, or just coming.

A snatch of breakfast, and it is time to go to church. We find the white church on the shore of Lele already occupied by a thousand people. The king leads the singing. The most blasé visitor must feel a tingle run along his ribs as these thousand trained voices take to the air. The volume and beauty of it is so great that one would not be surprised to see the sheet-iron roof go sailing off into space. Then the native minister, in high-collared white drill suit and bare feet, preaches. Through the open windows we can see the ship, waiting for stevedores. The stevedores are all in church. The service is long. When the last prayer is finished and we make to rise, the king, who sits beside us, whispers, "Now, Sunday school."

No one leaves. It is not until nearly one o'clock, after three hours of services, that we pass out and some of the men answer the insistent whistle of the steamer. But they must work fast, for there is another service at three and another at five. Double pay cannot induce them to miss a service.

There seems to be nothing fanatical about Miss Hoppin. In fact her creed appears to be solidly grounded in gastronomics, long recognized as one of the foundation stones of religion. Jesus fed the multitude. Every native who comes to Miss Hoppin's house gets fed. Incidentally, he always brings something to feed Miss Hoppin . . . so it works both ways. The natives have converted her to their interests as thoroughly as she converted them. She has become their champion against all injustice. Several petty officials were discharged because of her complaints of their harshness toward the natives. One, sent back to Japan, committed suicide. After that she complained no more. "They do the best they can," she said. So, instead of lodging complaints against them, she fed them too.

One night during our stay twenty native boys had to get off on the tide in their canoes at three in the morning to return to the mission school on the other side of the island. They could easily have eaten a cold snack before they set out—or a native woman could have risen—but no, the seventy-year-old missionary lady was up at two preparing a hot breakfast of rice with coconut cream, hot biscuits and coffee. Of course we can all be big-hearted now and then, at fit and proper times, say between nine and five; but I know that for me at least, two A.M. would be altruism's zero hour.

Two other extraordinary American ladies of Kusaie were the Misses Baldwin, large, strong-faced women whose fortitude belied their ages of seventy-six and seventy-eight. They were in charge of the mission school where eighty-eight young men and women ranging from thirteen to twenty years in age were being taught reading, writing and religion. We paddled the eight miles to see them.

The school was a dingy barn of a place perched on a hilltop with a magnificent view of lagoon and sea. It had the feeling of being completely removed from the world and all its wiles. Magazines did come from America but all pictures of women in low-necked or close-fitting gowns were clipped out before the journals were allowed to reach the eyes of Kanaka youths. The cult of the throttle-necked and ankle-length Mother Hubbard prevailed. The missionaries had not been off the island in twenty-five years. In 1911 they went to America and got a dress pattern; the dresses of the girls have been cut from it ever since.

My wife made a break.

"How much material does it take for one of the girls' dresses?" she asked.

"Six yards," replied the elder Miss Baldin.

"Oh, that must be expensive. One of my dresses takes only three yards."

Miss Baldwin stiffened. "It is never expensive to cover the body," she said.

Two hundred and fifty phonograph records of the lighter sort were sent by well-meaning friends in America. The missionaries took them to an upper room, locked the door, removed the horn from the phonograph so that no sound might escape from the room, and played the records through. Then they dispatched them by boat to a point far outside the reef whose bottom is said to be a good mile down, quite beyond the reach of the best native diver, and consigned them to the deeps.

Although reared in the liberal Congregational tradition, the ladies were won over by the mysterious island silences to the conviction that the second coming of the Lord was close at hand. In a world of increasing wickedness, they saw all the prophecies being fulfilled.

The ship needs stevedores. But this is Sunday, and the stevedores
are all in the little white church on the point.

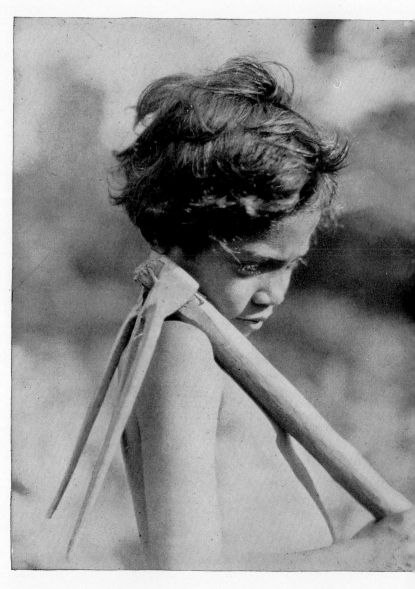

The Japanese have impressed native labor without regard to age or wage.

"Apart from the world on this little island, we feel that perhaps we can see such things more clearly than those who are in the midst of the false teachings."

Far be it from us to cavil at their beliefs. They may be terribly right. The folk of Sodom and Gomorrah scoffed, and were sorry for it. I do not seek to caricature but only to portray these two remarkable personalities; and to make a truthful portrait there are some important strokes of the brush still to be added.

One is that both these devoted women have given their lives for Kusaie, and the elder has given her eyes as well. She translated the entire Bible into the Kusaian language. She broke her glasses and sent the prescription to England to be refilled. In the meantime the proofs were ready to read. She felt that the natives must not be made to wait for their Bible. So she read the proofs . . . and went blind.

The book was manufactured at the school. The girls set the type, the boys printed it. The hand-sewing alone took two years. Only three copies could be bound in a day. But the great work was completed and the Kusaians had their Bible. The blind translator placed her hand upon the great three-inch-thick volume, her monument, and in her peaceful, unseeing face there was no regret.

She went on translating—arithmetics, grammars, Bible helps. Her sister read aloud the English version and she dictated the Kusaian. Of course in addition to these cloistered tasks there was the school-work to supervise—the daily guidance of eighty-eight inquiring minds. The curriculum might be lopsided, the pedagogy faulty, but the devotion was superb. A flaming object lesson for the Japanese official, or for any other official for that matter who is supposed to exist for the good of the people.

What have been the achievements of this mission school and other missionary work in Kusaie in the last half century?

XXXVI:

The Isle of the Angels

ONCE an island dreaded for its savagery and brutality, where shipwrecked strangers were sure of prompt death, where a king and his henchmen were carried in their canoe to a great hole and buried alive, where American whalers murdered and were murdered, where American ships were sunk in the harbor, where disease and violent death reduced the population from two thousand to two hundred, Kusaie is now an unbelievable isle of twelve hundred angels.

In olden times murders sometimes scored one or two hundred a year.

"How many murders a year now?" I asked the king.

He smiled. "There has not been a native murder in my lifetime," he said. The king was sixty years old.

"How about minor offenses? How many cases of detention in your jail in a year?"

"Jail!" exclaimed the king. "But there is no jail!"

"Well," I said, "whatever you call it. You must at least have some place to put the tipsy ones until they sober up." In all islands that I had visited infraction of the liquor law was the most common offense and the jails were always well patronized by alcoholic convalescents.

"But there is no drinking on Kusaie."

I thought he meant relatively none, only a few cases a month. But he went on to explain that no native had been known to taste alcohol in the past thirty years.

"I myself drank and smoked when I was a young man," he said, "but not since. If anyone drank now every man's hand would be against him."

"And smoking is under the ban too?"

"Tobacco does not sell well here, although I am sorry to say that a

218

few of the young men smoke. I have told my sons that if they smoke I will throw them out of the family." He said it with a broad smile expressing his easy assurance that it would never be necessary for him to carry out his vow.

Marriage is a sacred institution on Kusaie. Divorces are unknown. I am speaking of course of the natives, not of the Japanese newcomers.

There is no house of ill fame. There is practically no disease. There are no native medicine men, no charms or other superstitious devices to ward off illness, and the Japanese doctor goes fishing. Native physique is splendid. Poling develops the arm muscles; and standing braced in the canoe, the leg muscles. When the Japanese came, wrestling matches were staged between Japanese and Kusaians. Such matches are now forbidden, for the native men always won and the rulers lost face.

I think it may be included among the moral attributes of these people that their women are splendid cooks. And also there are ethical implications in the fact that more soap is used per capita than in any of the other islands. A ship no sooner casts anchor in the harbor than canoes surround it, fruit is passed up and soap is passed down. Kusaian faces sparkle. Smiles reveal flashing teeth. Betel-chewing is out, dentifrice is in.

Every day is Christmas. Gifts flow back and forth with the regularity of the tides. A taro pudding goes next door with compliments and a five-pound crab comes back. The visitor shares in the bounty. No one would take a penny for board, for the canoe that we sailed, for any of a hundred favors. But gifts were expected and accepted. Unaware at first of the custom, I lent my best shirt to the king when his had been soaked by the rain. He assumed it to be a gift, and wore it on the day we left as a special sign of his appreciation.

Service is exchanged for service. I build your house and you deliver my child. I do your fishing as well as my own and you do your farming plus mine.

Poverty is not allowed. Those who have give to those who have not when typhoon wipes out a plantation or accident deprives a family of its providers. Orphans are promptly absorbed into other homes.

Christian Kusaie even sends out missionaries to heathen islands round about. A native evangelist had been dispatched to Palau and another, during our stay, was waiting for a ship to take him to Enewetok. He ate at our table daily, toothlessly, explaining that he was saving his false teeth to use in primitive Enewetok where the foods are so hard.

In our Micronesian voyage we had found Americans on no other island. The fact that an American planter and several American missionaries were allowed to remain on Kusaie was fair indication that no great strategic importance was attached to that island. However, when Miss Hoppin went to America in 1939 she was not allowed to return. And the others were forced to leave early in 1941. Possibly since that time the defenses of the island have been tightened up.

The harbors are of small value. The chief one, Lele Harbor, has an entrance hardly a cable wide (600 feet) and a basin a half mile in diameter. The deep-water part of it is just adequate for one large ship. Several newspaper columnists have referred to the "formidable Kusaie base." It does not exist. The port was the snuggest we had entered anywhere in Micronesia.

There are two other still smaller harbors, Coquille on the northwest coast and Lottin on the south.

And yet there may be some danger of underestimating the strength of Kusaie. That strength lies not in its harbors but in its heights. Heavy guns mounted on its peaks or on their protected slopes might control not only the whole island but also a wide belt of the surrounding sea. Kusaie is roughly six by nine miles with an area of fifty square miles. Its central peak, Mount Crozer, is 2,064 feet high. Mount Buache, directly dominating the chief harbor, stands 1,946 feet high. There are three other peaks exceeding 1,500 feet. Kusaie is the last of the volcanic islands of Micronesia. The Marshalls next to the east are coral atolls.

An airfield may have been constructed on the flat island of Lele— but the mountainous main island is not suited to such use.

In short, Kusaie is a defensive outpost rather than offensive. It cannot launch either ships or planes at an enemy. But it will probably tot up a pretty good defensive record for itself when attacked.

The population of Kusaie in 1935 was 1,200, of whom only thirty were Japanese. Since the Japanese were few and weak, they stepped rather warily. Several times they applied torture to wring "confessions" from recalcitrant natives, but in each case a threatened uprising made them back down.

The king refused to allow his people to work for their Japanese masters on Sunday. Japanese officials argued with him in vain. One Saturday they undertook to wring consent from him by force. He was detained all day in the government office and subjected to "questioning" which is accompanied by the liberal use of burning cigarettes applied to the flesh. The natives gathered outside the office and were about to rush the place when an official came out on the porch, saw the crowd, and hastily reported to his superiors. The king was released.

His people still went to church on Sunday.

The king's blood was truly royal. For centuries his family had provided the people with kings. The result was an inherited poise and manner, a regal gentlemanliness, in contrast to the brisk, brusque ways of some foreign petty officials of common family who had been trained but not bred.

Anyone who wishes to take a few lessons on how to do the right thing upon every occasion should visit and study King John of Kusaie. We saw him three times a day at least, for he dined with us in the thatch house on the two-hundred-foot isle along with Miss Hoppin, Fred Skillings of English-Kusaian parentage, shark-hunter Jon Makoelun, and old Caiaphas who was an improvement upon the high priest after whom he was named. The queen was in the kitchen, a little thatch structure on the shore, from which emanated savory odors and ravishing foods concocted of breadfruit, bananas, taro and coconut cream. Our royal cook never appeared at the table, since Kusaie women do not eat with the men, but thanks to her delicious dishes we were more conscious of her than of anyone else. Often Miss Hoppin introduced New England delicacies into the menu. The king was at home on any subject or in any dish. He wielded knife and fork with as much skill as his paddle—and that is saying a great deal.

When he operated a canoe the canoe seemed to be a part of him. It is the office of a king in these islands to be able to do everything superlatively well. King John, although sixty years old, was powerful, broad of chest, and could swim, spear, paddle, with the best.

The native canoe is no birch-bark zephyr. It is a hollowed log, heavy and unwieldy. It would turn over in a twinkling were it not for the outrigger. This looks like a second canoe of miniature size, riding on the surface about five feet from the boat on the starboard side and connected with it by horizontal poles upon which a small platform is laid. The king lent me a sailing canoe and the natives warned me solemnly of the danger of capsizing. It was a strange craft to me, for the canoe of every island is different and a law unto itself. The canoes of Pingelap and Ponape carry lateen sails, and it is a merry task in a heavy sea to tack by carrying the sail from one end of the canoe to the other, making the stern the bow. The Kusaie sail is more like that of the Western cat-boat. But the canoe has no centerboard and its hull is as round as the bole of the tree from which it was made, therefore safety depends entirely upon the outrigger. The sailor must hold both the sheet and the steering paddle, keep one eye out ahead for shoals, another eye on the sail, and both eyes on the outrigger! If the miniature boat skimming alongside shows a tendency to leave the surface in imitation of a hydroplane, sail must be instantly slackened and the sailor's weight thrown to starboard, otherwise the outrigger will soar five feet up and the skipper will find himself a fathom down.

What lent piquancy to the situation in my case was that a shark of unconscionable length loafed alongside, apparently as interested as I was in the uncertain behavior of my craft. I had passed through a break in the reef into the open sea. The waves slapped smartly into the boat and I had no third hand to wield the calabash. Occupied with keeping the outrigger from soaring, I failed to take thought of the alternative danger. A sudden gust lifted the float, I leaned to starboard, the gust failed and the float sank, plowing like a submarine beneath the surface, going deeper and deeper, caught by the nose. Only another gust arriving at the opportune moment righted the boat and sent a shark home supperless.

To regain the lagoon I must furl sail and paddle against the wind. Accustomed to the light, swift Indian canoe of the Canadian lakes, I thought nothing of it—until I tried it. It was like paddling a mud-scow tied to a dock.

And yet the king could make that tree skim over the surface as if it were a leaf. He taught me much and, having a royal humility, was eager to learn. But I could show him nothing except the familiar north-woods knack of paddling a canoe without continually shifting the paddle from one side of the boat to the other, as the Micronesians commonly do. However, the American Indian knows nothing compared with the islander about canoeing in rough water. It was a treat to watch King John sail the open sea, lagging to let a great roller pass or shooting ahead of it at motorboat speed, or balancing on its crest like an acrobat on a tight-rope.

The king clung to the old ways, with one exception.

He had a pocketful of calling cards and delighted in handing them out. He gave me one. On it was printed, "K. J. Sigrah." Sigrah was his family name.

"What does the K. J. stand for?" I asked.

"King John."

And when the first Yank lands on Kusaie I can wish him no better luck than to be handed a card bearing the noble name, "K. J. Sigrah."

XXXVII:

Marshalls, Gilberts, Wake, Rabaul

WE HAD now visited all important groups of the Japanese mandate except the Marshalls. They did not fit into a difficult itinerary and we did not see them.

Any information I can give concerning them must be secondhand, gathered from the missionaries, natives and Japanese of neighboring islands. It may be said however that there are no better authorities. Many of the officials we met had served in the Marshalls. The natives, as before noted, were not daunted by long canoe trips over the open sea. And the missionaries were constantly in touch with, and sometimes changed places with, their colleagues on other islands.

The Marshalls were Miss Hoppin's home for twenty-five years and Carl Heine was there almost as long. They and a Dr. C. F. Rife were probably the only Americans to see these islands from the time the Japanese took them in 1914 until American airmen flew over them in the raid of January 31, 1942.

The Marshall Islands are the outermost Japanese wall facing Hawaii. This wall is seven hundred miles long, about the distance from Seattle to San Francisco. It is really a double rampart, consisting of two chains of islands, the eastern being called the Radak (Sunrise) Chain, the western the Ralik (Sunset) Chain. The two chains are about a hundred miles apart. Together they compass thirty-two large atolls and 867 islands and reefs.

Nowhere does the land rise more than 33 feet above the sea. During severe storms the lower islands are entirely inundated by the waves. The people clamber into the coconut palms while the sea roars beneath them. Sometimes houses, palms, people and all are swept away.

Any volcanic islands which the reefs may once have encircled have long since been submerged or worn away, and nothing remains within the atoll but a calm lagoon. The reef at some points is narrow; at others it widens to form an island. These perfectly level islands make good air strips. The calm waters of the lagoon are ideal harbors for surface ships, submarines and seaplanes.

The Marshalls were discovered by the Spaniard de Saavedra in the sixteenth century. Because the natives were picturesquely tattooed he called the islands Los Pintados, The Painted Ones. English captains later visited the islands and they were named after Captain Marshall, who explored them in 1788. But the British government took no interest in them and they were annexed by Germany in 1885. Japan picked them up in 1914.

That is the official history. Unofficially, it was the Americans who actually had most to do with the islands before the Japanese came. Not that the American record is one to be particularly proud of. Syphilis and tuberculosis were the gifts of the whalers. They made drunken murderous forays upon the natives. American ships became most unwelcome and many were destroyed by the angry islanders. Innocent crews suffered along with the guilty. An unoffending captain was picked up bodily by a great chief and his brains dashed out against a rock. Sailors were decapitated.

Then the ship named *Morning Star* arrived. It was a beautiful sailing clipper, but with auxiliary steam. The captain called for canoes to tow the ship into the lagoon against the strong tide. The natives dutifully performed this service, craftily planning later to destroy the ship and kill all on board. But the king intervened just in time. He had heard of the *Morning Star*—it was the ship of mercy paid for by the pennies of Boston children, and its passengers were the first missionaries to the Marshalls. That was in 1857.

The missionary, whether he intends to do so or not, always opens the way for trade, and it was not long before American trading ships were making regular calls at the Marshalls. The business methods of these trading buccaneers were often more shrewd than honest.

"He businessed me," became a current saying among natives, meaning "He cheated me." And since American whalers and traders were always fighting, a native threatening another would think it appropriate to say, "I'll Merikan you!"

The traders came to Miss Hoppin: "Don't let them use those words that way. It's an insult to our business and to Americans."

"Why don't *you* stop them?"

"They mind you. They won't mind us. How could we stop them?"

"By changing your business methods," suggested Miss Hoppin. She took the sting out of it by placing before them a bowl of hot candied bananas baked in coconut milk.

The net result of American influence upon the Marshalls has been more favorable than we would have a right to expect. A Japanese official complained to me "The Marshalls people can't get their minds off America. They call it their adopted country." The governor of Jaluit said, "Until we can stop American mission education and replace it with Japanese education, we can never turn the natives our way." And a native chief commented, "When the Japanese don't treat us right we go to the Americans. They talk with the Japanese and fix things up."

Small wonder that no more Americans were allowed to come in, and those already in were finally expelled.

But it may be taken as certain that the Japanese, left to themselves, have not won the love of the ten thousand natives of the Marshalls, and the people of this great archipelago next door to Hawaii are as well disposed as the Hawaiians to closer association with the United States.

Before these lines are in print the Marshalls may or may not be in Allied hands. In either case, a brief description of their chief atolls may be of interest.

The headquarters island is Jaluit. It is by no means the largest of the group, yet its deep lagoon is thirty-eight miles long and twenty-one wide. Fifty islands are strung along the reef like the pearls of a necklace. Several are of good size, one twelve miles long. Beside the southeast channel is the administration village, Jabur.

Although Jaluit has an immense fleet basin and serviceable airfields, some of the other islands are still better bases. Enewetok (Brown Atoll) has only twenty miles of sea-room but it will be found to have been highly developed as a defensive stronghold, perhaps because its nearest neighbor to the north is Wake. Wotje is a crescent moon—with the anchorage inside the curve and airfields on several of its sixty-five islands. On Maloelap has been made a splendid air base with well-paved runways, large hangars and fuel storage tanks. The Mili lagoon varies from twelve to twenty-three miles in diameter and this base has already withstood a lot of punishment.

The largest atoll in the Marshalls is Kwajalein, with a deep-water lagoon no less than sixty miles long and from ten to twenty wide. Our raiders find it well filled with cruisers, destroyers, tankers, submarines, flying boats, and airplane tenders. One of its islands, Roi, is a strong air base.

Close to the Marshalls on the south, outside the borders of the mandate, are the Gilberts, where American marines suffered severe losses when their landing boats struck coral reefs and the men were forced to swim ashore, a distance of eight hundred yards under merciless fire. There has been a tendency to criticize those in charge for miscalcula-

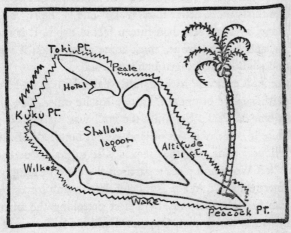

WAKE

tion. Why did they not know in advance that the tide would be low on these reefs?

After seeing how often the Japanese themselves miscalculated the behavior of wind and tide in the *Nanyo* lagoons with which they had had two decades to become acquainted, one is not disposed to quarrel with the explanation of Secretary Knox that a sudden shift in the wind lowered the water, causing the boats to hang up on the coral. Indeed the marines will be in rare luck if the same sort of disaster is not many times repeated in the devious, devilish and quite unpredictable currents and shoals of Micronesian lagoons, especially those of Ponape, Truk and Palau.

Also outside the mandate, but of grim significance in connection with

227

it, are Wake, four hundred miles north, and Rabaul eight hundred miles south. At this writing they are in Japanese hands. There is no particular risk in prophesying that they will soon be Allied bases from which a pincer attack may be made upon the important bases that lie between them, Truk and Ponape. These pincers will support the main drive which may be expected to come from the Marshalls and Gilberts.

Wake will live in history because of the heroic stand of the marines in December, 1941. Otherwise it is of slight importance. The Marshalls alone contain thirty atolls better than Wake. The Wake lagoon, though four miles long, averages less than fifteen feet in depth. It is useless for surface craft, and even seaplanes must come down upon it warily lest they crash on slightly submerged banks of coral.

The Wake atoll encloses three islands, Wake, Wilkes and Peale. All of them together cover no more than two square miles. The airport of the clippers was on Peale. Certainly the atoll was useful as a halfway station because it is the only dot of land within hundreds of miles. But one may seriously doubt whether it was wise to make "defensive improvements" on Wake and place a garrison there—to be slaughtered by the first comers. In short, Wake is indefensible by any forces placed on Wake. It can be defended only by a fleet patrolling the surrounding waters—and is not worth that. Our naval and air forces could capture Wake overnight; but would then have to stay constantly on the job lest the Japanese do the same. Therefore Wake will probably not be touched until Japanese naval power has been pretty well broken or has been distracted to other theaters. Then Wake's airfields will serve as useful springboards against the mandated islands.

Of far more significance is Rabaul. This powerful offensive and defensive base, only eight hundred miles from Truk, consists of a magnificent harbor called Blanche Bay cut into the end of New Britain Island. On the shore of this bay is the lovely town of Rabaul, and its name has been used in the dispatches to cover the entire region including the bay and the four great airdromes that surround it. The bay is six miles across and deep water extends within a few yards of the shore. It is girdled by mountain ranges. Above the town looms volcanic Mount Mother which in very unmotherly fashion nearly destroyed the

228

town in 1937. Nearby are the North Daughter and South Daughter. The whole region is explosive. Matupi Crater joined the Mother in showering ash and pumice upon Rabaul and killing several hundred persons. Vulcan Island, which was created in a single night by an eruption in 1878, suddenly flew into the sky on May 28, 1937. When the

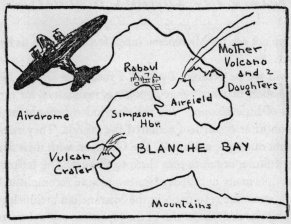

RABAUL

eruption was over the formerly flat island was a cone six hundred feet high.

Rabaul is once again being visited by eruptions, now coming from above rather than below, and more than one of them has been announced as a "crushing and decisive defeat."

"I think we have broken its back," said General MacArthur after the sensational sinking of more than a hundred ships and the destruction of 177 planes in October, 1943. Maybe so, but the snake continues to squirm after its back is broken, and hardly a week passes without another attack upon Rabaul. Its capture will be one of the major achievements of the Pacific war and will open wide the side door to the Japanese mandate.

But however valuable the side door may be, more important is the front door. That is from Pearl Harbor straight through the Marshalls.

XXXVIII:

What Are the Islands Worth?

W<small>E DID</small> not ask for Micronesia. Japan forced it upon us by making war.

What will we be getting? By "we" I mean the United Nations or whatever nation that body may appoint as mandatory for the islands.

"Islands of little account" was the description brought back by explorers soon after Spain had acquired the islands. They remained of little account during Spanish rule. The Germans, with their flair for scientific agriculture, began to turn them to account. The Japanese multiplied this effort many hundreds of times and have accomplished nothing short of an economic revolution in the Micronesian archipelago.

In nothing else does the genius of the Japanese people show to greater advantage than in agriculture. They have been trained for the conquest of the soil in their own tight islands. The Spaniards surveying barren Saipan could hardly visualize rich fields of sugar cane twenty feet high billowing in the breeze. Now the island produces six million dollars' worth of sugar every year.

One of the finest sugar canes in the world has been developed here. Java cane was formerly used. Unsatisfied scientists blended it with other canes from all over the world, producing endless varieties. The final result of all this polygamy was the birth of a remarkable half-caste, a blend of Java and Formosa, which thrives in the soil of Saipan. It grows to great size and has high sugar content.

The Japanese sugar executives have given the same unremitting attention to their job that their misguided militarist brothers have devoted to the science of war. The manager of the Saipan sugar mill spoke to me in good English and explained that he had been in all the sugar countries and had worked for years in a sugar mill in Cuba.

As for copra (the dried kernel of the coconut), its production has been quickened by improved breeds and scientific methods. The government has stood ready to give any copra farmer an iron roof, free of charge, to put on his drying house in place of the thatched roof. Under the latter, the wind dries the copra in about ten days. When iron is used the wind is supplemented by the sun's heat beating upon the roof, and the copra dries in five days.

Most encouraging is the recent success of tapioca. It is the answer to a hard problem—how to use barren uplands. Apparently just nothing would grow there. Not because of lack of rain—for on Palau, Ponape and Kusaie there is a daily deluge. The good soil is washed into the sea. Many plants will not tolerate such a drenching. Now, what would flourish in poor soil, and at the same time defy the downpour?

Tapioca. Wild specimens of it were found here and there growing to tree size. But they contained only 16 per cent starch. World-ranging explorers for the agricultural department fixed upon Java tapioca and brought it back to Micronesia. It yields 35 per cent starch. Large plantations have been put in. Mills have been built in various islands for grinding the roots into a white powder. The cake and confection industry of the world is a ready market for all the tapioca the South Seas can produce.

Even the natives are stirred up over it. True, the reactions of some of them are not quite what one might expect!

"It will be the ruin of our young men," was the point of view of an old chief on Ponape. "They are forgetting the value of leisure. Leisure. You in the West are trying to reduce working hours to increase the hours of leisure. That is best. Life was meant to be lived." Words that deserve more than a passing thought. But the chief's son had three hectares of land and he was planting it to tapioca.

"The tapioca company will send a truck to help clear the land," he said. "They will furnish seedlings. And they will advance one hundred yen—to be paid back later in tapioca. They will pay ninety sen a bag, and they say I can get two hundred and fifty bags of tapioca from one hectare. And I have three hectares. So how much do I make? I figured it all last night but I couldn't get it to come out the same way twice."

231

So we figured it together. Schoolteachers say that arithmetic is the Kanaka's weakest subject. Perhaps that is because he has had little use for it. It is due to become stronger now that he has begun to figure his profits.

On islands other than Yap, pineapples have been extensively planted so that it is no longer necessary to carry a can when going on a picnic. The government encourages the farmer by giving him a reward of ten yen for every hectare planted to pineapples and cared for for two years. Twenty-five yen goes to the native who gets up the energy to plant a hectare of coconuts and take care of it for three years.

In Palau everyone is feverishly raising pigs, for the government will not only lend pigs for breeding purposes but will reward the farmer with six yen for every pig born. In the same way, goats, cows, chickens carry prices on their heads. Cattle raising was introduced by a young Japanese who brought thirty cattle from Japan. Most of them died. This disaster, coupled with the disgrace he felt because he was living with a native woman, gave him such an inferiority complex that he attempted to commit suicide. He was stopped by a German missionary, Mr. Lange.

"Now I suppose you'll try to convert me," bitterly said the man who was a failure in everything, even in suicide.

"What you need is a wife!" said Mr. Lange.

There was no eligible Japanese lady in primitive Palau. But by the "picture bride" method, not uncommon among the Japanese, correspondence was begun with a Japanese widow in Hawaii. Portraits were exchanged. In due time the lady came to Palau, was married and provided her husband with enough money to set him up anew as a rancher. He bought better cattle and managed to make them thrive and calve. He accumulated one hundred, the largest herd in the South Sea islands. And, although he remained a good Shintoist, he contributed regularly to the German mission!

The Japanese farmer who needed land could get it from the State, three years rent-free, thereafter paying one yen rent per hectare. Or he could buy it at twenty yen a hectare.

The government found itself in possession of plenty of land that no-

232

body else wanted—barren, rocky or sandy soil. It began rehabilitating this land. Rich soil was actually sent by the shipload to the bleak coral atolls of the Marshalls. On certain rocky islands a tree known as the *soshiju* from Formosa was planted. It twines its roots around a rock and grows thirty feet high in three years. Its falling leaves and decaying logs make a soil where almost none existed. Of course the job would take some time. When I asked the Palau agricultural director how long, he replied brightly, as if promising something for tomorrow morning before breakfast, "I think we will have these islands fit for farming in one hundred years."

But he went on to point out that a century is a brief period when you consider the untold ages these islands have been lying unused and useless.

Phosphate from Angaur is being used to regenerate the land on other islands. Another pulmotor for exhausted soil is the lemon hibiscus. Yam-growing tires out the soil in ten years. But it has been found that if the fast-growing hibiscus is allowed to perforate the hard dry ground with its labyrinth of roots, within a few months there is light rich soil ready for another decade of service.

One problem, ever present in the tropics, is to keep the jungle out of the garden. It crawls in, smothering everything with weeds and creepers. But it cannot get through a vigorous thicket of bamboo. So the government, while preparing the land for farming, shuts out the jungle with walls of feathery bamboo.

Frequently some of this State land is presented to a village whether it wants it or not. The village is invited, compelled if necessary, to cultivate the land. All work together under the direction of the king (and he under the less obvious direction of the local policeman). The resulting plantations of pineapple, tapioca, vegetables and many fruits, formerly unknown to the islands, belong to the village. Any family wishing to use some of the food makes its purchases from the king, who keeps the money as "village money" to be used for the extension of plantations or for a clubhouse, a community fishing boat, piers, roads, or other public works.

The heart and core of the whole agricultural revolution in the South

Seas is the government experimental farm. These stations were begun by the Germans and continued by the Japanese. There is one on every important island. Here miracles are performed.

The vegetable was practically unknown in Micronesia. Experts had said it could not be raised there because of the heat and moisture. But on the experimental farms of Yap and Palau the following vegetables, imported from Japan, have been coddled until they have been made to feel perfectly at home in the tropics: cucumber, eggplant, tomato, radish, okra, lettuce, napa (a cousin to lettuce), carrot, onion, squash, pumpkin, melon, watermelon, ginger, cabbage, kohlrabi, peas, beans, spinach, mitsuba, potato, sweet potato, sugar potato, and eight-headed potato.

And fruits, flowers, exotic trees! One might imagine himself in the Garden of Allah as he wanders through the experimental farm at Ponape. Here are plant immigrants from all lands. It is like a world convention of growing things. They were brought here by the world-scouring agricultural scientist, Hoshino, who, bluff, hearty, rubber-booted, accompanies us as we walk about.

He points out corn from Kansas, chestnuts from Polynesia, cashew nuts from India, cloves and nutmeg from Celebes, alligator pears from Hawaii, lichee nuts from China, Brazil nuts from Brazil, oranges from California, jackfruit from Malaya, mangosteen and pomegranate from Borneo, aloes from Africa. Java has sent many delegates: the sapodilla plum, coromandel gooseberry, vanilla, pepper, cinnamon. And here are rubber trees, mahogany, teak, sago palm, oil palm, peacock palm, sugar palm.

There is a whole garden of drug trees—caiupute, tamarind, benzoin and the like. "When I have some small ailment, I don't need to go to the drug store," says Mr. Hoshino. "I come here and fill my own prescription with some bark or sap or leaves from this pharmacy."

Altogether in this farm there are two hundred and thirty-eight fruits, vegetables, grasses, shrubs and trees that have not formerly been native to Ponape—but are now! Nothing is kept that does not become indigenous, that has to be pepped up by new supplies of seeds from abroad.

Many of the plants are synthetic, Burbanked or Hoshino-ized. Rice, for example. Rice needs dry weather when harvested. But there is no such thing as dry weather in Ponape. Rain falls every day throughout the year. Japanese rice simply gives up under such conditions. However, the rice of India is accustomed to a wet harvest period, but it lacks other qualities of the Japanese variety. Mr. Hoshino took us down to flourishing rice fields.

"Here," he pointed to anemic rice that looked up disconsolately into a black sky from which great drops were even then rattling on our helmets, "is Japanese rice. This is a patch of Indian rice, not much better. But all the rest of the field is the cross-breed of those two."

The child was half as tall again as either of its parents, and had fine, heavy kernels. It combined the good breeding of the Japanese rice with the rain-defying hardihood of the Indian.

All the wealth of good things developed by the trial farms is available to the native. Some rather brutal persuasion is employed at times to get him to make use of his privileges. Village delegations are brought to the farm, instructed and supplied with seeds, and an expert goes back with them to see that the seeds are used. Every school has a farm, equipped from the trial farm, and agriculture is the chief subject in the curriculum. Selected graduates are sent for a post-graduate year on the trial farm, free of cost, and go back to their villages with the necessary seeds and tools.

But the chief professor of agriculture in the South Seas is the policeman!

While we sojourned in one jungle village we heard, daily, the sound of a hammer ring through the forest. That is an unusual sound, for the Kanaka house is tied together with coconut fibers, not nailed. But a Japanese house was being built. It would be occupied by the king's overlord, the Japanese policeman. That worthy now governed by means of infrequent trips from the port-town miles away. It was thought better that he should live within his district.

So one morning we saw a motorboat come up the lagoon towing a barge full of household effects—everything from a sewing machine to large framed portraits of the Emperor and Empress. The whole village together with the king, his nobles, and the two foreigners escorted the policeman and his wife to their new house. He invited everyone in to inspect it. What appealed to us especially was the bath. He insisted that we use it, and we had our first hot bath in three weeks.

The policeman was a pleasant fellow, with none of the officiousness that sometimes characterizes police in Japan. In fact his training and his duties were not at all those of the ordinary police. He was a graduate of an agricultural college! And his chief task was not to apprehend criminals but to teach agriculture! The mild-natured Kanakas commit few offenses. They do not need punishment so much as guidance. Therefore the South Sea policeman is trained in first aid, treatment of simple diseases, sanitation, the construction of better houses, road-building, educational methods, Shinto principles of morality, and, chiefly, farming.

"A good man," acknowledged the king. "But we do not need him. We know more than any stranger about cultivating the soil of these islands. And our gods will be angry if we follow new ways."

Polite and obstinate natives . . . opposed to a tactful and firm policeman. But it is the policeman who wins. Not by force, for he is only one against many if the scene is a remote island. There may not be another Japanese within a day's canoe-trip. It is remarkable how meek and good-natured a Japanese official becomes when there are no guns to back him up and his very life depends upon winning the good-will of the natives. He must forget his authority and go to work in his own garden, showing by example what can be done. He must travel about from one native's farm to another, carrying seeds and tools; and be always ready to bend his own back and get his own hands into the soil in order to demonstrate his teachings. Of course any young natives who have had agricultural training at the school or trial farm are his able supporters. And as the irreconcilables have died and the youngsters have come on, the revolution has gathered speed.

There is nothing altruistic about this program. Japan's object has been to improve the islands economically—and that could be done only by increasing the productivity of the workers.

Even greater treasure may come out of the sea than out of the soil.

236

"The possibilities of the islands are limited; of the sea, unlimited," said Governor-General Hayashi.

The sea area of Micronesia is thirty-six hundred times the land area. And nearly all varieties of fish may be found here, most of them in abundance. The export of dried bonito doubled in a recent year and tripled in the next. Marine products to a total value of well over two million yen are exported every year. Most of the export has gone to Japan, but from there much has been relayed to all parts of the world. Japanese canned tuna entering the United States has caused not a little worry to the fishing industry on the Pacific Coast.

First among the marine products of the southern sea is bonito.

Daily peril is the lot of the bonito fisherman. He must go outside the reef, in the open sea. He cannot wait for good weather. In waves that would shake an ocean liner his small boat drops like a descending elevator into the hollows and is tossed skyward on the crests.

The native canoes are now being supplanted by motorboats. These are not much safer than the great canoes, being only some forty feet in length. But they are much better for bonito fishing since they are able to go rapidly to the point where the school of fish may be seen leaping from the sea, too preoccupied in fighting among themselves to notice the approach of the swift craft.

At some islands, sardines are used to bait the hooks. At others, feathers. But the best bait of all seems to be a gasoline motor!

The sound of the motor brings the fish. In a motorless canoe, the fishermen pound on the boat in order to attract attention. The government has been so eager to develop bonito fishing that it would provide a motorboat free of charge to any group of thirty or forty Japanese (that number could be accommodated in one boat) who would undertake fishing. The men then owned the boat jointly and carried on work as an association.

Whatever may have been the adventures of the bonito in the sea they are nothing to its odd experiences while being prepared for market. It is boiled, the head is cut off, and the body is cut longitudinally into four. It is turned over to the bone pullers, armed with tweezers, who know exactly where each bone is located. The fish is then dried over fire for a few days and smoked for two weeks. Then girls manicure off the rough, smoky exterior with sharp knives until the fish takes on the appearance of polished red mahogany.

It is stuck away in damp sheds to mildew. The mildew gives it that choice tang. When it is thoroughly blotched with the gray growth, the mildew is wiped off and the fish is sunned, only to mildew again. For the best results this process is repeated from three to five times. Thenceforth the fish will be practically immune from mildew. It will keep indefinitely. There are said to be pieces one hundred years old. Many stores in Japan offer pieces ten or twelve years old. Like wine, it improves with age.

It is as hard as wood. To the foreign visitor in a Japanese store, a tubful of *katsubushi* (as it is called) looks like a collection of clubs or blackjacks, the purpose of which it is difficult to imagine.

The Japanese pay a high price for *katsubushi* and one piece will last the average family many months. For it is used as a flavoring rather than as a food. Thin shavings of it are put into the daily soup. Foreigners in Japan soon learn its value and its use is being extended to America and Europe. After the islands cease to be Japanese its manufacture might well be continued, for a little publicity would make a ready sale for it in many countries.

Millions of the buttons on the world's cotton garments come from the South Seas.

From the green, translucent depths within the lagoon of Truk a brown diver came up bearing an iridescent shell. He put it into our dugout canoe, then adjusted his goggles and went down again. A few months later that shell would gleam in the form of mother-of-pearl buttons on women's clothing in England or America.

We could see him plainly as his sinuous body glided to the coral floor, six fathoms down. He was helped to descend by a heavy iron which he held in his hand. One end of a cord was tied to the iron, the other end was fastened to a thwart in the canoe. His companion stood in the canoe holding a spear, ready to hurl it instantly if a shark should approach—for there are many of them in these waters, great savage white sharks, tiger sharks and blue pointers from twelve to thirty feet long. A nearby break in the reef made it quite possible that one might enter the lagoon.

Upon reaching the bottom, the diver began exploring. The shells are not easily found. They are the homes of an exclusive snail which does not care to have its house out where any roving sea pirate may find and attack it. So these gorgeously decorated residences with their unpleasant householders are concealed in rocky caves. The diver fairly stood on his head, his feet trailing toward the surface, as he peered beneath rocks. He never groped without looking, for those dark crannies are also the homes of other creatures not so harmless as snails.

He got two shells, then released his hold upon the sinker, shot to the surface and emerged, gasping for air. The iron was drawn up by the cord.

He repeated this performance many times until the floor of the canoe was covered with a rainbow of shells. His companion was bored. It was monotonous, standing there watching for a shark that never came.

Then suddenly things happened, all in a flash. The diver was rising, a long gray shape was approaching, the spear was flying through the air. It missed! The shark turned on its back to strike. With a yell the boat-boy leaped from the canoe and landed squarely on the shark's white belly. So startled was the fish that it turned aside and righted itself, dumping its rider into the sea. Both boys scrambled into the boat in great haste. They concluded that they had enough mother-of-pearl for that day.

These waters yield pearl as well as mother-of-pearl. The latter, of course, does not deserve its name. It is no relation of the real pearl, not even the most distant cousin. Ten thousand pearls a year come from Palau to the jewelry cases of Japan and the West. These are the famous Mikimoto cultured pearls. They can in no sense be called imitation pearls, for they are thoroughly genuine. But the oysters which made them were encouraged—subsidized—by man. Because of this encouragement the pearls can be produced in great numbers and are therefore much cheaper than accidental pearls. But they are identical in composition and in beauty.

The difference is only this: an oyster adventuring on its own may pick up a bit of shell or stone, and, unable to expel the irritating fragment, will cover it with a lustrous, calcareous concretion, thus gradually forming a pearl. But for every oyster that suffers this fate, ten thousand may escape it. At the pearl farm, laboratory experts open oysters and introduce a bit of shell into each, so that every oyster will produce a pearl.

From that moment on, it is up to the oyster. The process is exactly the same as in the case of the accidental pearl. The annoying bit of foreign matter is sheathed in layer after layer of pearl. The gem is completed in from three to four years (half the time required in the Japan pearl farms where the water is colder). During these years the oysters are kept in wire cages suspended in the lagoon.

When the oyster has had time to do its work it is taken into the laboratory and the pearl is extracted.

There is nothing artificial about the pearl. Even the particle at its center is the same sort of fragment that might be picked up by an oyster from the sea. But since a vain world pays for its gems, not according to their beauty but according to the difficulty of getting them, the accidental pearl will always cost more than the cultured.

The Palau gems are of unusual size, many of them from a quarter-inch to a half-inch in diameter. Most are white. Rarer and therefore more costly ones are black. A few are a lovely mauve.

Turtles grow to great size in these southern waters. Occasionally hunters find a turtle as heavy as a horse, five hundred pounds. To catch it is a difficult matter. One day on a small island two of our native friends saw a huge turtle emerge from the bushes where, we later found, it had just laid about two hundred eggs in the sand. It waddled toward the beach.

"Quick! Where's your rope?"

"I left it in the boat."

So there was nothing to do but try to capture the turtle with bare hands. An effort was made to turn it upon its back. That proved impossible. Then each seized a hind flipper. But the turtle, plying its fore flippers vigorously, tore across the beach and through the shallows, then dived into deep water, towing the tenacious natives after it. They were forced to let go and came to the surface, sputtering laments over the loss of two hundred yen—for the shell was of that value.

With a rope, the animal could easily have been noosed to a tree. It would then be killed on the spot, or else turned over with the help of improvised crowbars and taken home alive.

Turtles frequently sleep afloat a foot or two beneath the surface of the sea like slightly submerged islands. If a canoe approaches without the least sound of voice or paddle, the turtle may be speared before it wakes. Of course great care is taken to send the spear through the fleshy shoulder, not through the valuable shell.

The tortoise-shell industry depends principally upon the great hawk's-bill turtle of the South Seas. The animal's shell is made up of sections known technically as "deep belly," "light belly," "brown mottled shell," "brown shell," "black shell" and "yellow hoof." The last-named, a beautiful translucent yellow or cream shade, is the most valuable. Skilled artisans make beautiful tortoise-shell articles ranging from buffets, tables, vases and jewelry boxes down to combs, hair ornaments and cuff links.

In contrast with the beautiful turtle is the repulsive bêche de mer, or sea slug, the next most valuable marine product. This animate ooze is like a great snail, a yard long at its best, and four or five inches thick. We scooped one from the shallow sea bottom, put it on the slatted floor of the canoe, and forgot it. We looked half an hour later to see a pond of slime on the floor. In the midst of it the sea pudding, as it is well called, had mushed down through all the cracks between the slats so that there was about as much slug below the floor as above it. To separate floor and slug by force was impossible. Therefore suggestion was used. The floorboard was taken out and suspended in the water. The effect appeared to be soothing, for the slug gradually relaxed its hold and sank once more to the bottom—where we severely left it.

When the bêche de mer is cured, it shrinks from a yard in length to a foot. It is sent to China. Before use, it is placed in a chemical which restores it to its original length. It is sliced, cooked, eaten with great relish by the Chinese.

Sharking is always exciting, whatever method is used. Wholesale sharking is done by schooner. Six lines on each side of the ship pass through floating boards so arranged that the first tug will turn the white upper side of the board down and the black side up. Then the watchman blows his whistle. The men rush to the line and pull in the fish to the strains of a chantey. The line passes through a block in the rigging. The fish is drawn up to the block and dangles above the deck, its tremendous tail thrashing about to the peril of any who come near. The official executioner, perched in the rigging, thrusts a spear into the shark's forehead. Those on deck cut open the stomach, spilling the blood and viscera on the deck to the accompaniment of a terrific stench. When the shark is dead it is dropped to the deck. Many of the carcasses will list the ship, for the fish weigh from four hundred pounds to a ton.

Jon Makoelun, splendid old native of Kusaie, has sailed much of his life on the sharking ships.

"The best time is at night," he says, "especially between seven and nine o'clock. We've sometimes taken aboard a hundred and fifty sharks during those two hours.

"We use a manila line as big as your thumb and about five fathoms long. A very long line is not necessary; the sharks chase you, you don't need to chase them. The line ends in a length of wire cable and a big hook a foot long and four inches across the bend. The best bait is a piece of pork. It takes about three men, with the help of block and tackle, to haul one fish aboard.

"The five fins are cut off, dried, shipped in bags. Also we take out the liver. We squeeze it in the hands to break up the tissues, then put it in a strainer in the hatch with a barrel below. The sun shining on it causes the oil in it to drain out into the barrel. It must be kept draining for two weeks. It smells to high heaven. So do the sharks' carcasses. They can't be thrown overboard—that would frighten away the sharks. We take them ashore on the nearest island and bury them. You'd be surprised how they make the coconut trees grow."

The fins go to China as table delicacies, or for use in making gelatine. The oil has excellent lubricating qualities and does not get gummy, but it does have a slight odor. Much of it has gone to San Francisco—thence into the interior workings of sewing machines, bicycles, watches and fine machinery. Shark skin is used for shoes and bags. Because the skin is covered with small, pointed, calcified papillae, cabinet makers use it under the name of "shagreen" for smoothing and polishing wood.

The natives make a carnival out of mullet fishing. The mullet is a blunt-nosed gray fish one or two feet long, much prized for its taste.

The whole village joins in the sport. Men, women, even the babies, clamber into the boats. We paddled out with a fleet of about thirty canoes, which indulged in an informal canoe race on the way to the fishing grounds. Once there, all but the infants went overboard into the shallow lagoon.

Now the idea of mullet fishing is to put a fence around the fish. They try to leap over the fence, and are caught in it.

The fence is made up of vertical nets, huge rectangular affairs perhaps twenty feet long and eight feet high. They are placed end to end in a great circle often five hundred feet across. Their lower edges touch the sea bottom, but most of the fence is above the surface, projecting high into the air. Those who hold the nets begin to walk in, making the circle smaller and smaller. The caged fish swim madly about, seeking a way of escape, and finally become so exercised that they take to leaping in an effort to jump over the fence. Some succeed, clearing the fence with a magnificent bound of five or six feet. Others fall short and are caught in mid-air by the meshes of the net. Instantly there is someone at hand with a club to kill the fish with a blow on the head and toss it into a nearby canoe.

As the circle tightens the excitement increases. The fish may be leaping into a dozen nets at one time and the shouts of the men, laughter and screams of the women and the shrill treble of the flotilla of children echo back from the mountains in a merry pandemonium.

Fisheries in the mandate have annually yielded marine products to the value of about seven million yen. The yen's buying power in Japan is about equal to that of the dollar in America, therefore these products if put on the American market would be worth approximately seven million dollars.

And the possibilities of the Micronesian seas have barely been tapped. The phosphate annually mined in the islands would be worth four million dollars in the United States, the copra two million dollars, the sugar twenty-four million.

Micronesia will not be an economic burden upon the nation or nations made responsible for it. Not if anything like the Japanese skill is applied by the new landlords. For the islands have regularly been producing far more than they consume. In 1939 they imported goods to the value of thirty million yen and exported goods worth fifty million. That means that Micronesia is self-supporting, and better. The new proprietors will take over a going concern.

All this is aside from the strategic value of the islands. Even if the archipelago were economically a complete loss, it would be invaluable as a watch-dog against future aggression in the Western Pacific.

XXXIX:

In Time To Come

LET us briefly consider the three futures of Micronesia—the immediate, the postwar and the far.

The immediate future will see Micronesia playing its role as a road to Tokyo. This road, as suggested in the first chapter, may turn out to be a two-lane highway on which two lines of traffic may move simultaneously in the same general direction, toward Japan.

One line has already begun to move from Hawaii into the Marshalls. Thence it may be expected to proceed by easy stages five hundred miles to Kusaie, then four hundred to Ponape, four hundred to Truk, six hundred to Guam, one hundred and fifty to Saipan, eight hundred to the Bonins, five hundred to Japan.

The other line of traffic directed by MacArthur, who has promised to return to the Philippines may move by equally short stages eight hundred miles from Rabaul to Truk, eight hundred to Yap, three hundred to Palau, five hundred to the Philippines, four hundred to the China coast, and six hundred from the airfields of Chekiang province to Japan.

Let me say again that I am no prophet. These are reasonable routes, but variations from them are not only possible but likely under constantly changing conditions. Such routes may be recommended, not prophesied. They seem the best because (1) they would open a direct sea-road to China and end the present extraordinary situation which requires us to go most of the way around the world and over the Himalayas to give aid to Chiang Kai-shek; (2) they would cut off Japan's lifeline to Malaya and the Netherlands Indies whose resources are essential to her war effort; (3) they would block Japan's stream of supplies and reinforcements to the lands down under, cause military stagnation there and make the ultimate reconquest of those lands a good-sized mopping-up rather than a major campaign; (4) they are the shortest and most direct practicable routes to the Japanese mainland.

Micronesia having served as a warpath to Japan, what shall its postwar future be?

Hugh Byas, whom I have previously quoted with hearty agreement, I disagree with just as heartily when he says, "The mandate now held by Japan should be summarily transferred to the United States."

We have no warrant to deal "summarily" with peaceful and lawabiding populations no matter how small. They cannot be passed about as one would pass the butter. True, they have been. Neither the Spaniards, the Germans nor the Japanese consulted the natives before seizing their islands. The United States should be the nation to stop such violation of ordinary human rights. Nothing would do more to allay the suspicions of Asiatics who, prompted by Japan, fear that America and Britain mean to extend their imperialism over all Asia.

Unbridled self-determination is, of course, impossible. If each island of two or three thousand people were to constitute its own government we would have a myriad of sovereign nations in the Pacific; the result: chaos and constant war.

Self-determination is an impossible and even criminal ideal. No individual may determine his conduct to suit himself; it is determined largely by the needs of others as set down in constitutions and laws.

Nor has any group of people, calling itself a nation, the right to conduct itself regardless of the rights of other groups or nations.

The doctrine of self-determination has spread much false hope and bitter disillusionment. It should be replaced by some such term as world-determination. Only the general good of the world may ultimately determine the behavior of the individual or the nation. But I fear that such an expression as "world-determination" would never be popular, because it does not offer you and me the liberty to do as we darn please.

The Micronesian is perhaps a little more advanced than we in his social thinking. He realizes the inadvisability of self-government if by that is meant a separate government for each island or even each small group of islands. I asked many of the chiefs about this. Their views were pretty well summed up in the opinion of a Ponape chief: "When we ruled ourselves, every chief was at war with every other. It is better to have some higher authority."

A plebiscite might be held to learn the desire of the Micronesians as to what that higher authority should be. At the time of the Versailles Conference an American missionary who had served in the Marshalls stated his belief that if a plebiscite were taken the people of the Marshall and Caroline Islands would ask to be placed under American administration.

That may be the solution of the problem. It would not be entirely satisfactory. The United States did not enter this war for territorial gain. She cannot afford the taint of imperialism if she is to get on well with Asia in the postwar era and avert a world-destroying Color War which may even now be seen on the horizon. Asiatics would suspect that the plebiscite had been "fixed." Certain dissenting islanders would rise in rebellion (as in the Philippines in 1898) and we would have to use American troops to put them down.

Moreover we would not have an easy "out" as we had in the Philippines. There we could get out of it by granting independence to the Filipinos. We could hardly grant independence to the Micronesians within any reasonable time because they could not use it. The islands are so widely scattered and communication between them so difficult that an over-all native government would be hard to organize and harder to maintain. The almost inevitable result would be a split-up into hundreds of small and conflicting suzerainties.

With our hand in the bottle and full of islands we would be unable to get it out again. Better not put it in.

Moreover there is no warrant for regarding the Western Pacific as an American ocean. It is the crossroads of all the nations bordering the Pacific. Micronesia is four thousand miles from our West Coast but only a few hundred from China and to-be-Chinese Formosa, from British possessions, from Australian mandates, from a Holland more important than Holland, from French Indo-China and from the soon-independent Philippines. It lies athwart the trade routes of all these states. In case of war it is, as we are now finding out, the very kernel of strategy in the Western Pacific. It is of international concern.

Why should it not be internationally controlled as a benefit to all and threat to none? Japan has taught us our lesson as to the possible abuses of the mandate system if the mandate is exercised by a single power. I am aware that French-British condominium over the New Hebrides has not worked well. It would be absurd to deduce from this that condominium or international control cannot be made to work. The United Nations in their joint military government of occupied territories and joint direction of the armed forces have illustrated clearly not only the possibilities but the advantages of co-operation. Certainly the United Nations will govern Micronesia during the interim between the capture of the archipelago and the end of the war; and what could be more natural at that time than that the international authority already exercised be passed on to whatever world organization may then be established?

Japan would not immediately be a member of such a world council and would therefore have no part in the management of the mandate. Only after a long period of probation, covering perhaps many years, would she be admitted to the association of nations and share in its responsibilities.

Whether the island mandate is held by one nation or by all, the worrisome question arises: What is to be done with the Japanese?

247

There are now 100,000 Japanese in the mandated islands as against only 40,000 natives.

As shown previously, the high birth rate of the Japanese means that, even if no more Japanese were admitted to the islands, the Japanese population would steadily and swiftly increase.

We know enough about the Japanese to be very sure that they would expect to rule any land in which they were numerically predominant. There would be constant friction. Japan would champion her colonists. The situation would invite a new war.

The obvious remedy may seem drastic but it is probably unavoidable if there is to be any chance of enduring peace in the Pacific. Every Japanese person, man, woman or child, in Micronesia should be sent back to Japan.

This is not so colossal an undertaking as it might seem. The movement of 100,000 persons to Japan would not compare for a moment with the migration in 1922-24 of 1,350,000 Greeks from Asia Minor to Macedonia and Thrace. That dislocation, painful enough at the time, has resulted in great ultimate satisfaction to both Turkey and Greece.

The argument that Japan is too crowded to accommodate these persons is not valid. One hundred thousand will hardly begin to take the place of the three million men Japan is estimated to have lost in war since 1937. In a population of seventy-five million so small a proportion as 100,000 can be accommodated without difficulty. And even if it were done only with great difficulty, still it should be done.

While the Japanese have complained of lack of space, they have declined to populate their own island of Hokkaido. It is north of the main island of Honshu and a bit cool—rather like Wyoming. It does not have the rather precious miniature beauty of the Honshu landscape. The Japanese, who like small things, do not feel quite at home there. But it is a richly fertile country of broad plains suited to large-scale agriculture. It has an area of thirty thousand square miles, a population of only two and a half million, and room, according to Japanese authorities themselves, for twenty million.

If the Japanese of the South Seas were Chinese the case would be quite different. Chinese making their homes in other Asiatic countries adapt themselves, intermarry with the inhabitants, take on the ways, customs and loyalties of the new land. The Japanese remain a race apart. They look back to Japan. Then let them go back to Japan; they will be happier there and the world will be happier to have them there. So long as Japanese are allowed to remain in Micronesia it will be a hotbed of intrigue and springboard of new attempts to dominate southeastern Asia.

How should the brown men of the islands be governed after the Japanese regime is finished?

Well, we should not be too proud to learn from the Japanese. Their system has worked. It did not originate with them but has been followed more or less in other Pacific mandates.

The Japanese have found that the easiest way to govern the natives is through their own kings.

The South Sea king may seem "small punkins" when viewed from afar but he looms great at home. He is highly respected as having a hereditary right to rule. The people accept no kings other than from the recognized royal strain. There is no room for pretenders or usurpers. A king is not asked whether he cares to be a king, nor can he abdicate, nor can he be deposed. If he is wicked or incompetent, the people may go their own way without consulting him, but no one may take his place as king. In such reverence is the office held.

The Japanese have taken advantage of this regard of the people for their hereditary rulers. Instead of dethroning the kings they have simply given them government jobs as *soncho,* or district heads. According to the importance of the king he is paid from one yen to thirty-five yen a month. Such incomes, which seem princely to the islanders, smooth the way to obedience to government orders.

The *soncho's* duty is as before, to be the direct governing head of his own people. Of course some unaccustomed tasks are added to his old ones. He is expected to report births and deaths and many other facts and figures to a statistics-doting government. He must bring new laws to the notice of the villagers. He must marshal his men for the building of water tanks, roads and piers. Government officials rarely go past him—mainly because the people would be reluctant to obey instructions that did not come from their traditional chief.

The king's authority is buttressed by the rule that he who disobeys him will be punished with two weeks of hard labor on the roads. Greater punishment than this, the king is not allowed to inflict. He cannot pass judgment upon criminals. They must be turned over to the police department and the courts.

It is a delicate business when the king, however satisfactory to his own people, is unsatisfactory to the government. Perhaps he cannot get the modern point of view, will not recognize the need of sanitation and the virtues of hard work. Then the Japanese consult the people and, if possible with their approval, otherwise without it, they appoint another man *soncho*. The king remains king, but without authority. The *soncho* is chosen from the king's family, otherwise he could never hope for obedience. Thus within a single royal family there may be two rulers, one with honor, the other with power.

The superior officer of the king is the Japanese policeman. Usually the village police station is built next door to the house of the *soncho*. The latter has a desk in the police office. There he is an employee, outside he is a monarch.

He serves without being servile. More than once the kings have risked their own safety in championship for their people.

The structure of the South Seas government is, in brief, as follows. At the base are the natives with a degree of self-government through their own kings or *soncho,* under a Japanese police officer. The entire mandated area is divided into six "Branch Bureaux," each supervising a group of islands. The six governors of the Branch Bureaux answer to the Governor-General of the South Seas Bureau who is stationed at Palau. And the South Seas Bureau, in turn, is superintended by the Ministry for Overseas Affairs in Tokyo.

The new international administration may well follow some such form. The native should be allowed to keep his king. Some of these rulers are backward—a school for kings might be worth while. Branch Bureaux are almost necessary because of the wide separation of the islands and difficulty of communication. The governors of these bureaux, if the control is international, should be chosen regardless of nationality—British, American, Australian, Canadian, Chinese, French, Russian. The Micronesian himself should certainly be eligible for this position. The only criterions would be merit and ablity to confer with colleagues in a common language. The over-all executive officer might be a governor-general, of whatever nationality, appointed for a definite period by the United Nations or whatever world association may take its place.

The far future of the Micronesian islands may see them emerge from mandate status into a completely democratic self-government, perhaps in conjunction with many other island groups of the Pacific. This cannot happen now, not because the native is an ignorant savage—he is not, and his knowledge of democratic ways is surprising—but because of the isolation of the islands from each other. Yap and Truk are more distinct than the United States and Russia. A Chamorro family in Saipan talked to me about Broadway in New York and Piccadilly in London but could give me no information concerning the Marshalls.

This situation will change in time. The sea separates islands. The air will unite them into one continent. It makes no difference to the airplane whether it flies over land or water. The enormous impetus which the war has given to aviation, the frantic building of airfields in all island groups, the suitability of lagoons as landing fields for seaplanes, all are harbingers of the day when every chief or well-to-do copra farmer will have his plane. Instead of waiting a month for a boat from Truk to Yap and then taking four days for the trip, he may get off at any time on ten minutes' notice, make the trip in two hours and get home the same day. What seems fanciful now will be commonplace in fifty years. Daily postal service between the islands will integrate them and the improvement of the radio and the radio-telephone will have the same effect. A newspaper, either printed in one place and distributed throughout the entire area by plane, or transmitted page by page by wire-photo and printed locally, would help all the diversified peoples of the Pacific to have the same thoughts every morning. And it is only when people think together that they will act together.

But the radio, the telephone, the newspaper, ease of communication, will be of no use without a common language.

When we say that the islanders should all be taught English there are some who will charge us with a sort of linguistic imperialism. They will say, "Respect the cultural traditions of the native. The Kanaka should learn to speak, read and write the Kanaka language."

But there is no Kanaka language. Or, rather, there is a different language for the Kanakas of every island. Saipan cannot understand Yap; nor Yap, Palau; nor Palau, Truk; nor Truk, Ponape; nor Ponape, Kusaie; nor Kusaie, Jaluit.

Democratic unity is of course impossible with such diversity of tongues. If every state in the American Union spoke a different language we would probably have forty-eight nations instead of one.

A localized language stunts mental growth. Few of the islanders read. It would be of little use at present to learn, because there would be nothing to read (except, on some islands, the Bible, translated by the missionaries). No commercial publisher could be persuaded to print newspapers, magazines and books in a language read by only two or three thousand people. It would not pay. Hence a literature in an island language is impossible. The natives' only hope to tap the literary knowledge of the world is to learn a language in which the world's literature is published.

Another consideration: the Palau language contains only 6,000 words, the Truk language 3,000, the Yap language only 1,000. The English language includes well over 600,000 terms. A few eating-and-sleeping words did well enough in the isolated tropical isle. But times have changed. Making shift with a small coconut vocabulary in this modern, complex world into which the native has been introduced would be like paddling a canoe in a motorboat race.

New words make new horizons. The mind is expanded as it finds new ways of expression.

But assuming that the schools of the Pacific teach the islanders to speak, read and write a common language, why should it be English? Why not Japanese, Chinese or Malay?

Malay is not a great world-language. Chinese is, but it comes in

252

nine different dialects and is very difficult to learn. It would draw the Pacific toward China but would cut it off linguistically from the rest of the world. Japanese is also a very difficult and exceedingly provincial language. The Russian language is split into dialects. French, the "diplomatic" language, is spoken by some 70,000,000 persons, German by 98,000,000, Spanish by 115,000,000. The English language is spoken by 260,000,000 people.

English is pre-eminently the language of world communication. According to figures presented by the National Geographic Society in 1943, three-fourths of the world's letters are written in English, half of the world's newspapers are in English; announcers for three-fifths of the earth's radio stations broadcast in English. Its use is more widely distributed over the world than that of any other language. It is the closest approach to a world-tongue.

Moreover, as Christopher Hollis has said, "The English language is the language, far more than any other, in which the story of freedom is told." That is of importance if we look forward to ultimate democracy in the Pacific.

The propinquity of the islands to Japan means that they will always be affected, as will all Asia, by whatever influences come out of that country. Whether those influences shall be democratic or undemocratic, depends chiefly upon the outcome of this war. If the defeat is total and the military caste utterly discredited, there is some hope that a liberal Japan will emerge, ushering in an era of co-operation or at least of tolerance in Pacific affairs.

XL:

No Turning Aside

TIME is of the essence. There is much to be said for getting to Japan as rapidly as possible without delaying now to pick at the Japanese appendages in the Indies and Malaya. The best way to make sure of the death of the arms and legs is by striking not the arms and legs, but the heart.

There is a disturbing possibility that we may be turned aside into devious and difficult ways resulting in a prolonged war and a final stalemate.

We cannot be too happy over the statement of a staff officer representing the Southwest Pacific command at the Cairo Conference. After referring to a possible drive for the "isolation or recapture" of the Netherlands Indies, he said, "I think we can beat Japan without landing an expeditionary force on the Japanese mainland."

He is probably right if by "beat Japan" he means win the present war. Japan might beg for peace if shorn of her conquests. But just so surely as we spend our strength in the lands down under and refrain from attacking and occupying Japan itself, we shall have another Pacific war on our hands within a few decades.

Militarism must be crushed in Japan, not merely in the Indies and China. It is the proud boast of Japanese militarists that Japan has never been invaded. Her wars have always ravaged other lands, not Japan. Until the Japanese people feel the full brunt of war, defeat, and complete occupation of their country by Allied troops, the myth of Japan's inviolability cannot be downed.

The danger that we shall slip into the pitfall of easy victory is very real. The chief interest of the British is naturally in the reclamation of Burma and Malaya; the Japanese homeland is rather outside their sphere. The Dutch want the Indies but have no ambitions in the north-west Pacific. The United States feels responsibility toward the Philippines but has no territorial ax to grind in or near Japan's main islands. China wants China, not Japan.

Therefore the temptation will be great to let Japan off lightly. Especially if we waste our substance in riotous warring along the equator and fail to approach Japan until the "period of drag" four or five years later, war weariness may persuade us to accept postponement rather than peace. With Holland back in the Indies, Britain in Malaya, the Philippines redeemed and China restored, what more can we ask?

We can ask that this shall not happen again. The German people were told by their militarists in 1918 that they had not lost the war. They believed it because no enemy foot had touched German soil. They were willing to try again. It was an adventure in which apparently if they did not win, at least they could not lose. Much the same psychology prevails in Japan. The self-righteousness engendered by two thousand years of unbroken military success will not be destroyed by conciliation, appeasement or a negotiated peace.

Nothing but the most crushing and bitter disaster involving the demolition of Japanese cities and the sweep of United Nations forces through the land from Nagasaki to Tokyo will make war distasteful to the Japanese people and shake the traditional belief that it is the ultimate destiny of their *Tenshi,* Heavenly King, to rule the world.

Island Names

Many different names have been applied to the islands of Micronesia. Some equivalents are given below. Since various names have been used locally and for brief periods, this list is not complete. The order is from north to south.

Ryukyu, Luchu, Loo-choo
Bonins, Ogasawara, Munin, Bunin
Peel, Chichijima
Marcus, Minamitori Shima
Marianas, Mariannes, Ladrones, Islas de las Velas Latinas, Isles of the Lateen Sails
Guam, Guajan, Guahan
Yap, Uap, Guap, Wap, Yappu, The Land
Palau, Pelew, Balao, Palao, Parao
Babeldaob, Babelthaob, Babelthuap, Baberudaobu
Koror, Korror, Corrol, Kororu
Arakabesan, Ngarekobasan
Malakal, Marakaru
Eil Malk, Makarakaru
Peliliu, Peleliu, Periryu
Angaur, Village of the Dead
Uleai, Ulie, Woleai, Wolea, Mereyon
Enderby, Endabi, Puluwat
Pulap, Pourappu
Truk, Ruk, Hogolu, Te-Fan, Torakku
Moen, Haru (*shima,* island, may be added)
Dublon, Toloas, Natsu (shima)
Fefan, Aki (shima)
Eten, Take (shima)
Uman, Fuyu (shima)
Udot, Getsuyo(to)
Fala, Falat, Kwaiyo, Kayo(to)
Tol, Suiyo(to)
Ponape
Chokach, Jokaj, Jokaji
Kusaie, Valao, Strong's, Ualan
Lele, Rere
Eniwetok, Enewetok, Brown

Index

257